PRAISE FOR CAUGHT IN THE PULPIT

"The new edition of *Caught in the Pulpit* extends and reinforces the message of the first: that many who preach religion do not themselves believe what they preach, for the good reason that they have more insight into its vacuity than those to whom they preach. Some are tragically trapped in this hypocrisy, some choose to keep living the lie: but knowing this adds to our sense of the lie that is religion itself. This is an important book, because it reveals an important truth."

—**A. C. Grayling,** Master of the New College of the Humanities London and author of *The Good Book: A Humanist Bible*

"To believe or not to believe. That is the agony of many of the very leaders of organized belief. Before Daniel Dennett and Linda LaScola, who could have predicted that so many ministers, priests, and rabbis no longer believe and yet continue to lead congregations? Atheists in shepherds' garb. When they put on the robes of their faith, these men and women don a false self at the core of their personal and professional identities. How do they live with such a mask? They tell the authors, and we hear their voices throughout these pages. In the extraordinary profiles of these clergy, Dennett and LaScola show us an unknown terrain in vivid and heartbreaking detail. This is a book that should be announced from every pulpit and read by all concerned with the unholy place religion still commands in our world."

—**J. Anderson Thomson, Jr., M.D.**, author of *Why We Believe in God(s): A Concise Guide to the Science of Faith*

"Profound, honest, and revealing. I was also going to write 'surprising,' but I am not surprised. As a former preacher myself (who has since abandoned supernatural beliefs), I know exactly what is going through the minds of the clergy who are struggling with faith and reason. What I most admire about this book is the careful, scientific approach to the topic. . . . I know I am biased, but that does not mean thi

—**Dan Barker**, copresident of the Fr ... ation and author of *Life Driven Purpose: H*

"People often ask me, 'How could you become an atheist when you were a pastor?' I always answer, 'Exactly by being a pastor!' *Caught in the Pulpit* was one of the first books I read during my Year Without God and nothing I read for the remainder of the year was more relatable. In some cases I felt like I was reading my own story. This book is essential reading for anyone wanting to understand the process of losing faith. Though these stories are about clergy, their feelings and experiences will resonate for anyone who has been down this road."

—**Ryan J. Bell**, former pastor and writer, Year Without God

"Over a century ago, William James pioneered the study of religious experience, focusing in particular on people whose lives had been transformed for the better by coming to faith. In their lucid and poignant study, Daniel Dennett and Linda LaScola explore the experiences of those who have moved in the opposite direction—the leaders of religious communities, who, having lost their faith, courageously rebuild their lives. With care and sympathy, Dennett and LaScola bring light to some darker corners of the religious life."

—**Philip Kitcher**, John Dewey Professor of Philosophy, Columbia University and author of *Life After Faith: The Case for Secular Humanism*

"Reading *Caught in the Pulpit* is like listening in on intimate conversations, even confessions, of clergy who doubt the very beliefs they are paid to teach and support. Dennett and LaScola address their subjects with both skill and compassion, yielding expert philosophical and sociological analysis. A fascinating read."

—**Mary Johnson**, author of *An Unquenchable Thirst*, secular activist, and former nun

"Not all pastors who harbor serious doubts about what they're preaching can just walk away from it all, but in *Caught in the Pulpit*, Linda LaScola and Daniel Dennett share with us what's going on in those pastors' heads. Why don't they just come clean to their congregations? How have their sermons changed to reflect their uncertainty? This book provides remarkable insight into a silently growing demographic."

—**Hemant Mehta**, editor of FriendlyAtheist.com

CAUGHT IN THE PULPIT

Leaving Belief Behind

Expanded and Updated Edition

Daniel C. Dennett and Linda LaScola

Foreword by Richard Dawkins

PITCHSTONE PUBLISHING
Durham, North Carolina

Pitchstone Publishing
Durham, North Carolina 27705
www.pitchstonepublishing.com

To contact the publisher, please e-mail info@pitchstonepublishing.com.

Congruity edition published 2013
First Pitchstone edition published 2015

Printed in the United States of America

10 9 8 7 6 5 4 3 2 1

Library of Congress Cataloging-in-Publication Data

Dennett, D. C. (Daniel Clement)
Caught in the pulpit : leaving belief behind / Daniel C. Dennett and Linda LaScola ; foreword by Richard Dawkins. — Expanded and Updated Edition.
pages cm
Includes bibliographical references.
ISBN 978-1-63431-020-8 (pbk. : alk. paper)
1. Ex-clergy—United States. 2. Christianity and atheism. I. Title.
BL2747.D46 2015
200.92'273—dc23

2014037616

Cover photography by Bryce Vickmark / vickmark.com

CONTENTS

FOREWORD

Richard Dawkins

What must it be like to be frightened of your own opinions? If asked "What do you think about X" most of us enjoy the luxury of reflecting: X, well yes, what do I think? What is the evidence bearing on X? What are the good things about X, what are the bad? Maybe I should read up on X before formulating my opinion. Maybe I should discuss X with friends. X is interesting, I'd like to think about X.

Imagine being in a job which forbids any of that: a profession to which you have vowed your life with solemn commitments; and where the terms of the job are that you must hold certain rigid beliefs about the world, the universe, morality and the human condition. You are allowed opinions about football or chimney pots, but when it comes to the deep questions of existence, origins, much of science, everything about ethics, you are told what to think; or you have to parrot your thoughts from a book, written by unknown authors in ancient deserts. If your reading, your thinking, your conversations, lead you to change your opinions you can never divulge your secret. If you breathe a hint of your doubts you will lose your job, your livelihood, the respect of your community, your friends, perhaps even your family. At the same time, the job demands the highest standards of moral rectitude, so the double life you are leading torments you with a wasting sense of shameful hypocrisy. Such is the predicament of those priests, rabbis and pastors who have lost their faith but remain in post. They exist in surprisingly large numbers, and they are the subjects of this fascinating, sometimes harrowing, sometimes uplifting book.

Other jobs might make demands on your skills, but if you are deficient you can do something about it. A lumberjack or a musician can improve with practice: try harder. But lumberjacks and musicians are not required to *believe*. You can't change your beliefs as an act of will, in the way you can decide to improve your skills with chainsaw or keyboard. If the evidence before your eyes doesn't support a belief, you cannot will yourself to believe it anyway. This, incidentally, is one of the many arguments against Pascal's Wager: No matter how you rate the odds of immortal salvation, you can't decide to believe in God, as if it were a decision to bet on Red or Manchester United.

It is hard not to feel sympathy for those men and women caught in the pulpit. It is for this reason that a group of us set up The Clergy Project. I originally even thought of trying to raise money for scholarships—retraining clergy as carpenters, say, or secular counsellors. That proved too expensive. But we did provide apostate clergy with a Web site where they can secretly go to talk to each other, in confidence, protected from parishioners and even from family by pseudonyms and passwords: a safe haven where they can share experiences, advice, even metaphorical shoulders to cry on. Dan Dennett and Linda LaScola were involved in The Clergy Project from the start: Indeed it was largely inspired by their pilot study, together with the experiences of the pioneer apostate Dan Barker. LaScola and Dennett's pilot study involved five Protestant ministers. Four of them are founder members of The Clergy Project. Subsequently The Clergy Project grew and grew, and it now numbers more than 500, including Catholics, Protestants, Jews, Muslims and Mormons. The sheer numbers are heartwarming to those of us who see religion as unfavourable to human welfare and positively hostile to educational values. But the figures also imply a level of human misery on the part of the unfortunate clergy themselves, and the gentle kindness of Dan Dennett and Linda LaScola shines from every page of this book.

Their expanded study looks in detail at thirty individual cases. Some of these men and women believed passionately for many years before losing their faith. Others seem to have been already skeptical while still in seminary, but went ahead with their priestly career for reasons that need to be explored—and are. These are human beings, every one different, and the victims are allowed the space to tell their own stories, woven together with intelligent and insightful commentary by the two authors.

The book is a collaboration between a patient, sympathetic social worker and one of the world's great philosophers. It will surprise as it fascinates. If, as I hope and expect, the 500 apostates now in The Clergy Project turn out to be the thin end of a very large wedge, tip of a reassuringly large iceberg, harbingers of a coming and very welcome tipping point, this book will be seen as—to mix metaphors yet again with pardonable glee—the miner's canary. It will help us to understand what is happening as the floodgates open, as I hope they soon will. I also hope it will be widely read by still-believing clergy, and that it will give them the courage to join their colleagues who have already seen the light and walked away from the dark shade of the pulpit.

Oxford, UK
November 2013

PREFACE TO THE EXPANDED AND UPDATED EDITION

Daniel C. Dennett

The phenomenon of clergy who don't believe the creeds they profess from the pulpit has probably been around for centuries, unacknowledged and unimagined, except by those who were living through it. We brought it into the daylight less than two years ago when we published the first edition of *Caught in the Pulpit: Leaving Belief Behind* (in November of 2013). Much has happened in the world of religion since then, and everywhere we go, we are asked for the latest developments in our participants' lives, and in our own understanding of the phenomenon we sought to bring to public attention. It seemed important to us to take a second look at where we stand.

We were able to recontact many of our participants, and this expanded edition provides an update on their remarkable trajectories. Among the readers of the first edition were some who told us they couldn't stand the suspense. What on earth could these nonbelieving clergy do? Where could they turn? How would they handle their precarious situations? We found out a lot, and discuss the ongoing struggles some of them have, the peace some have made with their situations, and the major life changes some have experienced.

Anybody interested in religion and what it has in store for us in the coming years will find arresting insights in the candid revelations of our participants, often speaking for the first time in their lives in deepest confidence about their most closely guarded secrets. We think that this update will be particularly valuable to clergy who have found kindred spirits in our participants and must be wondering if they themselves should stay closeted, as some have done, or come out, as others have done.

In response to readers' interest in hearing more personal stories, we've added two additional sketches: Sherm, the Orthodox rabbi, and Stan, the military chaplain, and also included our original 2010 article, "Preachers Who Are Not Believers," as an appendix. The article has five sketches of its own, bringing the total number of sketches in this edition to twelve.

We've also added a new final chapter, "What's Next—A Response to Requests for Our Study's 'Conclusions.'" In this chapter we have used our analysis to ground some suggestions that we hope will persuade more readers than they enrage. All religions are in precarious positions these days, and hunkering down and hoping it all will pass may be the prevailing choice, but it may not be the wisest. Thousands of religions have been born, lived for months, years, or even centuries, and then gone extinct, and the pace of change seems to be accelerating. Leading, not just reacting, may be the key to longevity. Meanwhile, another generation of would-be clergy is entering seminaries and encountering the tender trap that will shape their lives for decades, if not irrevocably. They, above all, should read this book.

Tufts University
Medford, MA
December 2014

I. INTRODUCTION

Daniel C. Dennett

Preachers Who Aren't Believers

This book is about men and women who entered the clergy with the best of motives and intentions and have come to recognize that they no longer hold the beliefs their parishioners think they do. Half of the people interviewed still have a congregation awaiting them each Sabbath, trusting them to speak the truth from the pulpit. They come from various backgrounds and have made different decisions about how to deal with their lack of belief in what they think somebody in their position ought to believe.

The present study, made in collaboration with the clinical social worker and qualitative researcher Linda LaScola, is a continuation of our 2010 pilot study of five male nonbelieving Protestant ministers.[1] Our main objective: to explore, through in-depth interviews, the disconnect between what closeted nonbelieving clergy believe and what they preach, and the impact it has on their personal lives, their congregations, and society.

Most people who participated in the present study first learned about it through the media attention the pilot study received. This time there were thirty new participants, including women, Catholics, Jews, Mormons, a wider spectrum of liberal (mainline) and literal (fundamentalist) Protestant denominations, a few current or former theology students, and three mainline Protestant seminary professors. We included the seminary professors to learn how their students react to academic and historical perspectives on the Bible that may be quite different from what they learned in Sunday school. These professors teach Old and New Testament studies to beginning seminarians. Their personal religious beliefs were not known in advance and were not explored in the interviews.[2] To get a better sense of liberal clergy beliefs and thought processes, we included two active, believing, Episcopal clergy. Follow-up interviews with all the clergy from the pilot study and many from the continued study are also included. As with the pilot study, the interviews were done in confidence, with names and identifying details changed.

The interviews—all of which were conducted by Linda—varied in number, length, and setting. Though most were conducted face-to-face, some were done by Skype or phone. Only a few people were interviewed once; most were interviewed two or three times over several days, in discussions lasting an hour to an hour and a half. All active clergy were interviewed three times, allowing Linda to follow up on important issues and giving the interviewees time to reflect more deeply on their experiences and emotions. All in all, 90 interviews were conducted in more than 120 hours of conversation. (For a complete list and categorization of the participants, see appendix A.)

We had planned to assemble a diverse group of participants; the reality turned out to be more diverse than we guessed. People didn't fit into the neat demographic boxes we had prepared for them. Some had changed denominations during their careers, moving from literal to liberal (never the other direction) before dropping their beliefs altogether. Some who were active clergy "came out" unexpectedly a few weeks or months after they were interviewed, prompting follow-up interviews. Two participating clergy were on leaves of absence when they were interviewed, so their futures were up in the air.

An intervening event that surely affected some participants' subsequent behavior was the establishment of The Clergy Project, in March of 2011.[3] The Clergy Project, a confidential online community for active and former professional clergy who do not hold supernatural beliefs, is separate from our study—although both of us were among its founders and there is considerable overlap of study participants (twenty-four) and project members. It was the culmination of years of discussions between Richard Dawkins, founder of the Richard Dawkins Foundation for Reason and Science, and Dan Barker, copresident of the Freedom From Religion Foundation. Dawkins had long wanted to provide assistance to nonbelieving clergy who wanted to leave the church. Barker, a former evangelical minister, often encountered other former clergy who urged him to "do something" for people who, like them, had made such a dramatic, life-altering decision. The first fifty-two members of The Clergy Project came from lists of people Barker had met over the years and people who had participated in our 2010 pilot study or contacted us about it. It's important to note that while Linda and I are among the cofounders, we are not members, because we have never been clergy. Like all nonmembers, we have no access to the private Web site and take no part in the discussions there.

All current and former clergy and seminary graduates were asked about their childhood religious experiences, their decision to become clergy (or seminarians), their experiences in the seminary (if applicable), and their changes in belief and its effect on them and the people around them. As the interviews were ending, Linda asked two specific questions of the nonbelievers: "What have you gained as a result of your changes in belief?" and "What have you lost?" Their responses to these two questions comprise a section toward the end of the book.

Some Cautions

What is it like to be a practicing pastor or rabbi while not believing most—or any—of the doctrines of your faith? You may think you know quite well if you have read some of the many good autobiographical books and articles written by former clergy or nuns (*e.g.*, in alphabetical order, the work of Armstrong, Barker, Compere, DeWitt, Ehrman, Hurlin, . . . Johnson, Loftus, . . . Semple, . . . Uhl, ...). Or perhaps you have read *In the Beauty of the Lilies*, the heartbreaking novel by John Updike about the (fictional) Reverend Clarence Wilmot, a Lutheran minister who after years of struggling with religious doubt announces his disbelief and thereupon is plunged into a terrible downward spiral, losing his job, his respectable position in the community, and even his family's love.

Linda and I knew some of this literature quite well when we embarked on our research project. But, as usual, reality outstrips imagination. We didn't know the half of it.

There are very different ways of becoming a nonbelieving preacher, and very different ways of coping with the discovery that that is what you are. Our interviewees are not saints, anymore than you are, but they are in general good people: more conscientious and honest, we would hazard, than the average citizen, all trying hard to help their neighbors and not hurt a soul, trying not to lie or dissemble, but caught up in a web of tact, tradition, and subtly imposed expectations—a web trapping them in patterns of deceit that accumulate and threaten to immobilize them. Some respond more gracefully—which does not necessarily mean more honestly—than others. Some are bitter, feeling seduced and abandoned by their creed or angry at themselves for allowing their eagerness to go along with the program to trump their honesty. Some are wistful about what they will miss if ever they find a way out of their predicament. What they will miss is in some cases the wholehearted community spirit of their congregation; in others, the inflated respect and deference their position commands; in yet others, the limelight in which they exercise their considerable talents as preachers. These are people like the rest of us, succumbing to some temptations and stalwartly resisting others, with often unrealistic hopes and ambitions, sometimes self-deceived, sometimes depressed, sometimes aching with love of what they fear they will lose forever. And, yes, sometimes terrified of the financial calamity that will likely befall them if they lose their modest living. None of these people went into the ministry for money, that's for sure. If many of them now have a family to support, children to send to college, no equity in a home, who can blame them for considering money an important part of their problem?

I must stress these points from the outset, for our informants have already been subjected to ferocious criticism by religious leaders who read the article on our pilot project in *Evolutionary Psychology*. I find it a telling irony that out of the several dozen who posted commentary on the *Washington Post's* On Faith Web site, where our piece first appeared,[4] only Max Carter, a Quaker (whose tradition has no ordained clergy) and Rebecca Goldstein, a Jewish atheist, saw the torment of these clergy for what it is. The others seem to have forgotten Jesus' message about casting the first stone (John 8:7), responding for all the world like stage magicians infuriated by another magician's revelation of their trade secrets.

They were right to feel threatened. One of the moral quandaries Linda and I have faced in preparing this account is whether our revelations about the methods used by our informants to conceal their disbelief from their congregations will make the job of being a pastor much harder for all, believers and nonbelievers alike. We concluded that the membrane of deceit so often separating clergy from their congregations is on its way out in any event, and if we can hasten its extinction that's a good thing, even if in the short run it makes life more difficult for those intent on maintaining their positions with a careful self-presentation. They will just have to be more careful.

Stage magic has handsomely survived the rude subversion of Penn and Teller, whose amusing exposure of magicians' tricks has earned them accolades even from their fellow magicians, and it is quite likely, in our view, that after the initial shock wears off, churches that can put the stage magic behind them—or keep it on as explicit stagecraft, if they like—are likely to be healthier competitors in the Information Age of the 21st century.

Some are already there, such as the ceremonially "high" ("smells and bells ") but doctrinally "low" (believe whatever you want) Episcopal churches that hold their own in some parts of the country. Other, more "creedal" denominations have a harder road ahead, as their leaders well know. Evangelicals repeatedly warn that "if current trends continue, only 4 percent of teenagers will be 'Bible-believing Christians' as adults."[5] In 2009, one "postevangelical" spokesman declared, "We are on the verge—within 10 years—of a major collapse of evangelical Christianity,"[6] a prediction echoed and expanded more recently.[7]

Our decision to include the tricks of the trade in our account was not taken lightly. We realize that doing so may cause serious harm, making some benign effects of current religious practices harder to achieve. This is not the first time I have faced this issue. Many years ago, when I was researching the practice of anesthesia for an essay on pain,[8] I learned of the widespread use of amnestics by anesthesiologists. These drugs aren't painkillers at all; they are memory erasers, and anesthesiologists use them to wipe out any awful memories of pain that may have leaked onto the scene in insufficiently anesthetized patients. The use of amnestics makes their job easier and safer, since they don't have to anesthetize their patients as deeply (which is dangerous) to ensure an untroubled postsurgical result. But telling patients in advance that they might be receiving an amnestic only makes them more anxious and hence harder to tranquilize and anesthetize. (Now are you sorry you began reading this? There is more to come, so *caveat lector!*) I was importuned by several of my anesthesiologist informants not to reveal this awkward fact about benign subterfuge to the world at large, but I didn't take their advice, and now, forty years later, anesthesia is safer than ever. Perhaps this just goes to show how few people read my essay on pain, but in fact I have found that people who know all about amnestics are blithely unconcerned both pre- and postsurgically—certainly it hasn't bothered me in my surgical encounters. I suspect that anesthesiologists and church leaders alike are more fearful of candor than they need to be, and we will show you some evidence of that in due course.

Another worry of mine is that readers of this book may inadvertently render themselves immune to certain sorts of helpful intervention. When I was an undergraduate, I had a classmate, whom I will call Rob, who was both depressed (or had some other mental disorder) and obsessed with the literature of psychotherapy—especially the techniques. The obsession made him all but untreatable by the college psychotherapist. Rob would return from his weekly visit both morose and strangely triumphant: "He started by chatting me up about my coursework, and I responded with 'Gain your patient's confidence by engaging with him about a subject he knows well,' Jones and Smidlap, *How to Treat an Undergraduate*, p. 5,'" or words to that effect. He was just too self-conscious and savvy to let the therapist gain a foothold. I'm happy to say he survived his youthful funk and has had a productive research career as a psychologist. Will churchgoers who could use some spiritual counseling be similarly immunized and unable to respond to the best efforts of their pastors? Perhaps, but if that is the price to pay for saving some young aspirants to the clergy from falling into the traps our informants landed in, it will be worth it, in our view.

What We Did and Why We Did It

When I called for the scientific study of religion in *Breaking the Spell: Religion as a Natural Phenomenon,*[9] I drew attention to many of the obstacles to such study but urged readers to press ahead because of the importance of the phenomena and the urgency of learning more about them in an age when so many policies hinge in one way or another on getting religion right. I was soon approached by Linda, a professional qualitative researcher, who proposed to help me study closeted nonbelieving clergy—if we could find some. It turns out that we could, and the reaction to our pilot study encouraged us to expand our research and made it possible by inducing many other clergy to volunteer as confidential informants.

My collaboration with Linda has been my attempt to follow my own advice. Are the results "scientific"? Yes, in the important sense that we pursued our work with careful attention to the established methodological principles of research with human subjects, which always raises special problems. Chemists, geologists, and botanists can conduct their research without having to tiptoe around or whisper in the presence of their phenomena. They may even talk to the trees—or the rocks or the molecules—without worrying that in doing so they will subvert the objectivity of their experiments by provoking uncontrolled reactions in their materials. Research on animals needs more attention to these possible confounds, since animals are perceivers and perception is a gatherer and amplifier of environmental effects that are hard to keep track of. In the field, if you can't avoid detection altogether, you strive to avoid doing things that might perturb the normal behavior of your subjects, and if you absolutely must catch, tag, and release your study animals, you attempt to minimize both the trauma and the chances of creating dependencies between experimenter and subjects. (If they need it, nurse them back to vigor before releasing them, but don't provision them and don't warn them of approaching predators, for instance.) Moreover, there are standards of ethical treatment of animals that must be scrupulously followed.

Research on human subjects raises the bar much higher and introduces the need for special restrictions on experimenters, as well as care both in the choice of subjects (avoiding self-selection and other biases) and in how subjects are briefed and debriefed (if they're not simply observed "in the wild"). Institutional review boards must approve all research involving human subjects in advance, and issues of privacy and risk must be carefully assessed. With all these difficulties, it is still possible to do objective, controlled research on human subjects—even research on that most private phenomenon, human consciousness. What is it like to be a human being confronted with various stimuli, challenges, experiences, problems? We have a wealth of partial answers derived from more than a century of empirical research.

But consider the question *What is it like to be a religious believer? Or nonbeliever*? This is a perfectly reasonable and important question to ask, but if we want anything like a scientific answer, an answer that has some credentials beyond the respondent's reputation, we have to confront still greater obstacles to our inquiry. To see this, let's review the standard provisions for experiments designed to investigate human consciousness. This is the methodology I have called *heterophenomenology* (the study of other people's phenomenology, or conscious experience).[10] It requires the experimenter to communicate with the subjects, briefing them about what they will be asked and then getting them to express their beliefs about what is going on in their minds under the various conditions (which they often do by pushing buttons or moving joysticks, but these are still communicative acts, intentional and meaning-laden).

The only way of ensuring—and one can never ensure this 100 percent—that your subjects will be truthful or sincere is to keep them in the dark (they must be what the field calls "naïve subjects") about the point of the experiment. Thus they can't frame a desire, even unconsciously, to help or hinder the experimenter, and they will have no motivation to express anything but their candid, unvarnished opinion about what is happening in their consciousness.

Evaluation of many such experimental situations has also shown that experimenters often can't help biasing their interactions with their subjects or letting wishful thinking bias their interpretation of their data, so best practices involve a double-blind design, in which the person who interacts directly with the subjects also is as naïve as possible about the point of the particular experiment being conducted, and the person who categorizes the data is shielded from knowledge of which subjects had which preparation. (The same policy is followed in drug evaluation testing, where neither the administrator of the drug-or-placebo nor the subsequent evaluator of the effects on patients knows which patients are getting the drug and which the placebo, until all the interactions and evaluations are completed.)

Now ask how these well-supported rules for designing experiments interact with an attempt to probe human attitudes toward religion or to understand what it is like to believe in one God or another. There simply are no naïve subjects and cannot be any naïve subjects! Moreover, quite aside from any desire on the part of subjects to help or hinder the experimenter, there are a host of motivations to be less than candid, less than fully open, in responding to inquiries. Indeed, in some religions, such as Roman Catholicism, there is a sacred obligation always to profess the orthodox creed. Cardinal Ratzinger, before he became Pope Benedict XVI, composed a Declaration entitled "*Dominus Iesus*: On the Unicity and Salvific Universality of Jesus Christ and the Church," which was ratified by Pope John Paul II at a Plenary Session on June 16, 2000. Again and again, this document specifies what faithful Catholics must "*firmly believe*" (italics in the original), noting at one point what "the Catholic faithful *are required to profess*"—that the Roman Catholic Church is the one true church (italics in the original). Cardinal Ratzinger cites Paul's first letter to the Corinthians: "Preaching the Gospel is not a reason for me to boast; it is a necessity laid on me: woe to me if I do not preach the Gospel!" (1 Cor. 9:16). But this means that researchers have grounds for doubting sincerity whenever a Catholic claims to believe an article of Catholic doctrine.

Religious belief is a unique psychological phenomenon—not just hard to study objectively but often systematically elusive by design. For instance, we cannot know if Benedict XVI, now the pope emeritus, believes in the Trinity, because by his own avowal he would tell us he did even if he didn't, and there is nothing he could do to support his words with deeds. The best we can do is adopt the anthropologists' method of respectful but persistent inquiry and observation and make of it what we can. This can't take us far; religious beliefs, unlike beliefs about mundane matters (whether the horse in the corral is dangerous, whether these berries are good to eat, whether there are fish in the river), have no clear nonverbal manifestations in action.

When it comes to interpreting the religious avowals of others, everybody is an outsider. Why? Because religious avowals concern matters that are beyond observation, beyond meaningful test, so the only thing anybody can go on is religious behavior and, more specifically, the behavior of professing. A child growing up in a culture is like an anthropologist, surrounded by informants whose professings stand in need of interpretation. The fact that your informants are your parents and speak in your mother tongue does not give you anything more than a slight circumstantial advantage over the adult anthropologist, who has to rely on a string of bilingual interpreters to query the informants. (And think about your own case: Weren't you ever baffled or confused about what you were supposed to believe?) You may well be an insider, but you know perfectly well that you don't have any special insider's knowledge of the tenets of the faith you were raised in.[11]

The present study therefore did not adopt a strict double-blind experimental procedure, but we did what we could to neutralize our bias as experimenters. For instance, Linda didn't send interpretations of her interviews until I had read the transcripts and written up my notes, which I didn't share with her until she had finished drawing her own conclusions—though I sometimes sent her questions that needed answering. In interviewing, she made it clear that she was a researcher, not a therapist, and scrupulously refrained from offering advice or diagnosis, even when the subjects would clearly have welcomed it. In many cases, Linda was the first person with whom they had discussed these issues in such depth. They had not talked at length about their failed belief with their spouses, children, colleagues, close friends, or—needless to say—their church superiors. Their lives were, in this respect, supremely lonely, and their gratitude to Linda, a sympathetic interlocutor who helped them think things through in deepest confidence, was moving. Free at last, free at last—if only in their thoughts.

Quite independently of any official discouragement of candor by one's denomination, there are obviously many motivations to be less than truthful in responding to researchers on these topics, so the best we could do, ethically, was provide a setting that minimized these motivations. The mantle of strict confidentiality often encourages people to tell a researcher things they have never told anybody before, even their spouses and closest friends. For instance, would anybody confess to rape or murder to a researcher? Yes, in fact. University of Pennsylvania psychologist Adrian Raine conducted a strictly confidential experiment involving twenty-one "successful psychopaths"—people without criminal records, identified by their "passing" the standard test used to diagnose psychopathy in populations of convicts, an identification strengthened by brain scans revealing the telltale prefrontal-lobe deficiency in gray matter and other well-established markers of psychopathy. The interviewees were reassured by the certificate of confidentiality Raine secured for the experiment (a standard provision in research into topics where subjects could be at risk if their identity was revealed), and they readily provided detailed accounts of the crimes they had committed, including armed robbery, rape, and murder. Raine thinks there is scant chance that they were making any of it up, and he has perhaps more experience than any other researcher in talking with violent criminals. "Perhaps for the first time in their lives they could talk about their wrongdoings at length with a professional in full confidence and without risk—even getting into the nitty-gritty of rape and homicide."[12] Linda found her subjects just as willing, even relieved and grateful, to find somebody with whom they could discuss the ideas that had been roiling their brains for years, unexpressed and unconfided. Nobody, I daresay, has ever before confidentially interviewed so many practicing clergy about their loss of faith. There are inexpressibly sad moments, joyful moments, and moments when Linda uncovers self-deception that leaves an interviewee exposed—but not attacked.

Imagine what a momentous step it is to volunteer for these interviews. You have been conditioned not to unburden your soul, not to indulge in avowals with your parishioners or anyone else, and you have become adept at deflecting even your own attention from topics you know you can't handle. To let down your defenses and explain the inexplicable, admit the inadmissible, and acknowledge your own complicity takes courage. Their belief that by doing so, they would be helping others deal with their own entanglements with faith is a belief we intend to honor by helping some of them tell their stories, without distortion, without special pleading.

Our primary goal, however, has not been to help our informants but to learn from them. They are, both officially and in actual fact, research subjects in a project administered by Tufts University and hence approved by Tufts' IRB (Institutional Review Board, the human-subjects committee). As researchers, we are professionally obliged to respect their autonomy, preserve their dignity, minimize their exposure to risk, and do whatever we can to ensure that our research is properly conducted so that their cooperation yields valuable results.

A word on terminology: Oversimplifying somewhat, we use the term "literal" to refer to Judeo-Christian denominations that profess Scripture to be the inerrant word of God, a source of unvarnished truth on all matters. Literals profess belief in a personal God who created the world in six days and intervenes in the world, answering prayers and arranging for miracles. Jesus was literally the son of God and was literally resurrected. The term "liberal" refers to those who temper these claims with varying amounts of metaphor, holding that their function is symbolic or poetic. God is not a bearded guy in the sky—and maybe not even a person, and maybe not even a "being" at all, but something beyond our meager human comprehension. Pentecostals, Mormons, and Seventh-day Adventists are prototypical literals, and Unitarians and (most) Episcopalians are prototypical liberals. The literal/liberal opposition is best seen as a spectrum, with all manner of intermediate positions on specific issues, even within denominations; thus some Roman Catholics are adamantly literal about Transubstantiation and some are more liberal.

Agnostics are those who profess not to know—and deny that anybody *can* know—the truth about God's existence, or the divinity of Jesus, or the existence of miracles, and so forth. One of our participants, the Humanist rabbi, Jacob, introduced us to a term worth knowing and using: "ignostic." It was coined in the 1960s by the late Rabbi Sherwin Wine, a founding figure of Humanistic Judaism. He used it to refer to those who declare the question of the existence of God meaningless, in the absence of an agreed-upon definition of God, or (more brusquely) to those who just *igno*re religious doctrine, finding the issues not worth thinking about. Around the globe there are probably more ignostics than any other category, something we tend to forget.

Qualitative Research ("What Is It Like . . . ?")

Although it was not part of our study's explicit design, Linda, as a qualitative researcher (see appendix B), occasionally asks, "What was it like for you?" The answers are, typically, informative not only in what they assert but also in the way they assert it. Consider, for instance, Sherm, an Orthodox rabbi in his thirties:

> *Linda:* Was there a time during this process that you stopped praying, or your prayers changed, or what?
>
> *Sherm:* You can't stop praying, because, I think, it would become noticeable.
>
> *Linda:* But what was it like for you?, is what I'm—
>
> *Sherm:* Oh. Yes. Certainly in my head I've stopped praying. It's just words

to me. And I spend a lot of the time actually—I have other books open in front of me, other books of learning, and I study those. Those are, you know, Jewish things.

Linda: When you're supposed to be praying?

Sherm: Yeah. Nobody would really notice, because a lot of people do that. People learn while they're praying, they'll pray a little bit, a little quicker than everybody else, and while they're waiting, they'll read a line here, a line there.

Linda: From another book?

Sherm: From another book.

Linda: Like, a popular novel?

Sherm: Oh no, no, no [chuckle]. I actually, for the first time, saw somebody bring a popular novel to synagogue. But normally, no. It's a book of the Talmud, or the book of Mishnah, or even the Bible.

Here is Dave, a Baptist missionary in Asia, talking about his experiences teaching Bible stories to someone he hoped to convert.

Dave: And to sit there and explain to them about someone who died on a cross, then rose again; a donkey that spoke; and a snake that spoke in the Garden of Eden? Even back then, it's almost like, "Come on, do I really believe this?" But then I think, "Well, God can do anything," and then you teach it. Just not having to defend all that crazy stuff is a great blessing [laughs].

Linda: What was it like, saying those things to people?

Dave: Well, a part of you says it can't be true, but then God can do anything. God says it happened, so you talk yourself into believing that it really happened. I'll never forget, I was in my home church a few years ago and the pastor talked about, I think it was out of Judges, chapter 15, in relation to Samson. And something happened to Samson, where the Philistines wouldn't allow him to see his wife, so he went and caught three hundred foxes and he tied their tails together and he put a firebrand between their tails and sent them off to the cornfields, to burn up the cornfields. And I remember a woman . . . saying, "That's kind of hard to believe—that he rounded up three hundred foxes and sent them to burn up a cornfield."

> And I said, "Yeah, but with God's help, he could do it all." And she said, "Yeah, I think you're right." That was one of my first moments of "Wow, this is just a fairy tale!"

And here is Tony, a former Catholic priest, describing how he dealt with being gay.

> *Linda:* How were you thinking about sexuality? I know priests aren't supposed to have sex with anybody, but already knowing you're gay—what was it like?
>
> *Tony:* Yeah. I thought—there are a few different things I thought. Because I compartmentalized. I always knew that I'd been sexually abused; this all related into it. It's like there was this other me, or little me, that it happened to, but I was this super guy, straight-A, president of the class, perfect Catholic, perfect whatever, blah, blah, blah. So when I went into this whole priesthood thing, this celibacy thing, it was very easy to say to myself, "Yeah, I'm all integrated sexually. And all this counseling, all this growth that I have, and I accept all myself and everything, and blah, blah, blah." But then there was this whole other side of me—that I was just putting it all in the little closet inside of me, and there was a part of me that was thinking, "Yeah, I'll get ordained, and then it will all make sense." I really wanted to understand how celibacy worked. And especially . . . the last two years of college and the first years of seminary when I was with these priests that were hitting on me and using me for sex. It was confusing, because I had feelings of love and respect for them, and it was very difficult.

Linda and I don't just acknowledge the limitations of our methodology revealed by these observations; we wish to highlight them and stress that there is no feasible alternative if you want to study the experience of clergy who have to conceal their convictions. The best we can do is trust our abilities to engage honestly with our subjects and to detect the everyday signs of dishonesty as they might imaginably arise in these extraordinary circumstances. We're sure there are no impostors among our informants; relying on the well-known if far from exceptionless principle that admissions made contrary to interest are apt to be sincere, we judge our informants to be, in large measure, truthful. There are, of course, the occasional red flags of narcissistic recollection, of exaggerated self-pity or self-dramatization, a few tell-tale flashes of score-settling and gamesmanship, but repetition of pattern works wonders, and we eventually learned to recognize these moves.

Another limitation of our study is that our sample is self-selected and, as in all qualitative research, the farthest thing from a random sample. So no generalizations about clergy, or disbelieving clergy, or Baptist clergy, or liberal congregations are supported by our findings. One cannot learn all about what it's like to run a marathon by interviewing only those who drop out—but one can learn something. Like failure analysis in engineering, one can learn from a few mishaps what to look out for and where the weaknesses may lie. One can learn about the difficulties these individuals face and see patterns in them. One can learn about features encountered by all, or almost all, our informants in widely different religious environments and have some grounds for suspecting that these features are ubiquitous.

There is one question everybody is curious about that we are utterly powerless to answer: How widespread is the phenomenon we have been studying? At one extreme, is our sample close to exhaustive—are there only a few dozen such "bad apples" in a trainload of preachers? At the other extreme, have we uncovered a nearly universal affliction of clergy everywhere, with devout and sincere believers being the "rare birds" who survive today only in isolated pockets? Or is it much more likely that the truth lies somewhere in between? Nobody knows. Seriously, *nobody* knows. Our informants are generally sure they are the tip of the iceberg, but they have no way of testing that conviction. In all the commentary we have provoked from experts on religion or spokespeople for religion, nobody—as far as I know—has accused us of making things up or turning a molehill into a mountain. We can say that there are at least a hundred instances, since among the more than six hundred current members of The Clergy Project, there are nearly two hundred who still have a pulpit, still have a congregation. (The rest are all former religious professionals.) Since that private, confidential Web-based organization for nonbelieving clergy has grown to those numbers in four years, without advertising or canvassing, we can safely surmise that there are many more clergy out there who are in the same boat but haven't heard about The Clergy Project, or for various reasons would not want to join. Perhaps a nationwide confidential survey of clergy could give us a ballpark number, but the logistics of doing such a survey in a way that maximizes security and anonymity while screening out spurious responses is daunting indeed.

The purpose of qualitative research is to develop insight—in-depth understanding of attitudes and behavior in order to provide direction for further research. Because of the small number of people interviewed and the nonrandom method of recruitment, our findings cannot be evaluated quantitatively. It is important to remember this standard limitation of qualitative research while reading the sections to come. They are the truth about the people they are about, and not about anything else. They are anecdotal evidence, not statistical evidence. Make of them what you can.

II. SEVEN SKETCHES

Linda LaScola

Winnie, the Presbyterian Pastor: Wanting to Belong; Trying to Believe
Winnie was a Presbyterian minister for over ten years. She served two parishes, one as an assistant pastor and one as the senior and sole pastor. She is now a psychologist living with her wife in a major Midwestern metropolitan area. The Presbyterian Church was a central part of her life as a child.

> I grew up participating in every part of the Church, starting with day care and Sunday nursery school and then going on to Sunday school.

She especially liked the church her family attended when she was in her early teens:

> They had a guitar group, and they had an informal folk service. I was smitten; I wanted to be there all the time. My family sometimes wanted to go traveling on the weekends, and I'd say, "No, I want to stay home and go to church!". . . . I joined the adult choir there. I became very good friends with a couple that sang in the choir.

Her doubts about religion did not keep her from being active in the Church:

> I always had doubts—doubts about believing any of it. Does God really even exist? I remember walking our dog in the park at the top of our street that looked down on the water, and the wind and the sun, and

> I thought, "I don't worship God, I worship the sun." I love the sun, it's wonderful. Then I thought I may as well believe and join the Church, because millions and millions of people have been joining the Church for many years, and they can't all be wrong.
>
> As a thirteen- or fourteen-year-old, I would also go to adult-education classes, and I loved those. I just loved being accepted as an adult when I was a teenager—I thought it was cool.

It was then that she had the first sense of her sexual preference.

> I kind of thought all women got married but your best friends and who you got close to were other women. And you'd have your deep, emotional, intense intimacy relationships with them.
>
> I'm a lesbian, I realize now, but at the time I didn't. But I basically fell in love with this female pastor. I basically stalked her a lot of that time. So it was kind of a lot of awakening going on for me that year.

She also became aware then that women could become ministers.

> I didn't know women could do anything in the Church; I hadn't seen that before. So to see the female minister in her red robe and white stole just was totally enlightening. They used inclusive language—we'd cross out the words in the hymn book. Instead of "man," we'd use "human" or whatever. So all of that was just like this enormous awakening to me.
>
> At one point when we were having one of our many, many long, intense talks, the pastor told me she thought I was called to the ministry. And I was kind of stunned and didn't want to say anything. I had thought that to myself, but I hadn't said anything to anyone. And to have her confirm that perception of me—that it might be something I could do well—just floored me.

Years later, she told her parents about her interests.

> They basically said, "Well, you know, you'll never get married. You'll never have children. You won't be paid very much. You won't be respected, because women aren't respected much in the Church . . . . Do you really want to do this?" Then they go, "OK, if that's what you want to do, go ahead."

She looked to the Bible to support her decision.

> There are lots of passages in the Bible that say, "Leave your family and turn to God. Don't look back. This is the family of God; this is better for you."
>
> I'm called to do this. This is very important, even if they don't see it yet. God calls, God means it.

She spent a year in Israel before starting seminary.

> That was the year of really losing my faith. It's not just a desert, it's a spiritual desert. If you haven't been to Israel, it's a piece of desert that's rocky, dusty, hot, ugly, and it's the center of three monotheistic religions that fight with each other constantly. And it's in the middle of the trade routes. So it's an area that doesn't have any real reason to exist, except for those religions and because all the trade routes between Europe and Asia and Africa branch through there.

She was exposed there to many other kinds of religions.

> I took a tour of Sinai in October, and everybody and their uncle was climbing Mount Sinai. There's a church or a mosque or a grotto or shrine or something on every hill, nook, cranny, and cave. And most of the religious tombs and all the rest I found repulsive.
>
> I'm Presbyterian. I'm not Orthodox, I'm not Roman Catholic. I don't get into incense and smells and bells and icons. And that stuff is all over. You get Coptics and Russian Orthodox. You get dozens and dozens of types of Christianity that are nothing like Protestants.

After her experience in Israel, she questioned her commitment to the ministry.

> Well, I came back and I was really troubled, because I really wasn't sure I was Christian, and I really wasn't sure what to do.
>
> My ministers, when I was growing up, weren't hammering beliefs into us, but I knew I was supposed to believe that Jesus Christ was my Lord and Savior—I wasn't quite sure what that meant. And I don't see how you can have one God but three Gods—Father, Son, and Holy Spirit. And what are the End Times? I was hoping nobody would ever really ask me, because I really didn't know what to say.

While at a Presbyterian camp, she listened to the hymn "Be Not Afraid," with the lyrics "You shall cross the barren desert, but you shall not die of thirst. / You shall wander far in safety though you do not know the way."[13] She also encountered Mary Stevenson's poem "Footprints in the Sand," which concludes with "the Lord" saying, "The times when you have seen only one set of footprints, is when I carried you."

> I was very touched by those kinds of things. And I was kind of like, "Oh, I can do this."

Winnie went on to a prestigious interdenominational divinity school whose students came from various belief systems and levels of religious education.

> A lot of people take Old Testament first year, and the Old Testament lectures would throw students into the emotional, spiritual trauma that I went through in Israel. There are four sources in Genesis, and you know if there are all these different writers, then it's not all from God. And it's been translated, and it's been orally transmitted forever, and we don't really know what these words or those words mean today. . . . There's a phrase in the Song of Solomon that says, "Her hair was like a flock of goats on a hillside." And I thought, "Yuck!" until I was in Israel and I saw a flock of goats on a hillside, and they ripple. It's gorgeous! I realized there's so much we don't understand because we're in such a different culture and time.
>
> To me, it was fun. It was like a puzzle—I wanted to know this stuff. This was exciting. It didn't throw me at all. My parents had talked about this kind of stuff all the time, my church had talked about it, the adult group had talked about it. So I'd been exposed to a lot of that stuff. I didn't have the same reaction that a lot of my friends did, who were just kind of like, "Oh my God, what does this mean?"
>
> Fundamentalist students who hear this stuff never assumed that the Bible has multiple authors, or that it's dependent on the culture or the times or whatever.
>
> There were people who completely lost their faith. There were people who dropped out. There were people who weren't sure they were going to go on to the ministry—they changed what they were going to do.

Her doubts persisted, as did her desire to be a part of the Church.

> I wanted to believe in God; all those years, I wanted to. I wasn't sure if I really did or not, but I really wanted to.
>
> I felt like the Church was a family. It gave me a second chance, second home. I felt like there has to be something spiritual out there, and I wanted to be a part of it. And it gave me aim to my life, it gave purpose, it gave me direction, it got me out of my family. It was so comforting to know where I was going and what I was doing, and to love doing it. I loved it!

She enjoyed preaching in her first church, where she was one of four on the ministerial staff.

> Because I didn't have to do it very often, I didn't have to face my doubts very much. I would get to really spend a lot of time crafting a sermon, and I would pick something that was more of interest to me, that was talking about forgiveness or compassion.
>
> I would take a story in the Bible, and create some character that might not even exist, and tell the story from that person's perspective. People loved those sermons.

She eventually moved to a small, conservative congregation when its longtime pastor retired.

> When I got to my church where I had to preach every week, it was hell on wheels very quickly. . . . I was really stunned and shocked when a woman said to me, "I know what Jesus said in the Bible, because it's written in red." I remember just kind of sitting there, thinking, "Oh my God, what am I doing here?"
>
> I was not in a liberal church anymore. And when I talked about having doubts—because I've always shared my faith story with people and talked about my own struggles with it—the same woman looked at me and said, "Well, doubts are sinful. They'll make you go to Hell."

When asked her reasons for choosing such a conservative church, Winnie said she "admired their simple faith."

> I wanted to believe the way they did. I wanted that kind of fervent, deep, to your core, you-know-this-is-true.

She tried to make a go of it.

> I'd always agreed with Frederick Buechner's *Wishful Thinking*, his dictionary of faith, which defined doubt as "the ants in the pants of faith" that keep you moving.[14] So I always hung on to the idea that somehow you're not going to have the same faith you had when you were six, or when you were twelve, or when you were twenty-two. It's going to keep changing.

But she eventually left both that church and the ministry.

> I didn't feel like I could keep my integrity and stay in that church. I didn't feel like I could survive in that church. I knew I couldn't be me and be there. I know what they wanted to hear, and I couldn't give it to them.
>
> The longer I had to preach every single week, and lead Bible study every week, and deal with these people—it soured me on the entire thing. After living in a fishbowl for a while, I had no desire to be a pastor anymore.
>
> I was starting to realize I was a lesbian. The Church had banned the ordination of gays and lesbians back in 1978, before I finished seminary, so that being honest about my sexual orientation was never was going to be a possibility. And I just couldn't keep saying the words I did not believe.

She considered other, more liberal denominations, like the United Church of Christ or Unitarianism, but ultimately decided against making a change.

> I couldn't see switching denominations and having to take other people's exams, going through all those hoops again. I was done with that. And it would have required some of that, no matter what denomination I went to.

After working at a couple of counseling-related jobs, Winnie eventually went back to school for her PhD in clinical psychology.

> I think I get the best of ministry without all the crap of the Church. I really do. I mean, psychology is the study of the soul. I feel like I'm doing a lot of intervention with people in helping them figure out how

> to run their lives in a healthier way and get more of whatever it is they want.

She hasn't been back to church since leaving her pastorate. Her wife of thirteen years, a former fundamentalist, also does not attend church. At the end of the interviews, Winnie described her current views about religion.

> I believe there's something more than us, and I don't know what that is, and I have no way to define that. I don't want to put a label like "God" on it, because that has so much baggage for me.
>
> I missed believing in Santa Claus when I found out there wasn't one, and I had to fake it for my younger brother—and that's been the cycle. I wanted to believe, I embraced it wholeheartedly, and then I find out it's not true and I miss it. I look for something all-good and all-powerful and all-encompassing, and it's not there. I don't feel that I'm completely separate from any kind of spirituality. I would say that where I'm feeling it is in my gardening, being out in nature. I miss the fact that it doesn't have to do with community. But it really doesn't.

Carl, the Lutheran Pastor: Persevering Through the Pain

Carl is a mid-career Lutheran pastor of a liberal church in the Midwest. He has two children in college and a devoted wife who is aware of his lack of belief but does not share it. Carl describes himself as a "womb to tomb" Lutheran who felt called to the ministry as a young man.

> Part of my sense of call was a pretty emotionally charged thing, particularly at the camp. It was a place where families would come together for a week, and it was a very emotionally intense kind of experience. People would come in on Sunday and, over time, would sort of let their guard down, and there would be some pretty deep sharing that would happen. Typically, the Friday evening candlelight and Holy Communion services were pretty emotionally powerful events—lots of tears, lots of hugs, lots of good feeling. And it was in that environment that I had this strong feeling of being called to ministry—in addition to a discovery that my love of history connected pretty nicely with Church history, biblical studies, theology, philosophy, thinking about life in more than simply concrete ways.

He reflected carefully on his decision at the time, but has since questioned his reasoning.

> Who am I to be saying yes to this, and who am I to claim the Church's authority and to speak for God? It seemed—and still seems, at times—a bit overwhelming if a bit absurd, increasingly so, that a human being can claim to speak for God. I'm more and more skeptical of people who say, "God told me" or "I heard God say this to me." I've used that same language myself, but even when I used it at all, I used it sparingly. I might say, "Well, I think that this could be of God," or "I think this might be what was meant there." So I wonder, "Who am I to be doing this?" and I get a deep sense of my own humanity, my own imperfections. I think I'm a reasonably good, decent person, but in no way perfect.

When Carl went to seminary, after a rigorous academic and psychological acceptance process, he easily accepted the historical/critical method of studying the Bible and was interested in learning Greek and Hebrew, the Bible's principal original languages. This perspective "really unlocked some things that helped to make sense of what was going on." However, as he studied further, he had mixed emotions about what he was learning.

> The process of demythologizing Scripture was at the same time exciting and troubling, in the sense of looking, for example, at the two Creation narratives in Genesis and seriously saying, "OK, if they're not in fact true as people often define truth, then what are they? What's the purpose? Why are they important? What might be a different way of thinking about them?" The older I got—and I think this is true for a lot of people—the older I got, you look at those stories and you think it's ridiculous to think that this could be literally true in any way.

While he was "beginning to ask those questions," he continued "trusting [his] professors, who managed to hang in there with their own vows of ordination and teaching in a seminary of the Church."

> I was so set on this career path by then that at times I thought, "Well, you know, that's just the professor's perspective." Then at other times, I just took it in. And then at other times it was overwhelming.

He realizes the limitations of seminary training.

> Seminary's a place for a lot of questions, but it's also a vocational preparation school. Seminaries are in the business of providing pastors for the Church, which isn't to say that what we did there was superficial, because it wasn't. It was good scholarship, but finally, of the Church.

It was after years of repeating the liturgy and Bible verses that Carl began to read contemporary liberal Christian writers and revisit questions he had had in seminary.

> More and more, I paid attention to what's happening in the world, and I was having a difficult time squaring that with the problem of evil—the problem of bad things happening to good people, or bad things happening to people for no apparent reason. And then just sort of falling back on, "Well, you just don't understand," or "It's God's will," or "Only the good die young," or "God wants that person in Heaven." It begins to break down. So then I moved to really a pretty heavy focus on Jesus and who he is, and that's what drew me to the Jesus Seminar and Marcus Borg and Dominic Crossan and Bishop John Spong.
>
> I love the term that Spong uses—the whole idea of debunking supernatural theism. What does it mean if we begin to say, "OK, is there an interventionist God? And if so, then why do these things happen? And if not, then what?" Then how do we understand God at all—the concept of God, using the name of God?
>
> If I could have a completely candid conversation with Marcus Borg,[15] where he could be safe to answer, I'd like to ask him, "Do you believe in God at all?" And I don't mean that as a hostile question. Part of me would be comforted if he said, "No, this is a philosophical system. This is a system of finding our way through this world. But ultimately there is no sort of supernatural or cosmic other. This is what it is."
>
> I'd like to ask Borg how he has managed to keep his sanity with all of his writing and his teaching. He seems like a very mystical guy, but at times it does seem to me like he's putting it on so that he can still have a voice in the Church, because his whole thing is about what he calls "adult theological re-education": "precritical naïveté," deconstruction, and "postcritical naïveté." It's undoing childhood stuff and then going through a period of pretty profound deconstruction, but then reconstructing something at the end. It's like Paul Tillich's

> idea of God as the ground of being. Sometimes that makes sense to me; sometimes that sounds like gobbledygook. What does he mean, "the ground of being"? And how does one love the ground of being? I guess I'm not that smart.

Carl rejects "this understanding of God as this supernatural being out there" but still finds value in upholding Christian stories and traditions.

> More and more, I think Christianity has to do with living a good life. I think the lessons of Jesus are profound and apply to life, without needing any sense of "other." For instance, when I preach at a funeral of a lifelong faithful Lutheran, I think I need to be a good steward of the tradition. But I've pretty much rejected the idea of Heaven and Hell; it doesn't make sense to me.

Being a "steward of the tradition" and "an apologist for the Lutheran faith," as he put it, can be difficult.

> There's some dissonance because of my doubting. I'll say all the right words, do all the right prayers—sort of enter into it. But, yeah, it's tough for me.

Carl also expressed concern about being found out.

> If folks in my congregation knew I was having this discussion with you, it would not go down well, understandably. So maybe I'm looking for some answers myself, you know. Something about your study grabbed my attention and was intriguing enough for me to send an e-mail. But it's hard—it's hard for me.

He provided a typical dialogue showing how he approaches colleagues in the clergy about his concerns.

> When I've tested this a little bit—granted, a limited sample—it hasn't gone down real well. For instance [I'll say,] "Hey, have you read Marcus Borg's *Meeting Jesus Again for the First Time*?"
>
> "Oh, that guy's a heretic, and he's way out there, and he's a radical, wild liberal!"
>
> "OK, thanks. See ya."

He speculates on the reasons for his colleagues' responses.

> I don't think a lot of my colleagues are having the struggles I'm having, because they have simply chosen to compartmentalize it [their faith]. And for those who don't have the struggle, God bless them! I don't enjoy this. I hate it, actually. I wish it were easier for me. Most days, I wish I could just believe it and be done with it and go on. I haven't been able to do that.

Carl has a few friends he has discussed some of his concerns with: a group of retired Lutheran ministers and a buddy from seminary who didn't finish. This is how he paraphrases the advice from the retired ministers:

> Well, we long ago gave up on the idea that any of this is literally true, so what's the big deal? Why not simply appreciate the aesthetics of it and the meaning and purpose it gives to people. And if stuff seems like BS to you, well, don't preach it. You don't throw out the baby with the bathwater.

And that of the seminary buddy:

> You know, if this doesn't seem good for you or good for your health or good for whatever, why don't you do something else?

Carl says his response is to "kind of drop the subject and move on." Several years ago, he started a weeknight book-discussion group with parishioners. Their reading has included Borg's *The God We Never Knew*; *A New Kind of Christianity*, by the progressive evangelical pastor Brian McLaren; and books by the very liberal retired Episcopal bishop John Shelby Spong.

> Well, first of all, I say up front, "I am the facilitator of this group—I'm not teaching." Part of that, to be candid, is a little bit self-protective, but also I don't want to be seen as the authority, a pastor who is teaching from on high. I come prepared, and I ask questions, and I basically say there will be no judgment in the group. It will be an open discussion.

Carl has thought of leaving the ministry, and he applied for numerous jobs; however, he was not offered any he found sufficiently appealing.

> I think if somebody had said to me, "Here's a job that has nothing to do with God or deep thoughts or philosophy or anything having to do with the Church, and we'll give you the same amount of money," I would have taken it. But it wasn't there, so I didn't.

He has also considered becoming a minister in the Unitarian Universalist Church, which accepts nonbelievers both as members and clergy. Still, he feels the pull of his Lutheran roots.

> There's also the ecclesiastical sense of call. So there might be times when that inner sense of call is not very strongly felt, but you hear the Church calling. And it's embedded in my mind that the Church's call is God's call—that God is in the community, the spirit at work in and through the community. So when there have been doubts, the Church has always been there to say, "No, you're called to do this. You're good at it, you're good with people, you're a good public speaker, and so on."

He recognizes the positive role the Church has played in his life, and he fears the effect that his loss of belief could have if it were known.

> The Church has been my community all my life, OK? It's a place of meaning, a place of purpose, a place of affirmation, a place of wonderful music and relationships, a creative place. The community of the Church has been the thing that has supported me and been there for me through the best and worst of it. So to question, in a very fundamental way, the basic tenets upon which this institution exists, is, for me, enough to cause me to quake a little bit. . . . I have kids in college, so it's frightening to think that all that could be taken away if I ask too many questions or raise too many issues publicly, so I keep a lot of this in the closet. But I think there are times when I have physical symptoms. I don't like the term "anxiety attacks," but sometimes I'll read a hymn while we're singing it—a great old hymn that I've loved all my life—and take another look at the text and think, "That is absurd!" I love this music—bizarre language that I have sung with full voice without even thinking about it.

Carl decided he did not want to talk confidentially with other nonbelieving clergy because it would just "stir things up" for him. He plans to stay in parish ministry until his retirement.

Brian, the Lutheran Seminary Dropout: Dodging a Bullet

Brian is a government contractor in his thirties from the Midwest who calls himself "a naturalist, a materialist." We decided to interview him to get the perspective of a person who recognized his nonbelief before making a commitment. He contacted us after reading the 2010 pilot study—not to participate in the present study but to urge us on in our research, noting that:

> I fall into the category of those who dodged that bullet by deciding at the last minute not to continue on to seminary after college. I didn't realize at the time how much trouble I was saving myself.

Still, openly stating his views on religion ("I don't have a belief in the supernatural") is a relatively new experience for him.

> For the longest time, for many years, I didn't give it much thought, really. It was just sort of in the background of my daily life.
>
> On some level, not being religious was my default condition. As far as having the courage to acknowledge it internally, or even say it out loud to someone in a low-risk environment, like a coworker who I already knew wasn't a churchgoer, I would say it's fairly recently—within the past couple of years—that I really felt comfortable enough, as a fully formed adult, that I could demand basic human respect from people, that I didn't have to use the idea of religion to encourage them to accept me.

His Lutheran religious training allowed for some questioning.

> I was raised to believe that questioning our faith is natural—but not too much questioning. If you were having serious doubts, you needed to read your Bible. You needed to pray about it; you needed to reflect on how best to forgive yourself this fault and soldier on.

As a child, becoming a pastor seemed like a natural choice for Brian.

> I was brought up to believe that joining the clergy was one of the best things you could do with your life. And in conjunction with the fact that my particular set of inborn talents was uniquely appropriate for that duty, it seemed a natural progression for me, according to everyone around me. "Oh, he's so good at public speaking. Wouldn't he make a great pastor? He's so smart about memorizing Bible verses. He's so compassionate with his friends and his family members—isn't that a great quality for a minister?"

Brian attended a Lutheran high school and graduated from a Lutheran college with a double major, in communications and pre-seminary studies. Most of the hour-long Skype call with Brian was spent discussing his religious education.

> I studied ancient Greek and Old Testament Hebrew, and the contemporary Old Testament texts, and things like that. They're fairly frank there [at his college] about acknowledging how the Bible was put together in the first place. But no one at that school denied that it was all divinely inspired.
>
> Even in high school, we were already taught some of the historical information about how the Bible was compiled, and so on. There wasn't a moment in a college course when the professor shattered all my illusions about the divine inspiration of the Bible. It wasn't like that. It was just sort of a gradual, "Oh, OK, so you're just saying this or that book was included or excluded—that it was a political decision. OK. But you're also telling me that God made it happen that way because that's the way He wanted it to happen." It was all very self-justifying. It was an accumulation of knowledge, and then at a certain point you just realize and accept that God was an invisible hand guiding it all—or you don't. But, yeah, when I was a little kid I was taught that Moses wrote the Pentateuch and that it was directly inspired by the Creator. You're disabused of that notion fairly quickly, once you get into the meat-and-potatoes of religion classes, particularly at the college level.
>
> It was like, "Is your faith strong enough to withstand learning these things?" And the answers all around you are, "Yes, of course. Yes, obviously. We're learning more about how great God is—that He's able to achieve all this by these means. And the outside world, the secular world, won't understand, because they *can't* understand, and how lucky are we?"
>
> It's not an intellectual exercise. It's not an academic pursuit—it sort

of masquerades as one, but at its core it's a test of trust in each other. Are you or aren't you one of us? And woe to the one who doesn't toe the line. There's a lot of psychological pressure to conform, and when I was young it was too much for me. I was scared to look objectively at things, because I thought I was sinning by doing so.

I'm almost a little embarrassed now, looking back, that I didn't have the courage as a youth to stand up and ask the questions that probably a lot of people around me were thinking about too. We all just assumed that the faith that was around us was rock-solid.

After college graduation, Brian moved to another state to attend a respected Lutheran seminary, but he left after the first day of orientation.

I didn't feel that I could, in good conscience, be a faithful representative of the Church to people who were relying on me for their information about God. I had this overwhelming feeling that I was setting myself up to be a black sheep if I was too honest. Or alternatively, to be a self-loathing kind of creature if I stayed with the program, if I stuck to the talking points.

He had an explanation ready for his family about why he had changed his mind.

There's a code in the Church as to the calling: Are you [called] or aren't you? And only *you* know whether you're called. So I very simply just had to say, "You know, I didn't have the calling." A lot of information is conveyed in that simple phrase—to be called or to not be called—and it's enough for people. Now, they may ask follow-up questions, like, "Well, what do you think you're going to do?" But then it becomes a secular question, a logical question. The question of whether or not to join the clergy is a spiritual question.

Brian is now employed in a technical field for which he is well suited, and he is happily married. At the time of his interview, he and his wife had one child and another on the way. His wife is "culturally Catholic," and they plan to raise their kids that way.

I don't proselytize my son against religion. I put it in a cultural context, an historical context, for him if he has questions. So I expect that he'll be raised understanding the Christian tradition but not necessarily

> being a believer—unless, of course, he concludes on his own that it's the way to go, in which case I'll respect it. But I've got a real problem lying to my kids. I don't want to be a party to an indoctrination. I doubt if my wife would want that either, but she just sees it as a cultural heritage thing. She's not a hard-core Catholic, either.

He continues to be grateful that he did not pursue his seminary education.

> I would have been setting myself up for no end of misery had I gone into the clergy.

Glen, the Catholic Priest: Hiding among Those Who Damned Him

Glen is on an extended leave of absence from the Roman Catholic Church after ten years in the priesthood. He was raised in the United Methodist Church and as a young adult, became an Episcopalian and considered ministry in the Episcopal Church. He completed a doctorate in an unrelated field before entering a Catholic seminary. Glen felt drawn to clerical life as an adolescent.

> Even now it's hard to put into words this desire to be involved in the things of the church. . . . This desire to grow closer to God, and as you do so, to lead others to God. This desire to be involved in the liturgical and sacramental acts of the church. That was very much part of it. And I think even at that point there was an awareness of ministry as an opportunity to walk with people through the important events of their life. And that was very attractive to me as well.
>
> I remember when I sat down with my pastor and said, "I'm having these feelings that I can't quite put into words. It's almost like a calling from someone else." And he said, "Well, those are the right words to use: 'calling from someone else.'"

When Glen finished his undergraduate degree, he planned to enter Episcopal seminary, but he changed his mind after attempting to write his spiritual autobiography.

> I wrote one page, reread it, and thought, "This is the most ridiculous thing I've ever seen!" It was full of clichés and fluff and imaginative, overly romantic thinking about how God and I had been buddies all these years. I had an epiphany—that this is dishonest, and how can

> I pursue ministry when I don't have a concept of God, much less a relationship with God? And I just said, "Well, this will be past tense." And that ended my discernment in the Episcopal Church.

Glen remained an Episcopalian for a while before switching to a Catholic church.

> During my doctoral studies, I somehow fell in love with the Catholic Church. And how that all started I really don't know, other than that I was deeply in love with a guy who was Roman Catholic. So to get in good with him, I played the faithful bit. But I was rejected by him. And somehow I found myself really questioning myself, uncertain about myself, loathing myself as a gay man. I knew that the Catholic Church had some answers about morality, and about confirming that yes, there was something wrong with me.
>
> I could hide among those who were damning me. Oh, yeah, I had a lot of self-hatred, self-loathing. For the first time in my life, I had pursued a gay love interest, and it had gone horribly, horribly wrong.

The Catholic Church offered structure and safety.

> I thought, "This is a great solution to all of my sexual woes. I'll just be so good."
>
> I also sensed in the Catholic Church a more well-developed theology. I'm not quite sure why that mattered to me, but I understood it later in life: It provided answers, and I liked that; I needed that.

In the Catholic Church, the personal closeness to God that is a feature of the Episcopal faith seemed less important to him.

> In the Catholic Church, I could say that it's OK that I never fell in love with God, because I experience God through the Sacraments. I experience God through the recitation of the rosary.
>
> I may not have the warm fuzzies and the hugs that I need to live, but I will have the structure of having security. I will have the responsibilities. I will know my place, and everyone else will know their place, too.

When he applied to the seminary, he was not truthful about his sexuality.

> During my psychological evaluations, I was asked by the examining psychologist if I was gay or straight, and I said, "Straight." I lied.

Glen estimates that 50 to 75 percent of his fellow seminarians were gay, including "some who were not aware of it, so repressed that they never would have been able to access it." He recalled that the Church formally addressed celibacy but not homosexuality.

> Every year, we were required to have a sexuality seminar, where often we brought in an outside speaker and talked about sexual integration, about how to have healthy friendships, and how to be a happy celibate priest. But nowhere were things like homosexuality addressed. Masturbation was never addressed, other than to be laughed about.

In seminary, he encountered widespread social dysfunction.

> There was dysfunction among the faculty and the students. And I'm not excluding myself, either—I was certainly dysfunctional. There was severe emotional immaturity, severe relationship impairments.
>
> There was no expressed interest in getting to know people as individuals. I wouldn't ask, "How are you doing today?" I would ask, "Hey, have you done your rosary yet? Would you like to pray the rosary with me?" Or, "I hear your mom died. I'll do a novena to the Blessed Mother."
>
> There's a superficiality and social posturing in seminary that uses religious language to pat people on the head. People are trying to outdo each other in terms of piety and in terms of perceived socially aligned power relationships—for instance, "Well, my bishop is more popular than your bishop."

As for his academic experience at seminary, he enjoyed his studies even as he questioned some of what he was learning.

> A lot about Church history I just found fascinating! So much of it was new to me. And there is something about the complexity of Catholic theology that is really engrossing. But alongside the interest, there were also times in which I was troubled by something.
>
> We were studying atonement theory, and I thought, "Was there not a better way to save humanity than to resort to human sacrifice?" But

we were not encouraged to ask those kinds of questions. This particular professor mocked those who did ask those kinds of questions.

We learned about how the Bible was written and how it came to be. It's a mess! And when we study it semantically, we realize it's a joke—I mean, it is an absolute tragedy. It's just carryovers from other traditions; I could figure that out on my own. Then when there is repetition of stories within the Bible, the professor would say, "Well, these are just two different sources that were sewn together, but that's OK." There are always answers for these things.

Glen accepted the miracles of the New Testament without questioning.

The prophecy about Mary may have said "young woman" and not "virgin," but Christ also happened to be born of a virgin out of necessity—that he not be tainted by Original Sin, which is transmitted by sexuality. So it's taking some Scripture and Catholic theology and fusing them together to provide a nice answer. I thought, "Well, that makes sense! That's a nice answer!" I just wanted answers. I wanted things I could write down and regurgitate.

In Christology class, we learned the importance of setting aside scientific proofs when it comes to theology—saying there is scientific natural history and there's also God's supernatural history. And the Resurrection is the prime example of supernatural history that suspends the laws of nature. We cannot understand it in terms of natural explanations, only supernatural explanations. And I said, "OK, sounds good to me!"

Some seminarians would ask questions, being careful not to seem personally skeptical.

They would ask the question in class in just the right way to get by with it, such as, "Well, how do we answer those who say . . . ?" And that's the clue—"those who say." Then the professor would give the answer, and you could tell the person was still wrestling with it.

Glen described other ways that some seminarians dealt with their skepticism.

Often they became more and more entrenched in conservatism. They would study the Latin Mass and the saints. They'd read only the old

> authors. Maybe they immersed themselves in overly pietistic behavior. They retreated into the safety of hyperstructure, and I think I was guilty of that to some extent.

He didn't dwell on the theological explanations he learned in seminary until he became a parish priest.

> We don't have a lot of situations where we, as seminarians, are called upon to give these answers publicly to real people in real situations, and deal with their responses. It is such a controlled environment that the rubber never quite meets the road in a seminary.
>
> It wasn't until I got to the parish giving these same answers that I realized, "Boy, what bullshit!" There was a difference hearing myself give these answers to people who were genuinely asking. I felt like a fraud. I really felt bad.
>
> Sometimes I would convince people—not because of my language, but I think because they wanted to be convinced. When I was teaching Bible study in the parish, I would often use my seminary notes. I'd written down verbatim the nice way to say these things. And if you say crazy things in a nice way, most people for a split second will say, "Well, that sounds good." And then they'll be at home and they'll say, "Now, wait a minute! That doesn't sound right."

Giving sermons was easier for Glen than answering parishioners' direct questions about Church teaching. In his sermons, Glen found ways to deflect difficult situations.

> I never preached sermons that delved into the history of the Scriptures, because I was uncomfortable doing that. It raised too many questions in my mind, and I was afraid it would raise questions in parishioners' minds, and they would then ask me about it.
>
> I often would give sermons about life lessons that we can learn from the Scriptures as literary text. For instance, one Christmas I gave a sermon about the shepherds spreading the good news after they left the stable. And what was the most effective way to do that? To live a good life. Not necessarily to preach dogma but, as St. Francis says, "To preach the Gospel at all times, and when necessary use words."
>
> As time went on, I turned more and more to these canned, prewritten sermons that you can subscribe to for about $100 a year. They were actually pretty well done, using Scripture as the grounds for

> personal development. I would always adapt it to make it sound a little bit more like me.

There was one potential sermon subject that Glen carefully avoided.

> I never preached about homosexuality, ever. If I had said something against it, I thought people might think, "He doth protest too much." If I had said something in support of gay people within the Church, then that would probably have had ramifications—I might be called into the bishop's office.
>
> I never got a sense that people knew I was gay, but I'm not naïve enough to think that nobody figured it out.

Attempting to resolve parishioners' Church-related dilemmas was painful for him.

> A young, gay man comes to see me and says, "My partner and I have a child through a surrogate. I'm a practicing Catholic, my boyfriend comes to church with me often, and we'd like to have our child baptized." And my heart is breaking at this point. Everything I know as a human being says, "Baptize this child." If you believe in the theology of infant baptism, we're doing this for the child—to guarantee that he goes to Heaven. Plus, this is a practicing Catholic man whose partner comes to Mass often. But to my eternal—if there's such a thing—regret, I refused to baptize the child. I said, "Our Church loves you as a gay man, we support you as an individual, but we cannot support your lifestyle, so we cannot baptize your child." He started crying and pretty much stormed out, and I never saw him back again. That was the first major experience I had of realizing that what I did was harmful and disingenuous and fake.
>
> A parishioner asked if it would it be OK for his non-Catholic wife to take Communion. And both I and my superior said no, and the letter of the law says no. Here's a good woman, truly. She was raising Catholic kids, living a quasi-Catholic life. She would have converted in a heartbeat if it hadn't been for her family of origin. I still feel sick today about it.

As time went on, it became harder for Glen to accept his role as a representative of the Church.

> There were a lot of these experiences, feeling like a fake or fraud or

disingenuous, and they were increasing in power for me and really caused me to question. At first, I would never have admitted to not believing in the entire system. I'd think, "Well, this is just a crack in the foundation." But as time went along, I became more and more aware of cracks that I knew were there all along but just kind of pretended they weren't.

There's a horrible lack of humaneness regarding marriage and remarriage issues. There's close-mindedness to scientific progress beneficial to people—like birth control and condoms for people in Africa to combat AIDS.

I became aware of my own emptiness as a priest. Not just because I didn't enjoy it; I did enjoy some of the duties. I just couldn't effectively convey a belief system that was less and less real or believable to me.

After he told his bishop that he was unhappy and thinking of leaving, the bishop sent him to a retreat facility to "read and pray and reflect and do Mass." The psychotherapy he received while on retreat gave him additional insight.

Pretty early on, I knew that finding a different assignment wasn't the answer, because I would still be playing a role I didn't feel comfortable playing anymore and giving answers I didn't believe in. And I was dissatisfied with living an increasingly double life, going to Mass and saying, "Well, this is just a waste of time. Do people really believe this? Because I don't."

"It's true whether you believe it or not," was something I heard along the way. But I didn't believe that the bread changes to anything. My first awareness of my thinking was when someone dropped a Communion host and I wasn't at all alarmed. People will freak out if the host drops; a priest will take it and eat it. I would never do that; that's nasty. I'd throw it in the yard.

After much reflection, he accepted his unbelief.

I've wondered: Did my beliefs change, or did I confront a lack of belief that had been there all along? I think it's probably more that I refused to acknowledge a lack of belief because I so desperately wanted to believe. I needed the structure of church; I believed in the institutional Church and felt that was satisfactory enough. But the less I came to believe and trust the institution, the comfort faded. So I'm now left with the God that should be behind the Church that I don't really believe in.

I do not believe in the Christian God. I do not believe in the God that is recorded in the New Testament or the Old Testament. I do not believe in the God that is portrayed in the Christian creeds. I am fairly certain that there is no God—99 percent certain.

There's no God who is invested in our lives. There's no God who is by nature a relational being. The less than 1 percent of me holding out the possibility that there is would see it more as some kind of a vague force, an energy. But, again, in my mind it's so far-fetched and so remote a possibility that I really don't have a refined concept of what a god would be like if it did exist.

He considered the possibility that he had not believed for a long time.

I remember fairly early on in my priesthood saying to myself that I really don't think there's anybody listening. And I admitted to myself that I'm probably doing this out of a sense of duty, for some kind of psychological compulsion. I wasn't praying because I believed I was communicating with God, I was praying to assuage guilt for not doing it.

He started paying attention to information about nonbelief.

The very last year of priesthood, I read atheist writers like Richard Dawkins and Sam Harris. They just made sense to me; they hit my own logical thinking.

I remember watching episodes of *South Park* about the Catholic Church,[16] and thinking, "There is probably more truth in this than there is in all the New and Old Testaments—more truth about religion and the portrait of God that we humans have created for ourselves." Things like that, even though not scientific and not reason-based or particularly intellectual, still stuck with me.

When he decided to take a leave of absence, the first step in formally leaving the priesthood, his family was supportive but perplexed.

I didn't talk with my mother about it much, because I sensed that it just added to her confusion about why someone would walk away from a career they've trained for and seemed to enjoy. She has some Catholic friends who went to my parish, so she knows that I was well liked, well regarded. So for her it just doesn't make a lot of sense.

Now that he was away from the Church, preparing to reenter his pre-seminary profession, he reflected on how his life was changing.

> On Sunday mornings, I'm not quite sure what to do with myself. For quite a while, I did go to Mass, because I felt it was expected of me. But that was such an uncomfortable experience, internally and externally, with people seeing me there on the other side of the altar. I would force myself to go up and receive Communion, because I wanted to be seen receiving Communion. But I felt like a fraud doing that. So, I do miss the community. I do miss the being around people. I do miss having something in your life that you can count on taking place once a week for an hour.

As the last interview ended, Glen had a few final points he wanted to make.

> I want to help others—I believe that the kind of research you're doing can be very impacting.
>
> The breaking point came one morning when I was putting the clerical collar around my neck and I felt like I was putting on a shackle—you know, those old iron shackles? Leaving the priesthood was like taking the shackles off. It really was a sense of freedom, even though I was walking into great uncertainty.
>
> I knew of a priest who committed suicide and it came out afterwards how unhappy he was as a priest, as a person. I remember saying to myself when it happened, "Boy, I will never let myself get that unhappy."

Joe, the Mormon Bishop: A Hopeful Agnostic

Joe is a Mormon in his early forties, about halfway through his five-year term as bishop, or pastor, of his ward (congregation). The Church of Jesus Christ of Latter-day Saints does not have lifelong career clergy; instead, respected men in the community are called upon to act as bishops in addition to their secular occupation.[17] When their five-year terms are up, they leave that office—although they may be called upon again to serve the Church in one or another capacity. Joe has five children, the older ones in their teens, and a wife who is a stay-at-home mom and a dedicated church member. Both he and his wife come from families that have been Mormon for generations.

Joe's first questioning of his faith started a few years ago, when he became more active on the Internet.

> I think the Internet was a big factor, just beginning to research some of the questions about my faith and its origins.
>
> You know how you're on the Internet and something strikes your eye? You say, "Oh, that's kind of interesting. I'll just check that out—I'll just kind of browse." So I began to read some articles of an unorthodox nature that began to cause me to expand my perspective a little bit and help me to see things from a different point of view. I've always tried to be an open-minded person, so I began to see things from a different side.

One piece of information that Joe learned on the Internet particularly disturbed him.

> I was always taught that Joseph Smith had these gold plates and he had a tool to translate them with a scribe. Well, I come to find out that's not really how it happened. How it happened is, the gold plates aren't even there, or they're covered up in some way. He's got a hat, with what's called a seer stone, that he previously used to go treasure hunting with. He's got that in the hat, he's looking in the hat, and then this kind of dictating is coming to him. So I'm wondering, "What's the purpose of the gold plates, then." Right?
>
> The Church has no artistic representations of Joseph's face in a hat. And now I'm hearing about the hat, and I'm like, "I never heard about the hat. How come I never heard about the hat?" So, it's hard, you know—I mean, something like that is devastating.

Based on some of his Internet readings, he started to think of some Mormon teachings as being symbolic rather than literal.

> What goes on inside the literal Temple is kind of a macrocosm of what goes on inside your bodily temple. You are really the center, and how you create harmony and unity inside you is really what's more important than the actual, literal ordinances or sacraments or ceremonies. There was something about that that made sense to me and appealed to me. It provided more spiritual nourishment.

However, there are problems with the symbolic approach to Mormonism.

> The downside of that is that if you don't look at it literally, then you start to question what is literal and what is symbolic. Is there literally a God, or is that a symbolic thing? Is Joseph Smith literally a prophet, or is that more of a symbolic thing? So you start to examine those different points of view, and you start to question and wonder and examine what you believe.
>
> The Mormon faith is very black and white; there's not a lot of gray area that you can work with. Even my just talking superficially about the Temple with you would make a lot of Mormons feel very uncomfortable.
>
> There's no pathway that says doubt is a part of faith, from my experience in Mormonism. It's always "to know." "I know the Church is true. I know Jesus is the Christ. I know Joseph Smith is a true prophet." That's what you say every month in the Testimony Meeting. You get up spontaneously and you say, "I know these things are true." Nobody gets up there and says, "I have faith, I believe."

He also placed great stock in having spiritual experiences, until he learned more about them on the Internet.

> For Mormons, the idea of how you come to know that something is true involves having a spiritual experience where the spirit testifies to you or tells you that something is true.
>
> I've had some really special spiritual experiences—I would say that for me it transcends mere emotion. It's something I can't explain, necessarily. But then through my curiosity on the Internet, I began to find out that Mormons are not that unique. People who are Catholic, Protestant, Muslim, Buddhist, are having spiritual experiences, too.
>
> If God wants everybody to be Mormon because Mormonism is the true Church, why would He give other people spiritual experiences that would confirm their own faith tradition and send them out on that trajectory? It's confusing, you know.

Joe is struggling with his beliefs.

> It didn't feel good to me anymore to say that what I believe trumps everybody else. It's like the toothpaste is out of the tube and you can't push it back in.

I don't know what I believe anymore, you know. I don't know that I can hang my hat on anything. I do feel like there's love out there. I don't know that I can confidently, on a literal level, say that there's this Bearded Father that I'm going to physically embrace someday. The probability of it being exactly the way that I was taught is pretty low.

I'd probably label myself a hopeful agnostic, or a "possibility" agnostic. So probably leaning more towards theism a little bit—that something's out there. It's hard for me to let go of that.

His change of heart has been difficult for him and his wife.

You do a lot of crying. You try to talk to your wife about it, but she's still pretty orthodox, so it's hard on her. You're alone. You've got no one to talk to, because you're a bishop. You're supposed to be the leader of the congregation for five years, yet this is happening right in the middle of it. So it tears you apart, you know. You try to figure out a way . . . to carry on, because if you were to step down, that could hurt a lot of people's lives. It's hard, it's horrendous, it's painful.

The issues about the history, and some of the other things I talk about, are not a big deal for my wife. I don't think she thinks that deeply about it. The Church is a positive influence on her. It helps her to feel good. It helps her to feel connected.

Through all of this, Joe still felt like a Mormon and saw value in it for his children.

I will always call myself a Mormon. It's in my blood; it's in my DNA. It's my community on both my mom's side and my dad's side. Even if I'm not sure of the truthfulness or the literalness, I still have very positive feelings for the Church—so there's some loyalty there.

I think my positive experiences growing up Mormon tend to be more prominent than the part of me that worries that my kids are going to be in the same boat I'm in now. Yeah, they could be, but if they are, then I can be there for them.

He struggled to do right by his conscience and his congregation.

I love being able to help people through problems, to counsel them. That's good.

Some days are easy, some days are hard. I try to look for what's

> good. I try to look for how the Church is making a positive difference in people's lives. I talk like Jesus did, where everybody assumes I mean something in a literal way, and my meaning is more symbolic. I might say that I know that Joseph Smith is a true prophet of God. Now, on a literal basis, I don't totally know. But on a symbolic basis, I agree with Moses, who said, "I wish everybody was a prophet." And maybe everybody is, you know, for their own life.

When asked how he thought people understood what he said, he responded:

> I think they're taking it literally. Sometimes it's hard, because I worry that if they knew really what I was thinking and feeling, they'd be sad or angry or disappointed—devastated, maybe. But I always hold out hope that those things are true. I won't know it's literally true unless I leave this life and wake up and it's all the way I was taught. I think the probability of that happening is very low.

His changing beliefs made it difficult to carry out his duties as bishop.

> I'm in this really weird position, where a good bishop is supposed to try and bring people back into the fold. But at the same time, technically, I'm a lost sheep myself, from some people's point of view. So it's this cognitive-dissonance force, where it's just shredding me, and I want to talk with them so badly and say, "I know what you're going through." But I'm their bishop, too, you know, and I'm supposed to help them back in.

He would like to see the Mormon Church change.

> There are Mormons who want some breathing room, want some flexibility, want some reformation. They want to have that flexibility to be able to say that some things are not literally true, that it's more symbolic. I think there's a lot of Mormons who want to stay in the faith, but they want things to be a little bit different.
>
> If I'm talking to you right now, that means something. There are others out there. Maybe they don't talk about it, but I would imagine that there are some who feel the same way I do or have gone through what I'm going through.

In the meantime, he is waiting for his term as bishop to come to an end. He is glad to have an established way out and a secular career that provides financial support for his family.

> This is as far as I'm going. I decided I can't deal with the cognitive dissonance. It's too much being a leader—I'm barely surviving as it is. But I know there's a light at the end of the tunnel and that I'll be gone in the next two years or so.
>
> I'm fortunate. I know that those in other religions who have chosen ministry as a career have gone to divinity school. They've invested their whole lives in it. I can't imagine the pain they're going through. They don't have an easy exit. I'll have the opportunity to have a graceful exit, to go quietly. But they don't.

Stan, the Military Chaplain: In Search of Congruency

At the time he was interviewed, Stan was a thirty-eight-year-old, married military chaplain about to leave the service and the clergy to enter social work graduate school on the GI Bill. Raised in a fundamentalist faith in the South, he was ordained in a more liberal faith, the Disciples of Christ, before entering the chaplaincy. We met once via Skype while he was overseas and twice in person a few months later, at his final stateside assignment.

Stan had always been interested in work that focused on helping people. He had originally planned to be a pharmacist, but once in college, when he realized that science was not his strength, he became a religion major.

> At an early age I always felt that I would want to work in some sort of helping profession. I didn't know at the time what it would look like. And it just seemed that maybe the way was to help people out in the church community. It just seemed like a course of action that seemed congruent with my values growing up. I had a religious experience when I was about ten years old. I accepted the message of Christ and became baptized.

Stan was surprised by—and conflicted about—the biblical textual criticism he was learning in his Christian college, but he was determined to find a way to stay with it. So he went on to seminary, where he continued to vacillate until he discovered the field of institutional chaplaincy, which "was more about counseling and speaking with people and being with people."

Although he was happy with his choice of chaplaincy over pastoral work, he had trouble coping with an ongoing cognitive dissonance, both in seminary and later as a military hospital chaplain. (Stan also recounts some of his experiences in chapter IV, "From the Ivory Tower to the People in the Pews," which discusses the ordeals of several study participants as seminary students and later as working clergy, as their beliefs changed.) He described his feelings and his duties as a chaplain in a military field hospital as "quite intense emotionally."

> It's mainly being with patients, offering support. We have to find out their religion. If they need a priest or a rabbi, we can coordinate those visits. But for me, it's been about eighteen- or nineteen-year-old young men coming in with limbs missing.
>
> I'm thinking in terms of humanistic caring—in terms of helping people who are injured, caring for them—rather than just strictly in terms of my religious role.

He had to cope with his lack of belief as he comforted people who expected prayers and religious reassurance.

> It causes me some internal discomfort—but, again, I'm trying to combat it, because this is what they need. If someone is unconscious or on a breathing machine, I'm not going to impose my personal discomfort with prayer on them.
>
> I'm just aware that in those moments I'm being incongruent. It's an awareness that it's dishonest in a way. In the past, I've tried to process it, to get into the chaplain role. Now I find myself less and less willing and able to go there.

Despite his efforts to tailor his work to his talents and preferences and to provide the religious comfort that patients and families needed, about twelve years into his career he felt he had to leave.

> I realize I'm at a point in which the congruence can no longer be maintained. There's no point to me continuing being a symbol of, or affirming, something I have completely discarded.
>
> Staying in the clergy would be very difficult. It would be hell, I

> think—a feeling of just despair. Maybe that's a bit too harsh, but it would just be untenable, unworkable. I can't imagine continuing; I can't imagine it.

Unlike many other clergy, Stan was lucky to have a clear way out. He was young; he had funds to return to school; he had a wife with a lucrative and portable career who was supportive of his plans. He realized that he would likely react differently to his situation if all those factors were not in place.

> I can't say I've really been a theist for many years now. But I've hidden myself in the work of doing good and serving others. And I think given that scenario [in which leaving was difficult], I probably could create a reality where I'm holding it together. But it would be very, very difficult. In fact, it would probably be a situation where maybe my marriage would be a casualty, because I don't know if I could continue holding that together.

While pleased with his plans for the future, Stan also harbored fears about what people would think when they found out why he was leaving the clergy. He tried to analyze these misgivings.

> Maybe it's a fear of being rejected—by whom, I don't know—because I had invested so much time and so many years into going to school and being ordained. Maybe it's just a fear of the truth coming to light. I'm eager to let it out, and yet there's also the fear of what the consequences of that are going to be: professionally, personally, culturally. Maybe that's part of the fear.
>
> But I think part of it is living so long with this piece of myself hidden. There's just the kind of existential fear of letting it out and letting people see this is really who I am and how I feel. And so it may be just that sense of learning to say, "Hey, this is me. This is the truth," because it had been suppressed or hidden for so long.

He reflected on the factors that may have led him to this point.

> I know one big influence in my life was my maternal grandmother. She always admonished me to be, in her words, "a good boy"—polite and deferring to other people's wishes and demands. And the cost of that was kind of an internal struggle. And I think it also manifested

> itself professionally, [as in] "Well, I don't want to rock the boat," or "I don't want to give in to that." So a big process for me in recent years, personally, is to try to say, "Hey, these are *my* thoughts and feelings." And I think that also feeds into claiming this truth that I feel is truth.
>
> I really believe that everything that led me in this direction that I chose was out of a desire to do, or try to do, what I thought was doing good. And yet it felt almost like when I'm taking my cat to the vet and I've got to get him in the little kitty cage, and I trick him to get in there. And then he's trapped; he can't get out. So it's like a little trap.

While reluctant to tell his family or military colleagues about his upcoming career change, Stan was eager to tell some of his friends, and he was generally pleased with their reactions.

> Yeah, I've told my good friend, then I've told two people I went to college with. One is a Presbyterian minister, and he's very, very, very conservative.
>
> Another friend is a fairly religious guy. He did say—and this was kind of annoying—"I'm praying for you and hope that you'll return to your faith." To which I said, "OK. Well, thank you." But the context of the conversation was support. I think maybe they don't know what to say. I think they mean, "I care about you." I think they mean, "I wish you well; I want the best for you; I want to see you succeed." I think you can find all those meanings in that phrase.
>
> I think that a lot of my fear is unfounded. I think it was friends who were having a conversation about life, and it was more important to listen to each other and talk to each other than to go off and start talking about, you know, God or belief in God or the proof of belief. It was just kind of refreshing; it was just like friends talking.

He is putting off telling his mother, not sure of what her reaction would be.

> On one hand, I think she may be very supportive and interested, and on another level, I'm thinking, "Wow, she could start quoting Scripture!" And what if it does turn into that—into maybe guilt or judgment?
>
> Probably most of the anxiety I feel is coming from myself, because I don't anticipate anger or disappointment. There may be some of that, I don't know. I think she would just want me to be happy and feel I was being true to what I believe.

Now that he was about to start on his new life, away from religion, he was philosophical and accepting about his transformation.

> It was a process. It wasn't like one day ten years ago I thought, "This is crazy! I'm going to go be a social worker." It was almost as if I came to the conclusion that this is what I am. But it was a process of shedding the spiritual journey, or the religious piece. It just took time for me to take off those layers.

Sherm, the Orthodox Rabbi: Falling Out of Belief

Note: Unlike the preceding sketches, this one lacks detail regarding the subject's circumstances. This is to protect his privacy within the small community of American Orthodox Jews in which he lives and works and expects to remain.

Sherm, an Orthodox rabbi who has multiple roles and responsibilities within his congregation, describes his change in religious beliefs as "like falling out of love." He "fell out of belief"—didn't want to and didn't expect to. It happened naturally, during conversations with a member of his community who had a way of interspersing his own controversial beliefs with disturbing questions.

> He was introducing me to ideas of biblical criticism—or biblical scholarship, as it's called today. And also evolution and scientific theory, which I was brought up to think is ridiculous—that evolution could be true. It's ridiculous to think that the Bible is man-made. That's how I was brought up—extreme. I was actually brought up where even *midrash* interpretation of the Bible, which is completely far-fetched and never meant to be taken literally, was taken literally. I mean, things that would just blow your mind.
>
> So this person was introducing me to a whole new way of thinking. He never actually said it to me but he was strongly intimating that he wasn't really a believer, and it was like an introduction to a new area that I'd never been really involved in.

Sherm did not shy away from the challenges.

> Whether he presented me with biblical scholarship or scientific theories which were completely against the Bible stories, I had answers for all of them. I had ways of getting around it and living a fine observant, believing life without those problems.

He ultimately responded to his interlocutor the way he had been taught to answer this kind of question by the learned rabbis he had been exposed to in his many years of study and observance. He said, "I don't believe because I have proof or because I know there is a God. I believe because my father believed and because his father believed." Interestingly, he later found validation for this viewpoint among atheist writers.

> I've heard Christopher Hitchens and many other famous atheists say the exact same thing: If you were just to come out and say that there is no proof to all of this—that it's just that we believe because we were told to believe and they were told to believe, and so on—I'd have the most respect for a person like that. And Hitchens is right.

Although in my interviews with Sherm he stuck to the idea that his faith had simply fallen away, he realized, as they progressed, that he had also had doubts while in rabbinical school. He was able to satisfy these doubts at that time by checking early Jewish sources and learning that rabbis had found ways to reconcile science and religion.

> Even medieval rabbis had already said that if there is a scientific theory that goes against the Torah, you have to reinterpret the Torah metaphorically. That's how they explained it and that was fine with me. These medieval rabbis came up with this even before there was any science to refute.

As a student, he was also impressed by a modern Orthodox rabbi who was very clear about having accepted evolution.

> He has said straight up that he believes that the first eleven chapters of Genesis are completely metaphorical. He doesn't believe in the [Noachian] flood, and frankly it's ridiculous to believe in the flood. Modern biogeography would be impossible with the flood. You can't explain why kangaroos are only in Australia, for example. It doesn't

> really make any sense. And even though he's on the fringe, that was my one saving grace, I guess you could say. I clung to belief with this one rabbi.

He explained how Orthodox Jews can believe certain things without thinking about them.

> A lot of Orthodox belief is based on what's been accepted as the norm. Meaning it's been accepted that we don't accept evolution, so we're not going to accept it. My whole family, in its entirety is, you know, Young Earth creationist. Six days and that's it.

And he professed amazement at what intelligent people are willing to believe.

> It's interesting. In Orthodox Judaism a lot of people, very intelligent people—professionals, doctors, lawyers, who have had a decent education—believe some of the most strange things. I can understand that if you want to accept that the Torah is the word of God, you'll just accept it. But they accept things about the evil eye. They'll go to old women in Israel to get pots of lead—I'm not joking—boiled over their head, and it's stirred, and that removes the evil eye. I talked to somebody recently who seemed like an intelligent person, and he told me that his wife was sick and the doctors could not figure it out. His mother-in-law said it was *ayin hara* [the evil eye], and she said, "You have to do this, you have to do that," and within a week she was better. Intelligent people!

Still, none of this dissuades him from remaining within the Orthodox faith. He believes that Orthodox Jews have values that he will always "hold dear."

> They are universal: kindness, you know, not getting angry, getting control over your emotions. Values that I think any good person would want to instill in their own children. There are ways that Orthodoxy presents those things which is very nice—and even intellectually stimulating.

Sherm's wife, while firmly Orthodox, agrees with some of his thinking about science. He learned this when he began discussing his views with her.

> It started off with just me explaining to her why you don't have to believe the two theories about dinosaurs. One is that because dinosaurs existed in the flood, the extreme conditions made them look much older than they are. This is of course ridiculous, because we don't look at the bones themselves, we look at which level of rock they're in. And then the other one is that the dinosaurs were put here to test us. Thankfully, both of those things she thinks are ridiculous.
>
> Evolution she's not as keen on. It's very hard for her to grapple with it. Although she has never read a book about evolution, just the idea that the human being comes from something that looks like a chimpanzee is too foreign for her.

It was difficult for his wife when she asked—and he admitted—that he was a nonbeliever. He had not spoken about his lack of belief to anyone else, except in these interviews and with people in The Clergy Project (who did not know his real identity).

> My wife saw that I was getting to be less and less of a believer. She realized, I think, where I was going, and one day she just asked, "Do you just not believe anymore?" I said "No." That was the first time I said it out loud, actually. It was tough for her.
>
> To her, it's just difficult to grapple with. We have kids, and we're raising them Orthodox. She certainly would not be willing to give that up.

He hadn't given that up either—acknowledging that he was raising "Orthodox grandchildren" for his and his wife's parents. But he also felt good, as a father, to be exposing his children to a modern worldview.

> I'm very open with our kids about science. They don't even know that there's a contradiction between what the Bible says and science says, because we don't present it that way. I have books on evolution in the house, which I take out from the library all the time, and my kids see them, and they don't even think twice.

Sherm wanted to be clear that although he had by now absorbed a fair amount of atheistic and scientific information, his beliefs had changed before he started seeking it out.

> I watched lectures from Dan Dennett, Sam Harris, and others, but I really only started watching that after I fell out of belief.

These forays confirmed and deepened his convictions.

> Once you read that the scientific community has really good explanations of how things came to be, and what they don't know, they say simply, "I don't know," then the need for God slowly slips away.

He said that it's still easy to be perceived as being within the fold, since for Orthodox Jews practice is a much bigger focus than belief.

> It's easy to disguise yourself as an Orthodox Jew, because 99 percent of what makes you Orthodox is your actions. It's what you do. It's such a practice-based religion. I do everything that Orthodox Jews do. It's so systemic that I keep *shiva* [mourning period for close relatives]. I *daven* [pray] at synagogue, and I put on *tefillin* [two small black boxes strapped to the head and arm] every day. I do all these things. And nobody would ever think twice.

Later in the interviews, as he reflected on his having become an atheist (as he readily called himself), he expressed surprise that it had happened.

> Never in a million years. I mean, until two years ago I thought there was full evidence of divine revelation on Mount Sinai. There's a book that presents the evidence of how you can't fake a mass divine revelation, because it's just too hard for so many people to lie to their kids; it would never work.

When pressed to describe his feelings as his beliefs fell away, he strove to be specific.

> I can't really pinpoint the emotions. It certainly wasn't anger. It wasn't disappointment. It was just, "OK, this is another transition. It's another change I'm going to make in my life."
>
> One of the things I felt was a little bit disappointed—and kind of

> embarrassed, like I had spent an entire life working towards something and it's nothing. It's a little foolish—I felt a little foolish. But I wasn't angry; I wasn't angry at anyone. I still have a lot of respect for the religion and for religious people.
>
> A little excited, I guess—excited that maybe I've really latched onto something. Maybe that was the excitement. But it wasn't major. I think validation would be the most strong reaction.

He was comfortable with the tactics he was using to keep his secret and stay within his community.

> I avoid anything that could really get me into trouble. I think I could say something like, "God is evil." I don't have a good answer to that. And there are ways to say that the world is billions of years old and not be in any trouble. But I would never say that evolution is true, because that *can* get me into trouble.

He appreciated his interviews with me and his participation in The Clergy Project as the only outlets for discussing his new way of thinking.

> Joining The Clergy Project and coming here [to the interviews] are big steps for me. They're kind of like my rite of passage into this world.
>
> There is no one I feel that I can turn to about this. At least, no one who's accessible to me. And I don't think I would appreciate what they would have to say to me.

He was resigned to living this way for personal and practical purposes.

> Sometimes I feel it's a little ridiculous—a little bit like playing games. But right now I just tell myself that it's just part of my job.
>
> It's not so easy. A lot of what I'm doing, I believe, is just what it is: made up by farmers and barbaric, ancient people. It's just—strange.
>
> If I were to come out, I believe that my father would probably never talk to me. It's very, very possible. If he would, I would be shocked.

Though he intends to keep his beliefs secret for a lifetime, he hoped he was contributing to a more secular society in the future.

> One reason I'm happy to be part of the study is just for me. I ultimately

want to be on what I believe is going to be the right side of history. Down the road, people will look back at studies like this and say, "They got it right." That's what I'm hoping for.

III. BREAKING THE SHELL
Transparency and the Survival of Religions

Daniel C. Dennett

There was a great Hasidic rabbi who used to say that a Jew sees more on the subway in one ride from Williamsburg to the city than the Jews used to see in the shtetl—back in the early days—in their whole lifetimes.

—Sherm, Orthodox rabbi

The second law of thermodynamics tells us that everything wears out in the end—"In time, the Rockies may tumble, Gibraltar may crumble, they're only made of clay." Living things defy the second law for a while, extracting energy and materials to repair and renew themselves, and of course reproduce themselves, staving off death and extinction indefinitely. Religions, as self-perpetuating social institutions, similarly defy the second law, and they do it thanks to design features that bear a striking resemblance to the mechanisms of the simplest living things: cells.[18] In order to survive and reproduce, a cell needs:

1. a way of extracting and using energy—that is, a metabolism;
2. a way of reproducing—copying its particular solutions to the problem of staying alive into other, offspring systems;
3. a protective membrane to keep the good stuff in and the bad stuff out.

The membrane must have entrances and exits, of course, under the control of the inner machinery—not only to acquire the energy and excrete the waste products but also to acquire useful outside information to guide its trajectory. Here, too, the essential trick is finding ways of letting the good stuff in while keeping the useless and subversive stuff out, or else neutralizing or destroying the bad stuff once it gets in. Cells have evolved many ways of dealing with these requirements, including extra internal membranes to protect specialized modules, all manner of sentries to keep the enemies out, and inner patrols to keep the peace within.

Religions have rediscovered many of the same mechanisms. This is not really a case of Art copying Nature, since most of these features of religions had been in place for centuries before the discoveries of cell biologists. Rather, it is a case of convergent evolution. Similarly, dolphins didn't copy sharks when the dolphins' mammalian ancestors joined sharks in the oceans millions of years later; evolution by natural selection reinvented the hydrodynamic sharklike shape a second time. Good tricks tend to get reinvented again and again.[19] Looking at the plight of pastors through the lens of evolutionary theory yields a compelling sense of the Good Tricks that have culturally evolved to deal with the problems and forces that have shaped practices and traditions over the centuries. What the Darwinian perspective adds to traditional interpretations of these mechanisms is the recognition that Good Tricks need not have clever, devious designers; they may evolve by differential replication. There are reasons why the surviving variations work so well, but nobody needs to have appreciated these reasons. The practices and policies may have emerged by happenstance and been adopted with a mere glimmer of understanding, or even utter misunderstanding, but they then "paid for themselves" by enhancing the fitness of the institutions incorporating them.

It is well known that different religions handle the membrane problem in different ways and with different results. At one extreme are secretive sects and cults, highly xenophobic and isolated, prohibiting access to all outsiders and severely restricting the inflow of information from all media to their members. Less insulated but still heavily sheltered are Orthodox Jews; the Hutterites; Anabaptists, such as the Amish; the Druze; some varieties of Muslims, especially the women; some varieties of Buddhist monks; and Christian monks and nuns. At the other extreme are churches that advertise an open-door policy, welcoming all and attempting, with varying degrees of success, to render their members immune to all the alien material rushing in.

There is a systemic problem that all religions face, no matter which policy they adopt: Somebody has to monitor the external world to decide what to let in and what to censor (if possible). Moreover, some of what gets in needs to be detoxified somehow, and doing this means that somebody has to attend carefully to the dangerous material. How do these monitors protect *themselves* from the dire effects of the poisons? Not very well, and the task is getting harder every day. Does it ever happen, for instance, that a church leader gets to know the enemy in order better to combat it, only to be persuaded by the encounter that the enemy is right? Yes, indeed. Several of our clergy—Glen, the Catholic priest; Adam, a Church of Christ minister from our pilot study; and Harry, a former Lutheran and nondenominational pastor interviewed for the present study, for instance—sought out books by the New Atheists (Richard Dawkins, the late Christopher Hitchens, Sam Harris, and myself, among many others) only to find themselves persuaded by them.

The media have become well stocked in recent years with new expressions of disbelief, bringing taboo topics into general currency and confronting defenders of religion with a delicate choice. Should they avert their eyes and urge their flocks to do likewise, in the hope that these subversive themes will recede? Or should at least some of their members examine the new threats and try to disarm them, discredit them, extinguish them? Religions are not alone in facing this quandary. How much sex education do parents want their children to get, and when and how should they get it? And the problems are not new.

How 'ya gonna keep 'em, down on the farm,
After they've seen Paree?
How 'ya gonna keep 'em away from Broadway;
Jazzin' around and paintin' the town?
How 'ya gonna keep 'em away from harm?
That's a mystery;
They'll never want to see a rake or plow,
And who the deuce can parleyvous a cow?

How 'ya gonna keep 'em down on the farm,
After they've seen Paree?[20]

Religion's defenders (the monitors guarding the membranes) have had to deal with this problem in one form or another for centuries, but it has become much more severe with the rapid spread of electronic media. The Roman Catholic Church's notorious *Index Librorum Prohibitorum* (Index of Prohibited Books) was initiated by Pope Paul IV in 1559, in response to the rising tide of printed books in the wake of Gutenberg. It lasted for over four hundred years and was quietly abolished after the Church realized that it was not only ineffective but also counterproductive, inciting curiosity about the listed books. (Compare "Banned in Boston," an epithet once much sought by Broadway shows.) Books and other print media continue to storm the gates, but their role is beginning to be overshadowed by the electronic media. *South Park* had an episode about Catholicism that made an impression on Glen, the Catholic priest who has lost his faith. And the Church of Jesus Christ of Latter-day Saints decided to respond to the smash-hit Broadway musical *The Book of Mormon* (written and directed by the creators of *South Park*) by running an advertisement in the show's program, a wise concession to the obvious new truth: There is no effective way to reassert the traditional privilege of religions not to be treated satirically and critically. It is worth noting that the underlying problem also besets the best-intentioned news media: Should they broadcast a story about some evil hoax or urban legend sweeping the Internet? Won't exposing it have the unintended effect of rendering it more credible to many viewers who may not even have encountered it?

Why might a television cartoon be a more potent faith-breaker than a carefully argued book? There are many obvious reasons, but one that has not been sufficiently understood is the role of *mutual knowledge*. Whenever you read a book, there is bound to be, somewhere in the back of your mind, a sense of the many others who have read or will read it. Pulling a book from a library shelf and seeing by the slip pasted in the back that only one other person before you has ever checked it out has quite a different effect from seeing a long list of prior readers: The book instantly becomes more potent, in ways seldom reflected upon. Is the book now more authoritative, just because others have read it? No, not necessarily, but it can be seen to have been a bit more influential than the average book. It has attracted attention. Perhaps the book has been popular, unduly popular, with readers for bad reasons; perhaps it is notorious, not celebrated; but still, you are not the only person to have read at least some of the sentences in this book. You are not an audience of one. Why do advertisers pay such extraordinary amounts for twenty or thirty seconds on the Super Bowl? Because they know that hundreds of millions of people will be watching *and will themselves know that hundreds of millions of people are watching and will know that these hundreds of millions will also know that hundreds of millions are watching.* That is a spectacular amount of mutual knowledge, and it pays off in heightened credibility.

How so? Well, would you pay millions for an advertisement and then make claims in your ad that could be scrutinized for falsehood by hundreds of millions of potential whistle-blowers? What someone is willing to say "in public" has always had this added credibility, for good reason, and the electronic media permit the public arenas to be multiplied by many orders of magnitude. People don't need to reason it out explicitly; they can just find themselves being particularly impressed by what is said in public. This is a simple example of the reasons that can lie behind a practice that becomes popular and eventually traditional. Nobody has to have theorized explicitly about the added value of a public pronouncement in which mutual knowledge is maximized; once its success is noted, it will be copied and its success confirmed.

Imagine you're a Catholic watching the *South Park* episode on Catholicism. The fact that it makes your religion look ridiculous is bad enough, but that fact is multiplied by your realization that millions of people are laughing and those millions know that millions are laughing. Your religion is in danger of becoming a standing joke! How does the isolated viewer know that millions are not just watching but laughing? Because this is commercial television; if the program were too offensive, too obnoxious, it wouldn't be broadcast (note that this is manifestly not the case with Web sites). Apparently, your neighbors don't just tolerate this denigration of the tenets and practices of your religion; they may well enjoy it.

A television documentary provides another telling moment. Sherm, the rabbi, recalled watching a conversation between Richard Dawkins and the Nobel laureate physicist Steven Weinberg, in which Weinberg mentioned that he had a friend who was an Orthodox Jew and an atheist. This, in a way, gave Sherm permission to be an atheist. He wouldn't be alone—there were some really smart Orthodox Jews (friends of Nobel laureates!) who managed to be atheists. And now the world knew this—they talked about it on television, after all. It was an open secret.

Religions aren't the only institutions facing novel problems of maintaining their membranes, their metabolisms, their very lives, in the face of the challenging new environment into which we are thrust. The transparency of information engendered by electronic media has dramatically changed the epistemological environment—the environment of knowledge, belief, error, illusion, confidence—that we all inhabit. It threatens the security and stability of all institutions that depend on confidence and trust—which includes, besides religions, such disparate entities as newspapers, banks, hospitals, universities, and governments. If a reliable source of information loses its reputation for telling the truth, it may be out of business, no matter how scrupulously it checks the facts it promulgates. So a new arms race ensues, dealing in the manipulation of reputations for truth-telling, and its campaigns can be detected on all sides. Al Jazeera has an excellent and deserved reputation in most of the world outside the United States for truthful reporting. Will its recent acquisition of Al Gore's news Web site finally secure Al Jazeera's respectability in this country, or will it damage Gore's reputation? [As of this expanded edition, Al Jazeera is now widely available on American satellite and cable providers.] *Time Magazine* continues its print edition in the United States, whereas *Newsweek* abandoned its U.S. edition in 2012 and that edition now exists solely on the Web. In recent decades, both magazines tried bolstering sales by running favorable cover stories on religious topics: the Shroud of Turin, the Dead Sea Scrolls, the Gnostic Gospels, new interpretations of putative relics and archeological discoveries. They clearly saw the security of religious institutions as a possible lifeboat to cling to, but in retrospect it is not obvious that the choice was wise.

Oxford zoologist Andrew Parker has proposed, in his 2003 book *In the Blink of an Eye*, that the Cambrian Explosion of novel life-forms, which occurred some 540 million years ago, was triggered by a change in the chemistry of the atmosphere or the seas or both—a change that increased the transparency of these media, letting much more sunlight in, making vision possible for the first time. Suddenly it paid to have eyesight, with which to see your prey or your predators in the offing, and as eyes evolved so did all the devices and tactics that eyes enable. The result was an arms race of new ways of hiding and seeking, locomoting, and defending oneself that drove evolution into one of its most innovative and revolutionary periods. My suggestion is that we are entering just such an arms race today, thanks to the cultural evolution of all the new ways of obtaining and distributing information—and misinformation. Old tactics and defenses no longer suffice, and whoever doesn't redesign in a hurry is doomed to extinction.

Religion has changed more in the last century than in the previous millennium, and I predict that it will change more in the next twenty years than it did in the last century, for just this reason. The old ways, the traditional ways, no longer work in the new world of universal transparency. Faced with these changing conditions, institutions will either have to learn how to live with the greater transparency or how to shield themselves from it—going underground, in effect. As usual, those who guess wrong will soon be defunct. Our study participants are the canaries in the coal mine, sensitive harbingers of things to come. Consider the experiences they report as having contributed to the shaking or evaporation of their faith. Here are a few examples.

The story of Noah's Ark is a favorite Sunday school staple, for obvious reasons. It invites art projects and—except in creationist churches—provides a nicely indirect and innocuous way of introducing the idea that the Bible contains myths (without challenging any of the myths of Christianity). But for Tammie, a Methodist pastor, observing the Sunday school presentation of Noah's Ark became a particularly eye-opening moment, for she realized for the first time how depraved the story is.

> They did a few weeks on Noah's Ark. . . . They did this little sand art thing, and just pictures for me to put on my wall, you know, as little kids will do. And I thought to myself, "How horrible is it to teach a child about a God who would save eight people and then destroy the rest of the world?" Of course, as kids, we don't see it that way—we focus on the boat and the animals and the rainbow. But if you really think about it, it's a horrible story. It's worse than any horror picture out there. That makes God worse than Hitler.

Why did this perspective occur to Tammie? The story of Noah's Ark has been taught to children for centuries, but a new sensibility about genocide, about ethnic cleansing, is now much more apt to intrude on one's reflections than in earlier times.

The people at Disney face the problem of what to do with the vault of Disney classics that were innocent and charming only forty or fifty years ago but now make us uncomfortable. Are the Indians—excuse me, Native Americans—in *Peter Pan* acceptable, or racist stereotypes? What about the African Americans in *Song of the South*? Or (one of my all-time favorites) the jiving black crows in *Dumbo,* who sing about seeing an elephant fly? I find the parallel between embarrassing Bible stories and no-longer-presentable Disney films personally enlightening, since I remember how much I loved the Disney films as a child (and still do), and hence how mixed my emotions are today as I applaud, on the one hand, the progress we've made while deeply regretting that one price of that progress is the tarnishing of the treasures of my youth. I feel a touch of shame when I recall how oblivious I was to the racism in those movies—but then I reject that guilt; I was responding naturally and naïvely, as children do, to what is presented to them as benign by their elders. But then it occurs to me that I was enlisted, subliminally, in a bland conspiracy of prejudice—which I might resent, were it not for the reflection that the enlisters were in the main as innocent as I was. It was nobody's fault and everybody's fault, and now there is no turning back—no honest, innocent way of maintaining a pristine regard for the movies one has loved.

These mixed emotions assault many Christians when their attention is drawn in adulthood to Bible stories they learned to love as children. Pastors can't retire half the Bible to the vault, available for scholarly study but never again accessible to the general public, much as they might like to. They can only hope that benign neglect of those verses in the weekly Scripture reading and in Sunday school will allow the offending passages to recede into obscurity. But too many of the tales are too famous, too ubiquitous in world culture, to retire gracefully. For literalists, for whom the Bible must be avowed to be the inerrant word of God, this is a particularly vexing problem, a trap with no escape route. They may recoil in anguish from the prospect of denying their love of those verses, seeing it as a betrayal of their heritage, but they can no longer claim unaltered respect for and belief in them with a clear conscience. They may compartmentalize, trying to isolate their faith from their worldly knowledge, but at some level they know it is loyalty now, and not conviction, that evokes their professions of faith.

This phenomenon complicates the task of seminary professors. Winnie the Presbyterian recalls her professor giving the class some friendly advice about how to discuss the Virgin Mary.

> He said, "With Presbyterians right now [in the 1980s], the Virgin Birth is a really hot topic. And when you go out and interview with a church, you're probably going to be asked a question of what does it mean. So here's your answer: It's not a question of Mary's sexuality; it's a question of God's initiative—whom God chooses to do God's work in the world. God picks the weak and the foolish, not who you'd think would be picked. So someone like Mary, who normally would be stoned to death, is actually someone [to whom] God said, "Nope, you get to carry the Son of God." I thought, "Cool! Got that one!" And I used it in interviews, and it worked. People liked it when I told them that, because they'd struggled with that for years.

Then she added, "His assumption was that none of us assumed this is literal. To make that kind of statement to a theology class. And nobody raised their hand and said, 'No, you're wrong.' All of us were, like, 'Oh, good answer!'" One wonders: Weren't any of the students shocked by this tacit presupposition? Or had they all been initiated already, without ceremony or explicit acknowledgment, into the inner sanctum, the club of loyalists whose mission is to maintain the flock's allegiance to the traditional liturgy?

Every professor in every field is beset by the problem of having to adopt unexamined presuppositions in order to get on with the teaching, but seminary professors face an acute form of this quandary. If they are too candid too early, they risk alienating their students, so they are well advised to save the inside dope until the class is ready for it, but this requires them to be less than honest at the outset.

Movies like Bill Maher's *Religulous* and Monty Python's *Life of Brian* have a way of insinuating themselves under the skin of the curious faithful who dare to go to them—not surprisingly. But, ironically, some of the books intended to shore up flagging loyalty by offering new avenues for the expression of faith can inadvertently undermine it. A prominent series of video study guides, *Living the Questions*, may work well for many parishioners, but according to our pastors it can also shine a little too much daylight on the details. For instance, Carl the Lutheran pastor watched the programs himself and decided some of his flock couldn't handle them. Bart Ehrman's books are eye-opening surveys of biblical scholarship and church history, not intended to subvert faith but having that effect on some pastors and churchgoers. Then there are the respectful books by liberal journalists who are acceptably polite and apparently supportive of religion. These are some of the most corrosive items in the environment, as the fundamentalists recognize. Robert Wright's *The Evolution of God* and Nicholas Wade's *The Faith Instinct* are by journalists who are part of the "I am an atheist, but . . ." brigade, and they sometimes have the effect of hastening the evaporation of the last traces of conviction. With friends like these, who needs Dawkins and Hitchens and Harris?

It's not just that the current information environment has a broad spectrum of content explicitly inimical to religion: Even without it, the sheer accessibility of factual information on all aspects of the history and internal workings of religion endangers institutional creeds as never before. Just discovering, in a newspaper article, that most Christians don't believe in Hell can be unsettling, and, as Harry, the ex–Lutheran pastor, recounts, so can trying to explain the Trinity to foreign students who just don't get it:

> I remember trying to explain the Trinity in both languages, and then getting through my explanation and just looking at these blank stares and then finally getting a lot of pushback from them, saying "This makes no sense at all." And rather than agreeing with them, I remember trying to find other ways to explain the Trinity in a way that might make sense. But that was a seed that was planted a long time ago that kind of stuck with me, and I think maybe festered in a way—little things like that.

Tony, the ex–Catholic priest, was astonished to learn about Protestants in public high school: "I thought everyone who wasn't Catholic was Jewish, because that's the only other religion in the Bible." It is unlikely that young Catholics today can still grow up so sheltered.

The factual stew is growing and growing, and our study is doubtless adding to it. In today's world, studies like this must be accepted. They are perhaps radical, but they are not pornographic, treasonous, or violent. Their intent is to inform, not destroy. Churches must learn to live in a world where such discussions are rife, or they will go extinct.

IV. FROM THE IVORY TOWER TO THE PEOPLE IN THE PEWS

Daniel C. Dennett and Linda LaScola

Three Seminary Professors

Daniel C. Dennett

> *I tell them I think the Bible is the word of humans about their experiences with God. Those who can think can then realize that's perhaps not exactly the same as saying it is the word of God.*
>
> —Beatrice, seminary professor

This formulation nicely captures the tension of the encounter between the professor and seminary students in their first-year course on the Old Testament. Beatrice breaks the news gently: "Those who can think" will read between the lines, and any who can't think will not notice the difference. The message still comes as a shock to many of her devout but naïve students. Beatrice, who was educated abroad, says "I think I am a Christian. I believe in God." Apparently her experience in the United States has made her wonder, and she resents being forced by U.S. churches to be the bearer of bad tidings, a revelation that caught her off guard in her first semester of teaching

> these unpleasant truths. For some it's unpleasant—like [the fact that] Adam and Eve did not really live. I did not think anybody could think that they really lived and ran around in Paradise—I just couldn't have

> imagined that. So by now I've learned to be a bit more careful, just enough not to hurt people's feelings and take them a bit more slowly into this new way of looking at the Bible.

She herself attends a liberal Protestant church and is bothered by the way every Scripture reading is prefaced with, "Listen to the word of God."

> I think the Church is to blame a bit for the confusion the students have to go through, in that it does not make clearer that the Bible is a human document.

Beatrice is a scholar, steeped in the painstaking critical analysis of the texts and aware of the centuries of creative and political turmoil that went into the editing of that anthology we now count as the Bible. "I think it's much more exciting to see these differences—for example, contradictions in the Bible," she says. But many of her students are threatened, not fascinated, by these discoveries, and her enthusiasm is met by resistance, a problem she faces with a mixture of frustration and sympathy.

Beatrice is one of the three seminary professors included in our study. As noted in chapter I, we had no precise way of assessing what self-selection bias went into our small sample, but since the three who were interviewed provided strikingly different perspectives on how they handled student dismay, it's safe to say that their experiences are not unfamiliar phenomena in seminaries.

Portia, too, teaches Old Testament to first-year students at a seminary that takes in students from a variety of Protestant denominations, ranging from Unitarian Universalist to Pentecostal. She has come to recognize "that shell-shocked look I get, maybe, in those first two weeks of class," and notes that quite apart from anything she might say to them, their discovery of the sheer diversity of creeds among their fellow incoming students is often a rude awakening.

> Many students in their first semesters are actually shocked to learn that not all Christians believe that God sent Jesus to Earth to die for their sins. Although that is one common belief within the Christian church, it's not necessarily . . . the norm for all Christians.

Matthew has a somewhat easier diplomatic task than Beatrice and Portia, since he teaches New Testament to second-year students, mostly of mainline Protestant denominations. Still, although they've survived their first year, they are often upset by what he teaches them, and part of his reaction to their continuing naïveté is to seek refuge in the perspectives of postmodernism.

> As children of the Enlightenment, they tend to regard texts as valuable insofar as they speak about the truth.

His students still believe in truth and falsity and haven't yet learned to appreciate the sophisticated framings by which deconstructionism can evade those challenging judgments and transform troublesome text into a soothing miasma of metaphor and myth, since different contexts make for different messages.

All three professors in their different ways acknowledge that their seminaries face difficult times, in keeping with national trends. Seminaries that used to receive more than three-quarters of their total operating costs from their denominations now receive, on average, less than half. Enrollments are down for younger students, so that today's trained seminarians emerge considerably older than their predecessors and hence will have shorter pastoral careers.[21] After years of steady decline, enrollments nationally seem to have leveled off, or even increased slightly, but given the current economic situation, more students are relegated to online courses or evening classes after work at the seminary nearest their home, instead of attending—and living at—a seminary run by their own denomination.

A delicate task confronts the professors: Their students arrive at seminary with their heads buzzing with fervent aspirations and unrealistic expectations, and it falls to the faculty to bring them down, gently but firmly. Says Beatrice:

> Many of our students coming to the class think the Bible is true—for example, that the five books of Moses, the Pentateuch, are written by Moses, and the prophetical books are written by the prophets. Then, they have ideas about inspiration. Somehow, they think, it all comes directly from God. Most of them don't seem to have thought through exactly *what* they think. Many of them grew up with the biblical stories

> in church as if all these stories happened as they were told. . . . And then the historical/critical method tells them that's not the case: These writings were written in time, and by many different authors, and the story of Adam and Eve is a myth and didn't happen like that.

Not surprisingly, the students are upset.

> They really struggle with that, because some of them then think everything they believed was wrong. The first reaction of many is to reject what I teach. They don't like what I teach [laughs]. Different people react differently—it depends very much on their upbringing. Some of them reject what I say, and they close their ears and don't listen. More of them try to integrate it somehow. . . . They play cheap tricks in order to try to harmonize these [revelations] differently.

And just like that, many of these students take their first steps into the world of systematic hypocrisy that will surround them for the rest of their career in the clergy. What else can they do? Abandon their dreams on the spot? Hardly possible; first, they decide they must reserve judgment until they are sure. (Imagine arriving at Hogwarts School of Witchcraft and Wizardry and finding yourself enrolled in Introductory Card Magic: Sleight-of-hand and Marked Cards. "They must just be testing me," you think. "The good stuff will come later. I'll hang in there and see.")

It appears that the students don't have to be warned about not divulging what they're being taught. Portia notes that a common immediate reaction of her students to all this new information is to declare that they will have to keep it a secret. They do this spontaneously, from the best of motives: to protect somebody they love and admire. She puts it this way:

> When you inform a student that David didn't write that psalm, you're not just raising a question about the authorship of the psalm, you're challenging somebody's grandmother. . . . or you're challenging a pastor who may have been extremely influential to a person. . . . So, especially within the first year or so, there's a great deal of almost this sense of secrecy—that "I can't share this with people in my congregation. They can't handle it."

Self-initiation into the secret society comes naturally under those circumstances, but Portia tries to use this reaction to get her students to reflect.

> Well, that is kind of my role. . . . I try to do it somewhat pastorally too. . . . If you can find what the good news is in it for yourself and share what's liberating about it, what's useful about it, then most people in congregations, more people in congregations, are willing to hear it. . . . So, often I suggest to students that they've skipped a step by worrying about how they're going to share it with other people. They haven't taken the time to figure out what it means to their *own* faith. A lot of our students are so caretaking that they can actually hide behind other people and fail to own up to how disturbing it is to them. They'll say, "Oh, other people will be upset about this." "Well, did it upset you? Why? Why not? What does that mean for you?"

But does this work? Do her students pause to consider this carefully, or do they leave the question unconsidered and unanswered? Sometimes their circumstances make examination a luxury they cannot afford. Consider this heartbreaking case recounted by Portia.

> The lawyer who grew up, let's say, in a secular setting, finds a church, becomes very involved, decides she wants to work within the Church. Gives up the law practice, sells the house, . . . leaves the kids, and then begins to learn things that are different from what led her to leave her law practice in the first place. And now she's got a spouse and kids. . . . So it's hard for her to feel like she's got the freedom to explore diverse possibilities, because it's late in life. "I don't have much time. I need to get on with my training, and I need to get on with what I'm called to do."

Couldn't churches and seminaries find ways of giving an early warning to would-be seminarians in order to prevent such untimely disillusionment? Perhaps, but that only displaces the problem instead of solving it, as is shown by another painful case, recalled by Beatrice. In her first year, she taught a demonstration class for prospective students, to show them what seminary would be like.

> I chose that topic [the Book of Esther] on purpose, because I thought, "That is a book nobody cares about very much, and if I introduce them

> to the idea that it's not historically true or did not happen like that"—there was never a Queen Esther—"it will not upset anybody very much." We know that, because we know a lot about these Persian kings. We know all their wives' names, and there was no Esther, ever. So we're pretty sure nothing like that happened. So I thought I'd choose this story and then talk about how I think we can still look at these books and think about the theology they express. We had a big circle, with all these prospective students I didn't know, and I told them that this story never took place like that, but that is not the end point; we have to look at the texts, they are still valuable. . . . But afterwards a young woman, one of the prospective students, told me that the moment when I told her there was never a Queen Esther, her whole world broke down.

Liberal denominations don't often create this problem, since their Sunday schools tend to teach the Bible stories as wonderful stories, not necessarily as true stories. As long as conservative denominations persist in teaching the Bible as literal truth, they are playing a game of chicken with the minds of their young proselytes. It solves a short-term problem by laying down an easy rule to remember: Every statement in the Bible is literally true. And the challenge this poses for some young believers is usefully bracing; they revel in what they take to be their creedal athleticism. But what will it yield when an authority figure—a professor at seminary, a pastor in a different denomination, a biologist on television talking about 3-billion-plus years of life on Earth—calmly, matter-of-factly denies one of the unassailable truths they have been taught? Some have the temperament to hang on to their convictions resolutely. As Matthew notes:

> Some of them compartmentalize: "OK, I'll play the academic game so I get the degree, but I'll keep it in a safe compartment. I'll play the game as a game. But deep down, I'm going to be fundamentally the same kind of deeply conservative, perhaps even fundamentalist, believer as my people."

There do not seem to be any stable intermediate positions between defiant inerrantism on the one hand and, on the other, the sort of interpretation and appreciation of the Bible as literature which is available to any atheist. Portia discusses how hard it is for her students to get comfortable with an intermediate position:

> That takes a lot of practice, so it's not surprising that people leave seminary not fully excellent at it. That's why we really focus on "You've got to get continuing education, and you have to have support groups and peer groups."

She envies the ease with which more conservative Christians can get their message out.

> This is just a hunch, and I can't prove it whatsoever, but I think what's happened in the last twenty years in the United States is that fewer and fewer diverse Christian voices are making it into the media. And that the religious right has been extremely successful in getting a lot of press. What's happened is that believing and nonbelieving persons think the religious right speaks for all of Christianity. So I think it's harder than it was even twenty years ago to talk about, and even Christians can't agree on what "God" means. I do protest when they assume that the religious right is Christianity and liberal Christians are just a little footnote.

Liberal Christians have no difficulty saying what they don't (any longer) believe, but they find it hard to express a positive version of their message that can compete with the forthright, even defiant, claims of the literals. When asked whether her students believe in a supernatural God, Portia's difficulty with the question is more expressive than her actual words:

> That's not always a question I ask students. So the truth is, it's hard for me to know for sure the question you're asking. What I do believe, though, is they haven't moved from yes to no, or no to yes—that there's a lot of movement within their definition of what God is. So that's really why my question for you was, "Will this study interpret anything that's 'differently believing' as nonbelieving?" Or it might not look like the way they believed when they were seven or even twenty-five. So, how many go from no to yes, or from yes to no? I think that that's far less the case than more open-endedness and more diversity. . . . I think part of the reason they struggle so much is that they probably still don't have good language for what they do believe, so all they know to talk about is what they no longer believe. So you'll get students who say, "Well, I don't believe God's the big father in the sky." OK, great, fine: What *do* you believe about God? And I think that's [pause]— The seminary tries

> to work on that, but I think if we fail them somewhere, it's probably there. It's not that they don't believe, but they're not leaving with good enough alternative language to express what they do believe. So what it comes across as is, "Well, I don't believe that anymore, and I don't believe *that* anymore. I don't believe the Bible is the literal word of God." Well, OK, fine: What *do* you believe about the Bible? And often when students say, "Well, I'm not sure if I believe in Jesus anymore." Believe what about Jesus? You don't believe Jesus was a human being? You don't believe that Jesus died for your sins? You don't believe that Jesus was a model to follow for human example? I think also what students are aware of is that what they used to believe, they no longer believe—that they're not as articulate yet in affirming what they do believe. And most of them—I believe this—most of them actually still believe in God, still have a place for Jesus in their understanding, but they don't have good language. They don't have good, positive language.

She is confident that her students are wrong when they claim that nobody in their home congregations believes what they now believe.

> I hear this all the time: "Everybody in my congregation believes that; I'm the only one [who doesn't]. And how can I go to them and say I don't believe that?" Well, I can just guarantee that that's not true. Not everybody in a congregation believes the same thing. . . . I teach in churches some on the weekends, and preach. And often I'll go to larger Protestant denominations, where people can pay me to come. So I'll get a really intelligent adult who'll come to me after and explain to me that they don't really fit in here because they don't believe what everyone else does. Then the next person in line will tell me that same thing. And then the next person will say the same thing. And I think you're right: I think people are scared of having the conversation, because nobody wants to be left out, especially out of a voluntary group.

From Matthew we get some first-hand glimpses of the interface between academic theologians and the more straightforward creeds of many would-be pastors.

> What I try to do when I introduce the historical/critical method is to emphasize the difference in the social setting between the rules for reading in the church and the rules for reading in the academy. Identifying those different social contexts helps the students make the

> transition, so that they don't think they're being asked to learn a new set of dogmas that replace those that they use in the church.

What does Matthew advise his students to do about negotiating the passage between these two different contexts? He tells them what they shouldn't do: use the pulpit for instruction.

> But what I think is important in principle is that the pulpit is the least important place where teaching should take place. Preaching is much more about *ethos* and *pathos* arguments than it is about *logos*. . . . So that your sermon doesn't become the place of introducing strange concepts to the congregation—very bad teaching method.
>
> Should the young pastor then try to make it clear to the congregation that no truth claims are being made from the pulpit? I don't think that would work. If you were to announce the context in advance, you'd lose the sought-for effect. Preaching is a kind of theater, and just as actors strive to get you so involved in their words and deeds that you forget you're watching a play, preachers shun any expressions that might remind you of the hypothesis that they are purveyors of traditional metaphors—symbol-slingers, not teachers. If you tell the congregation that it is *ethos* and *pathos,* you lose them.

Like Portia, Matthew understands that when his students leave the seminary they are far from expert in the art of speaking in the special nonacademic style one should adopt in the pulpit. And like her, he has no quick fixes to propose.

> *Matthew:* When I use the term, "a little bit of knowledge," I mean it quite seriously. I mean, they learn enough to be able to use phrases and mouth slogans and, you know, play around with ideas. But they don't have the depth of learning to communicate to others what's really of value to them. . . . And that depth of knowledge, which we often think of as genius, is simply the capacity to have control over a huge amount of data and find the simplest route to expressing it, whereas people who are undereducated are manipulating sets of concepts that they don't fully understand in their actual relationships. So they mouth views, but they don't really grasp it themselves at a deeper level.
>
> *Linda:* This is what I've gathered—that they don't know what to do with the knowledge they have. They may understand it, but they can't

imagine going back to their congregations and talking with people about that, because they don't think it will go down well.

Matthew: But that's exactly what I'm trying to suggest—that the difference between my students and me . . . is not only that I'm older, it's that I've worked at this field long enough that I don't have to couch it in jargon. Remember I talked earlier about being an honest broker? I can teach about these things as simple metaphors, comparisons, analogies, common sense. Here's how the world works; think about your grandma. And it's highly sophisticated. It's the social construction of reality. I can go on and on about the theoretical bases of this—but what makes a good teacher, and a good preacher, is the capacity to take complex issues and render them simply. And they don't know how. That's why they're ill educated; they simply don't have the depth of knowledge to be able to speak.

So I'll give you an example! They've studied the Gospels with somebody and they've learned that Jesus spoke in parables but that the parables are very complicated and he may or may not have actually said this parable. They've read three books on this subject. And they get up in the pulpit, and they rehearse this infinite regress before they ever can say how simple this parable really is. So they're half-baked intellectuals, if you will. And that's what creates this anguish.

Linda: Let's say I was a good student. I got class time with all the best professors, and I'm mature, and I go into this congregation. I'm a good speaker, I'm a compassionate person. What do I do?

Matthew: I will say it's tremendously varied. There are churches that would be eager as all get-out to hear what you had to say. If you were in a UCC [United Church of Christ] congregation, if you were in a Presbyterian congregation, if you were in an Episcopal congregation, you're not going to find the problem. They're hungry for educated pastors, they love them. But—

Linda: Let me stop you a minute. They may be hungry for an educated pastor, but they may *not* be hungry for some of the information the pastor has.

Linda then asks him what she should do in that circumstance. What's an "honest broker" to do? Should she give them what they want, even if it means dissembling, and then do the innovative work away from the pulpit? Is the answer in adult education, Sunday school, seminars, conferences? If so, then what should she say from the pulpit?

But Matthew has no advice on that point. He is better on problems than solutions. He sees and deplores the "infantile" faiths of many churchgoers and even some of his students, but he does not articulate his "mature" faith, beyond saying that "ambiguity is the sign of mature faith."

> *Linda:* OK, faith in what?
>
> *Matthew:* In God.
>
> *Linda:* And what is God? I know that's another huge question.
>
> *Matthew:* But I can answer it. For me, God is the source of everything that exists, and the goal toward which everything that exists is directed. It's not an object among other objects; it's not thematic; it's not— As Augustine said, if you can think it, it's not God.
>
> *Linda:* What does that have to do with Christianity and Scriptures?

To which Matthew responds:

> Here's what it has to do with Scriptures and Christianity. In the 13th century, Aquinas, among others, developed a very sophisticated epistemology, a theory of knowledge with regard to things divine, and it said authentic theology has to be dialectical in character. It has to have three dialectical moments: The first is the moment of affirmation; this is what we'll see in Scripture. It tells stories, it gives commandments, it says that God is angry, God is loving, God is this, God is that. And there's a certain simple, mystic appropriateness to that language. We can't do without it—"Your mama loves you." But, said Aquinas, following Pseudo-Dionysius, to speak only at that level is to make an idol of God; it's to identify God with our own concept; it's to be incredibly intellectually immature. So the second moment of the dialectic is called the negative way; it is to deny the proposition. The Scripture says, "God is good." The first thing the theologian has to say is, "God is not good"—just like Christopher Hitchens says, "God is not good." And why? Because whatever God is, God can't be good the

> way that your mama is good. So, the third moment of the dialectic is called the analogical way, so that in analogy, points of similarities are found within points of greater dissimilarity. So that one says goodness is to God and goodness is to your mama, but you recognize that you're talking about something totally different.

It's hard to imagine what a congregation would make of any of that. Matthew's primary mission as a seminary professor, supposedly, is to prepare his students for the role of pastor, including their role in the pulpit, but he has no detailed advice on how to address "infantile" congregations as an "honest broker."

Portia puts the problem differently, and starkly, saying of her graduates, "Most of them actually still believe in God"—hardly a ringing endorsement of her seminary's success with its primary mission. You might expect that if this is a widespread pattern, religious leaders would be bent on examining it and considering reforms to alleviate it. One way would be to drop the requirement of seminary training for pastors altogether, and this has been a growing trend among conservative churches. But the problem of how to meld "mature" and "infantile" faiths gracefully almost never gets mentioned. The oft-cited 2008 Alban Institute study, *Becoming a Pastor: Reflections on the Transition into Ministry,* discusses the results of an ambitious "Transition into Ministry" program involving hundreds of Protestant seminary students moving into the profession.[22] Presumably this study was initiated and funded because of perceived shortcomings in the current practices of preparing people for their roles in the clergy, and while it goes on at length about the importance of mentoring once the novice pastor gets out of seminary, it doesn't mention the problem of an awkward mismatch between seminarians' newly developed beliefs and those of the congregations they hope to lead. Why the silence? This "dirty little secret," as one pastor put it, cannot be openly discussed, because—in the minds of most people who know about it—it would exacerbate the problem by having a devastating effect on everybody's morale.

This is not an unusual phenomenon in institutions, from corporations to the military. For instance, colleges with declining enrollments or SAT scores or acceptance rates tend not to publicize those ominous trends for fear of accelerating them. Portia closes her interview by saying that the question on her mind—a question she would like to put to her students—

is, "Are they really sure they can't talk honestly?" Probably they are not really sure, but they don't dare commit themselves to the experiment. Unlike Portia, who has a measure of job security in the seminary, their fates hang on the opinions of congregations who may, for all they know, be full of folks who share their beliefs but are themselves unwilling to stick their necks out.

What Happens in Seminary: The Students' Perspective

Linda LaScola

Until the advent of the Internet, objective information about religion was hard to come by except in higher education, where students specifically interested in religion, and perhaps wanting to make it a career, took courses in it. Most of us learned about religion from our families. We were indoctrinated. We went to the religious services that our families took us to as children, where we were taught to believe in a particular creed and eschew others. We were *aware* of other religions, and in many cases we had been taught to respect other people's beliefs, but we were not expected to share them. Times have changed. The huge amount of information available on the Internet has enabled people to learn about many subjects, including religion. Instead of being limited to the stories and doctrine heard from family and clergy, people can easily learn the facts and history of many diverse religions on their own.

Students who enter seminary, like any students who have committed time and tuition payments to specialized, master's-level education, are strongly motivated to complete their studies and succeed in their chosen fields. Like all serious scholars, seminary students have a thirst for knowledge and a desire to apply it properly. Most graduate students hope for ultimate financial security and some measure of respect from their community. Seminary students hope for that and more—a special place in society. They will be addressed as "Reverend" or "Father" or "Rabbi"; they will be perceived—among people who share their beliefs and even among some who do not—as representatives of God's word on Earth. They take their studies seriously, hoping to use their advanced knowledge to carry out their work. However, as we saw in the previous section, there are surprises in store for those incoming students who expect that their faith will be deepened, and for those graduates who expect that their flocks will appreciate their wisdom.

We found, among our interviewees, four more-or-less distinct reactions, in varying degrees, to the seminary experience:

1. fascination with and enthusiasm for the religious knowledge and insights they were gaining;
2. a deeply troubled sense upon exposure to the ambiguities and complexities of religious history and thought;
3. a recognition of the seeds of doubt that would trouble them later in their careers; and
4. an emphasis on diligence in pursuing their coursework, without much analysis or judgment.

Fascinated Seminarians

Tony, a former Catholic priest; Caitlin, an Episcopal priest; and Darryl, a Presbyterian pastor, all exemplified, in their seminary years, those students who thoroughly enjoy and appreciate the experience. Tony was especially enthusiastic.

> Oh, I was fascinated! I love to learn, and learning all this stuff—it was incredible! This academic approach—it all started to make sense to me, because all these black-and-white arguments never seemed right to me. "Do it because God told you to." How did God tell me to do this, you know? But learning about it like it was scientific—using the historical/critical method, or semantics and the hermeneutical approaches we were using—it was just fascinating and stimulating to me. And it felt very real to me, because we're putting all this time and effort into it, using our logic and our rationality.
>
> That's how I was trained. You've got to go back and understand not only how the Scripture, the teaching, was formed but what it meant, in the time, for the people, and what the Church was trying to say at that time, and . . . how it was supposed to be used for those people, in that time. You can find how to say how it's supposed to be used. You can draw the parallel today. I learned that from my professors.

Caitlin had a similar gratifying experience while studying for the Episcopal priesthood. She recalled how much she enjoyed learning about and analyzing the formation of the early Church.

> In seminary, we were given license to pick apart things, with critical and traditional historical criticism. We could see how the Babylonian influence, and how the Judaic influence, and how the early Christian influence, and then the Constantinian influence, shaped Christianity. And then the early Middle Ages, with the Roman Church and the Celtic branch. We were allowed to tease that apart.

She was also open to a metaphorical understanding of the Resurrection.

> Oh, I think there was no doubt in my seminary that all of us believed in the Resurrection. And whether we believed in an actual, physical, bodily Resurrection—we fell along a spectrum of that.
>
> It didn't have to be true factually for me. I embraced it because it could be—it could have been—like that. And the mystery of it was— I loved the mystery of it! Sure, I think it could happen. Would I have been a person of non-faith if I didn't believe that it happened? No, I wouldn't. I would still be that person embracing the possibilities that it could have happened. So I think maybe I'd call myself a Christian person embracing the possibilities more than the factualities. I could work with that.

Darryl, who participated in our 2010 pilot study, spoke about how his Presbyterian seminary classes "blew open" Christian doctrine for him.

> In seminary, it wasn't black and white, it was plaid, polka-dot—there was just such a variety of thought that went in every different kind of direction.

Deeply Troubled Seminarians

Others reacted negatively to academic religion. As noted, Stan, who became a Disciples of Christ military chaplain, got off to a rough start in his Christian college, even before entering seminary.

> The school I went to was affiliated with a Pentecostal faith group, yet our professors taught us textual criticism, how the Bible was formed. So, yes, that came as quite a shock. I can remember taking one of the introductory classes and thinking, "Wow, this is not at all what I thought it would be!" At first it felt very threatening. I felt very angry—this is what I've always heard about so-called liberal theologians and denominations. And then after a while I really wanted to embrace

> it, because I thought, "Gee, this is genuinely how it came to be. This is based in history, literature, and archeology." It was the first time I felt that the myth I'd been told from childhood was shattered. It was the time I realized that there was a feeling of a shift from a literal understanding.

Stan considered changing his major at that point, but instead he continued his studies, because he figured he could "compartmentalize what I was learning in class, if I had more faith," or that he could become a professor instead of a pastor. Once in seminary, he was exposed to further factual information about religion.

> Now, the seminary I attended was pretty conservative, but we still learned textual criticism and the way the Bible was put together. We still learned what the academy taught. So even at this very, very, very conservative seminary, it was almost like the seeds of rational truth were still being sown.

During a seminary internship, he found his niche in the field of hospital chaplaincy.

> Spending one year in a hospital, it became clear to me that this was something that was unique—meeting people in a hospital. And that's where I began to see that I'd rather stick with this than be in a church.

He suspects that other skeptical seminarians have followed a path similar to his—away from church assignments and toward more liberal denominations.

> I think there are a lot of people like me. I haven't really met anyone in the military to have these conversations with as a chaplain, but I've seen a lot of my classmates leave and go into different denominations. Several became Episcopal priests. There are some that became Universalists. Some became United Church of Christ. I just came to, for me, a logical conclusion that [religious belief] is all ridiculous and doesn't make any sense.

Jeb, who attended a Southern Baptist seminary, openly questioned, both with other students and his professors, what he was learning there.

> We'd come back from a theology class and get into discussion. Then issues would come up, and I'd realize I wasn't the only one saying, "Well, if that is so, what about this?" In other words, if we know that lots and lots about the biblical story is not accurate, then in what sense do you say the Bible is inspired, that it has some divine stamp on it? It seemed to me that that's the fundamental question one raises, if everything you know about this is supposed to come from some authentic source. It seemed to me that the whole house of cards falls down if your source of authenticity is flawed.
>
> I got to know my professors very well, and mostly I didn't raise those questions in class. Mostly what I did was talk to them personally and say, "What do you think? Do you really believe, let's say, in the Virgin Birth?" Mostly, they equivocated. I haven't looked back on it for many years, because I've been out of it for more than forty years, but when I was struggling and I looked back on it, I would realize they didn't really give a good answer to that.
>
> One of my professors, whom I dearly respected and loved, almost admitted that were he not in the twilight of his career, he would no longer be a professor of religious philosophy, because he did not believe in an eternal soul. He didn't honestly think there was anything after this that was going to survive our death. And he almost said as much in class, but not quite—sort of guarded. I do remember asking him in private, "Why can't you go ahead and stand up and say that you don't think there's anything after death—that this is all we've got?" And once again it was a kind of equivocation, of saying, "Well, it's not certain, and it's just better to just sort of leave it as it is." Something like that. In other words, nobody would come straight out and say, "No. I think it's all a crock of shit, but this is how I make my living, so I've got to stick with it."

To avoid disappointing his deeply religious family, Jeb finished seminary and entered the ministry.

> I just thought, "Well, I'm good at this, and I want to help people, so I'll just try and put those questions aside and go ahead and plunge into trying to be the best people-helper I can be, in spite of the fact that I'm not sure all of this holds together."

Candice was so adversely affected by what she learned in a Roman Catholic seminary that she had become an atheist by the time she finished her master's degree. She abandoned her plans to work in the Catholic education system and entered a field unrelated to her graduate studies. Still, she initially reacted much like the "fascinated" seminarians described above. She liked her elective theology classes in college so much that she majored in theology.

> I enjoyed it [her undergraduate education] and I found it interesting—because it was so much new information, right? Learning about Augustinian theology and philosophy and then also looking at biblical criticism. I thought, "Wow, this is really interesting!" When I was a little kid I wanted to be an archeologist. I found that same kind of digging, the fact-finding, in biblical criticism, and that's what interested me, in that I'm going to find the answers. Because I had all those questions when I was a child, too. I don't really understand a guy living in the belly of a whale. And why is Eve so bad? I wanted answers to those questions even when I was a kid.
>
> In philosophy of religion class, we spent the entire year proving that God doesn't exist. Yet somehow—I don't know, maybe it's a uniquely Catholic thing—I was able to compartmentalize my belief into this little package, where I just didn't touch it. I let all these ideas swirl around, and I looked at them kind of the way a kid would look at images through a kaleidoscope—with awe and wonder. But I didn't think it could touch my religious belief, it formed my early life so much. It was just a given. Everybody believed in God, because it was an impossibility not to. Plus reading about the Old and New Testaments, and how they were written, when they were written, and what communities they were written for. First off, there was a barrier there that I didn't touch intellectually and kind of ignored. It was purposeful ignorance—it really was.

As her graduate studies progressed, her reaction to what she was learning deteriorated.

> The more I was studying, the more I just felt like I was wasting my time. And I felt like, "Well, I don't believe it," and actually started to look at that little package I had put aside, of beliefs. And I thought, "Well, I'm constantly rearranging it, and I'm constantly bringing in new information and trying to restructure, and it isn't sound." I had to accept that it isn't sound. I sat with that for a while, then I had to take a break from school for family reasons, so during that time I thought

> about the fact that I accepted that my belief wasn't sound. And then I just thought to the point where, "Maybe I don't believe this at all. So what does that mean? Maybe I believe in something else." Then I thought, "All right, let's look at other Christian denominations." So I tried out this church and that church—it was like changing outfits. And I felt I didn't really like that, either. It still made no sense to me.

Her goal then was to get out. She wrote her master's thesis and left quietly.

> I had no desire to tell anyone, mostly because I felt like I was going to waste my breath. And the other thing was that I didn't want to be ostracized. I already felt it enough internally, because I was so conflicted being there, and so frustrated by some of the classes I was taking. I just wanted to kind of slip under the radar. It wasn't purposeful, but I didn't want to get caught up in the messiness, and I knew it would get messy.
>
> I didn't want to get into an argument with people, and I knew they would make a really great argument for why I should continue to believe in God. And I didn't want to stand there and say, "You're having no effect on me, because I thought about this myself for a long time."

The Seeds of Doubt

Bill is an Episcopal priest whose initial awareness of his growing atheism—as he freely calls it—began in seminary.

> I had an internal dialogue. I had conversations with myself, and, looking back, it was not a systematic atheism that I was putting together in seminary but a systematic Christian theology that worked for me. And certainly a liberal seminary education provided the tools to do that.
>
> I was introduced to what is called form criticism, literary criticism—Paul Tillich, Rudolf Bultmann. It reinforces my progression to atheism. It reinforces it—I'm not there yet.
>
> It would be the wrong assumption to say that a liberal seminary is the defining moment in one's awakening to atheism. I believe that one would have to take the long look, the broad look.

Bill didn't talk to his professors about his wavering beliefs, but he did occasionally talk to some of his classmates.

> We would talk, but we were cautious. We were not completely honest. We would talk about how bold and courageous we were, to finally give

> up on a personal God. I think the academic exposure reinforced, for most of us, what we had already been processing and reasoning out and thinking through. And that academic arena gave us permission, but only to move by degrees, because now the problem is even more vexing. If not a personal God, then some kind of God. And for me, that was so bewildering. It was even more incredible for me, and I even wrote my senior paper on the problem of an intelligent being. As I recall, I began by stating emphatically that I cannot any longer find succor or comfort in a personal God, because that personal God has the power to say hello and yet never, never speaks. So I'm left with this even larger enigma: of a God somewhere that is responsible for all of this but yet, in all of that power, refuses to become personal. I ended the paper somewhere by saying that it's forcing me to continue down the road of doubt and unbelief.

Bill recalled getting an "A" on that paper.

Vince, a former Catholic monk, seminary teacher, and visiting parish priest in the 1960s, was similarly conflicted about some of what he learned in seminary.

> We were introduced to modern critical biblical studies because we got a new professor who'd just finished his degree in Europe. His whole approach was something totally different. We had never experienced anything like it. Instead of taking the Bible in a very literal sense, we began to look at it in terms of not only its literary composition but its historical setting. Not the more traditional idea, [which was] that the Bible was symbolized . . . by a traditional icon of the Evangelist writing with the dove, representing the Holy Spirit, perched on his shoulder, whispering in his ear—that type of thing. This man opened our eyes to the fact that the Bible was the work of men. It was the product of human beings and their age and their culture. That's when we start talking about, "What does this all mean? How do we deal with this?"

Vince and some of his classmates were also disturbed by the Church's attempt to keep them in the ancient confines of their religious order.

> Watching [contraband] modern movies made us more aware of the fact that we weren't living in the 13th century; we were living in this century. And at this point, if you were still thinking in terms of being an effective priest as well as a monk, we had to have a real feel for the

> life of the people we would be working with and the world we would be working in. If I was going to be teaching and preparing my students supposedly for the ministry, it should be for the ministry that was relevant to the world they were going to go out in.

He and many others in Catholic religious orders were hoping that the then-new Vatican II rules would liberalize the Church.

> I wasn't ready to decide that maybe I'd made a mistake, a serious mistake, and I should go seek something else. There was also a lot of hope that the changes that were being officially approved by the Council could make some really significant changes—not just in the Church but in our order.
>
> They allowed us to voice and write our opinions of what changes should be made to our rules and practices. Eventually—this was after I was already ordained, already on the seminary faculty—they did issue a revised rule, constitution, and the changes were totally insignificant, essentially the same document. It was about that same era that quite a number of other padres decided that was it, and left.

Vince decided to stay on in the Church. It wasn't until several years later that his experiences, which will be discussed in the next section, prompted him to leave.

The Diligent Students

Some of the clergy who eventually moved from belief to nonbelief were diligent students who were undisturbed by what they were learning about religion during their college or seminary years. Their negative reactions came later, based on additional learning and/or their experiences with their congregations.

Michael, a Seventh-day Adventist pastor, knew in high school that he would enter the clergy.

> I believed that's what God wanted me to do, so that's what I did. I went straight through high school and right into theology in college. I started seminary, went nine quarters straight through, and went straight into pastoring.

He recalled seminary in terms of the courses he took but not how they affected him at the time.

> There was some Reformation history. Biblical history would have been teaching the Bible as literal—just learning the stories of the Bible as literal fact. Not much as far as other perspectives go, when I think of how the Bible was formed and when I think of studying Reformation history and stuff.
>
> I took three years of Greek. Homiletics, preaching. Old Testament, which is just as it is written in the Bible. In seminary, we took a class on creationism, but it was basically *promoting* creationism. There was very, very little looking at other perspectives.

Harry, who went to a Lutheran seminary, spoke readily about his studies and his interactions with his classmates.

> I remember having great conversations. I remember loving the theological dialogue, the talk in the cafeteria about what we'd heard at lectures. I remember really enjoying that a lot.

His exposure to liberal, academic theology did not affect his beliefs while he was in seminary, and he was not troubled by doubts about what he was learning.

> I remember one Systematic Theology professor who was way on the left end of the spectrum, who flat-out said he didn't believe in subjective immortality—the continuing existence of you as subject after you die. And he was a well-respected, well-known theologian in Lutheran circles. That kind of shocked me, and I didn't believe that at that time. I totally believed that there was Heaven and everything. So I guess I was exposed to some of that in seminary, but I wouldn't say I had major doubts. I think I was fairly orthodox—unless I was just totally lacking in insight and just parroting the party line in order to get credentials and get ordained.
>
> I didn't see doubts being contradictory with my role, because I met so many professors who seemed to be fairly open-minded, and I thought if they could do this, I could do this, too.

Harry thought his approach to seminary was probably quite common among students.

> I think part of the deal is that most people go to seminary really not knowing a whole lot about the Bible. So you're so busy just trying to learn all the material, and you're studying Greek and sometimes Hebrew, that you're kind of taking it for granted. You went to seminary under the presumption of faith.

He had a logical explanation for how he and others could avoid thinking more deeply about the many questions that were raised during his seminary experience.

> You're just trying to pass tests and that kind of thing. And it didn't click; for some reason it didn't click.
>
> Most people did not go to seminary as seekers. They go because they're already committed to the program. You took this to be—in some way, shape, or form—the word of God, whether literally or symbolically or metaphorically or whatever, but at some level you believed that this was the word of God. And I think that that's why I had those blinders on. I just said, "Well, it's Scripture, so I'm accepting it." You do spend some time, when inconsistencies pop up, finding ways to explain them away. But after a while, spending any time with the Bible takes its toll. I mean, Christians don't even read the Bible—that's quite obvious to me.

Regardless of how these clergy responded in seminary, they found it challenging to apply their new theological knowledge and understanding to the people in the pews—to which set of challenges we turn next.

After Seminary: Preaching and Teaching

Linda LaScola

For most of our participants, applying their seminary-acquired knowledge meant working in a congregation. It was in this setting—in the pulpit, in study groups, in one-on-one meetings—that these freshly minted clergy brought their theological knowledge to bear and practiced their pastoral skills. It was here that they met with troubling experiences they ultimately could not reconcile. Many of our participants found that the people in the pews not only were uninterested in their pastor's advanced knowledge but actually eschewed it, instead favoring the naïve, feel-good aspects of faith.

These new clergy became disillusioned by dishonesty or corruption in the church hierarchy. Novel insights and information about their religion alarmed those who had remained believers in seminary, leading them toward nonbelief. They obfuscated, adapting their message to be more relevant to people's everyday life, while avoiding disturbing historical or doctrinal issues. Attempts to stifle their negative feelings became more difficult. They found their questions and discomfort growing instead of diminishing. They noticed that knowledge about science excited them more than religion did. Eventually, irrespective of the initial strength of their enthusiasm and commitment, their religious beliefs diminished until they were gone.

From Fascinated to Frustrated

Tony recounted his frustrations trying to apply what he'd learned in seminary to his interactions with his Catholic parishioners.

> These very cerebral professors would come up with these ways of still believing in the Resurrection—"Our faith is faith in their [the disciples'] faith." And I started to adapt those. But really, the popular theology in the pews is—I hate to say it in this way, but it's like a third-grade understanding of things, especially confession and sacraments and morality. It's this very childish way of understanding things—the black and white: "The Bible says it; the Bible tells me so."
>
> I got out of seminary, then into the priesthood, and then back out in the pews, where it's the popular theology, where everyone's just like, "Whoa! It says here that God destroyed Sodom, so gays are bad." And you're like, "No, no, it's all about hospitality, and the real sin was that they didn't welcome the homeless person and the alien from another land into their house, which really has all these effects on what we say about social justice in our country, and we really should be having open borders," and all this kind of stuff. And then they're like, "No, it's because gays are going to hell." And you're like, "My God, how do you get people to *grow*?"

Caitlin's experiences were similar to Tony's.

> I thought the seminary experience was wonderful, because it was so academic. But to move into an Episcopal congregation where people were thinking that Moses wrote the first five books of the Bible himself

> and did not want to hear you challenge that! Still, some people were interested, and we did lots of Bible study with some of those. Some people didn't want any part of it. So it was a mixed bag. People were more willing to accept that Moses didn't write the first five books of the Bible than they were to accept that maybe Jesus wasn't resurrected in bodily form. There's a real spectrum.

She learned, from personal experience and from her mentors, how the church was different from the seminary.

> People go to church for all different reasons. They go for comfort, just because that's what they always do, or they go because they think it's the right thing to do. They go for social reasons, or for moral reasons, or, you know—all kinds of reasons people go. But they don't necessarily go to learn the most current, critical, academic criticism of Scripture. They don't do that. So there was a rupture between coming out of seminary and what I discovered the people were interested in, particularly in terms of preaching. And what my clergy mentors would point out to me, over and over, was that people don't care about the intellectual piece. It's not that they only want the feel-good piece, it's that the academic piece isn't what preaching is about. That's what *teaching* is about. But that's not what congregational pastoral life is about.

Later, when Caitlin had a church of her own, she did an experiment with the Nicene Creed, the profession of faith most widely used in Christian services—an experiment that troubled some of her more traditional-minded parishioners.

> There was some set-up for this. I didn't just pop it on them. I asked people to recite the parts of the Nicene Creed that they actually believed. It got very quiet. There were only six or seven people there who recited the whole thing. It was very interesting. The people who recited the whole Creed were furious at me, because that's "what we do."

Darryl acknowledged that he was "still playing the game" of being vague about his beliefs with his Presbyterian church members.

> I've been surprised at some of the stuff I've been able to get away with

> in my sermons—either because the people listening agree with me or maybe it's not clear enough. It's not so much coming out and saying I don't believe Jesus is God—but in the bulletin I can take out a lot of the objectionable language in the liturgy. And there's lots of way to talk about Jesus, as being a follower of his philosophy of life, without using terms like "Son of God."

Darryl's situation is discussed in more depth in our section on the pilot study participants.

From Deeply Troubled to Desperate to Leave
Stan's work as a hospital chaplain contributed to his nonbelief.

> It was after realizing—I know this sounds very elementary—that people die in hospitals. I saw a lot of death, a lot of dying, and regardless of who they were, if people had cancer and it was inoperable—miracles don't happen.

Still, he found it rewarding to comfort people when they were in great physical distress. It was the time he spent leading regular church services that bothered him.

> I was a chaplain who hated going to church, who hated doing these things. And it's like, at what point is it insanity to continue to do this? There was one thing to being in a hospital, in a military unit, when you're out doing drills or maneuvers or you're out there with the troops. But when you're in the chapel, and you're doing all these activities and teaching classes and preaching, and you find, "Man, I absolutely despise this!"—it becomes such a misery, really.
>
> I would always try to make things relevant for people. But in terms of looking at these texts and trying to find something to preach from these texts, it was just really, really difficult. Because I'm not believing a word of the literal text, so how do I make this apply in some way to a motivational thought or something? So that's kind of where I found myself. Of course, being a liberal clergyperson, that's what I've been doing for a long time. But it just got to the point where I thought, "What am I doing? What am I doing? What's going on here?"
>
> I spoke a lot about love and community and encouragement and caring—and those attributes of caring for society and the poor and the needy and the marginalized which I felt, "OK, I believe this; this is

> good stuff." But when it comes to walking on water and miracles and this kind of stuff, I just think it's so much crap. So how do I reconcile this?

For a while, he found ways of coping.

> I do like people and being around people, and I tried to put the energy into thinking about just helping people in their life, and bettering their life, and having a sense of community. People need a sense of community, of belonging, activities for children. People came to chapel for those things, but it was because they had these beliefs in God, and many of them truly believed that.

But it was hard for him to keep up the façade.

> People would come to me, for instance, about homosexuality. "I have a nephew who's homosexual. Can you give me some advice on how to deal with his situation, because I believe he's sinning against God." And I would say something like, "Well, tell me more about that," instead of saying, "Oh, yeah, you need to go to this passage," and this and that. I felt afraid to say, "Well, is he happy with the person he's with? It sounds like he's just a homosexual, and that's OK, isn't it?" They're not wanting to hear that. They want to hear me give the answer that's going to help them to fix their nephew. And I just simply couldn't give them the answer they wanted.

So he finally decided to get out. Like many others, he left quietly.

> I feel that I'm at the point where, if I'm going to have a sense of integrity personally, professionally, I have to push forward—into what I believe and what I no longer believe. It's come to a point where it's dishonest—even if in my mind I can rationalize by attempting to say, "Well, I have a very sophisticated understanding of spirituality, and it's about social justice, and it's about community." But the people who are in the pews, the people who see you as clergy, don't make those distinctions, can't make those distinctions. So you get the dilemma of "What do I do? What do I do with my life?" I've chosen to go back to school and have a sense of congruency about what I'm doing.

When Jeb was still in the Southern Baptist seminary, he would try to avoid preaching.

> When I was asked to fill the pulpit at the seminary church where my fellow students and my professors were, I got to the place where I said to the senior minister, "Don't ask me to do that right now, because I don't have anything but doubts to talk about."

Later, when he had a church of his own, he attempted to preach with authenticity.

> By the time I finished seminary, since I had decided that I was going to try to stay in it and make it work, I just concentrated on how anything I had learned could contribute to the human condition.
>
> In the sermon, I would talk in general terms. I was still trying to believe there was something there. I could not, at that point, have said, "I am an atheist." I could not even have said, at that point, "I am an agnostic." It was just "I have tremendous questions about all this, and I'm not sure how much of it—if *any* of it—makes sense. But I'll just try to preach the part I think does make sense." And mostly that had to do with how we treat each other, and how we learn to be forgiving. In a Baptist church, you don't ever preach a sermon without Scripture. So you find a text, and, yes, some of the time it would refer to things that I now know are simply not so at all. But at the time I was trying to make something be so. So I didn't preach my doubts.
>
> I'm sure many of my sermons at the time were things that, once I finally left the ministry, I would say I knew at that time were not so. But I was trying to make myself believe it, so I could have something to say in the pulpit. I had lots and lots of angst and internal questioning of myself: "How can you be doing this? How can you keep on doing this when you've got such significant doubt?" But it's what I did.

Jeb was a successful minister in the eyes of church leaders.

> The church was growing. People joined. When they joined, they gave money. When they gave money, the church could add a new addition on. The reality is, the people who are the movers and shakers in the church want the church to grow. They want the money to come in. And if you can bring the money, they'll let you get away with a lot of stuff.

However, like Stan, he had difficulty continuing to do something he didn't believe in. He left after a few years.

> For whatever reason, if something doesn't make sense to me, it's just really tough for me to let it go and say, "Well, everybody else believes it, so . . . . " I really, really tried to do that. But that's not easy for me. My best friend in seminary ended up being a sterling minister, and it was hard for me to understand why, because when we'd be in conversation about this, he would mostly agree with me. But it just didn't seem to bother him that much.
>
> I was conflicted, and it was tearing my insides out. You know, "How can you do this? They believe it and they think it makes sense, but you don't believe it and you don't think it makes sense. How can you keep doing this?" That's what I finally ended up saying: "I can't do this any longer. It's just tearing my insides out."

Knowing what other seminary-trained clergy have been taught, Jeb thinks his understanding of the Bible is pretty common among pastors.

> There is a rather large number of real, educated, not just Bible-school-trained ministers who, if they were pinned down, would have to say, "I don't believe in an eternal Hell. I don't believe in a virgin birth. I don't believe in a Resurrection. I don't think the Bible is, in any sense except a poetic one, the word of God." Because if they're intelligent and have a decent education, you've got to look around and say this is where you come out.
>
> If you study the quotations in the Bible about the idea of a holy virgin shall conceive and bear a son—from Isaiah, you know—the word translated "virgin" simply means a woman of a marriageable age. It doesn't mean "never had sex." So the logical consequence from that is that if there was an actual historical person named Jesus, he was born the normal way. Somebody had sexual intercourse and we have a biological father.

He also thinks he knows why some ministers stay in the pulpit despite the questions that come from their advanced knowledge.

> Most ministers who have had some of those questions but have managed to stay in, by the time they get to be my age they don't want to revisit it.

Even though Candice left the Catholic Church after completing seminary, she still found herself in uncomfortable situations when asked about religion.

> If someone approached me and asked, "Why do you feel this way?" then I'd go into more detail and say, "You know, the Old Testament was written at this time, and there were two primary writers, but really four writers, who wrote the Old Testament. Mark is the first Gospel and not Matthew. You know, this document that we don't have is supposedly the inspiration for all the Gospels, because this, this, and this are in all four Gospels." I could get into that, but that's a very complicated response. And I've observed people who are listening to that response, and—I don't want to be judgmental, and maybe it's because they haven't had the exposure to it—but they don't have the intellectual capacity to understand it. It's because religion is placed in this little box that doesn't get touched and that most of them don't look at or study. It's all about how it makes them feel.

She learned to avoid such conversations.

> If I was talking one-on-one, I'd say, "Constantine, the Emperor of Rome, is the one who called the Council of Nicaea. He's the one who determined the dogma that we know. He's the one who said, 'These are the books that are going to go in the Bible, and these are the ones that are not.'" But I find that it tends to get people really angry, unresponsive, and they stop thinking when you start talking that way. And this is the last thing I want to have happen—for people to stop thinking.

Like Jeb, she has opinions about the religious beliefs of the people she encountered in academia.

> I don't think a lot of theologians worry about whether they'll go to Heaven or Hell. They're worried about making sure that they're in touch with God, they're in touch with that creative force in the universe, that inspiration. That's what they're longing for—that transcendent understanding of the world in harmony. And I say all this because I felt all that. I thought, "Wow, the world is this wonderful! This is such a cool place!" One of the hardest things about accepting the fact that I didn't believe in God was accepting that the world could still be this wonderful, magical place but without the deity.

She also has opinions about the Church's fundamental motives and priests' fundamental beliefs.

> I honestly think the reason the Church continues in this is because it doesn't want to give up this power it has on the world stage. It has nothing to do with perpetuating faith, hope, and love, but it's more about perpetuating itself. It's become an artificial organ, and it's trying to survive. And that's just my position on it. I honestly think that most priests—I know, because I've listened to the priests; I've gone to school with them—they don't believe the canonical stuff. They don't believe and they don't even go *near* the Trinity. They study it, but they don't necessarily understand it.

Finally, she has advice for young Catholic seminarians.

> I'd say, "Don't stop questioning." I mean, there were obviously questions that brought you to the point you are in your life. There were obviously questions that inspire you about religious language and religious ideology—all the beautiful, lyrical ideas espoused from the pulpit. But don't sit back on the laurels of those beautiful things. You need to make sure that those beautiful things that are said are matched by beautiful works, and that is not always the case. When there's something in your religious experience or your religious tradition that reflects the diminution of another human being or harms another human being, then you must recognize that it's not in the best interest of human beings. And it's not in your best interest to perpetuate anything that supports that position.

From Seeds of Doubt to Blossoms of Disbelief

Bill, who intends to remain an Episcopal priest until his retirement, acknowledged the atheism that grew in him in seminary several years later, when he accepted the finality of death.

> For me, the greatest anxiety was death. I knew I had held onto faith due to fear, and I really believe I somehow allowed myself to enter that darkness in an unlimited way. And I was not fearful. I really did have peace, and whatever remnant I had of God vanished. And then, although I was alone, I could quite literally say, "I'm a nonbeliever. I'm an atheist."

He believes that that acceptance has helped him minister to the dying.

> We lost a young man in our church recently, and I spent a lot of time with him, just having conversations. And as he came closer to the end of his life, he was more and more honest about his fear, his uncertainty. I believe that those are emotions that, once addressed and allowed to be present, lose their power over us. That was a really, really intimate kind of walk with him. I realized the value of what I had been allowed to do for my own self.

He spoke about how he has handled the issue of the Resurrection, in both preaching and teaching.

> I have said from the pulpit, "I don't know about you, but for me . . . the story is not about the resuscitated corpse. It's not about that." I would use language like, "It is about the presence of God among us." I believe that makes sense to people.
>
> Occasionally, mostly in those teaching opportunities, when you're gathering around, there's an invitation to conversation, and I'll ask, "What do you think [about a metaphorical interpretation of the Resurrection]? Is that good news or bad news?" People say, "What difference does it make, one way or the other?"

Bill says he is comfortable in his priestly role but acknowledges some continuing conflict.

> I know I am who I am. I know what I think. I know I'm not troubled by it. I don't lose sleep anymore, because, after all, accepting my atheism wasn't about God, it was about my fear of death. And so I would say that I play the role—put the collar on and say the prayers.
>
> We don't have a problem talking about the myth of the Virgin Mary. That's easy work among Episcopal and other colleagues who think that way. But to me, that's completely different from saying, "I'm an atheist."
>
> There's this whole issue of "I'm an atheist, I'm a nonbeliever." And yet I'm still using the language; I'm still helping people depending on where they are. But most are not atheists, or at least they're not admitting to being atheists. So I compartmentalize that conflict.
>
> I don't think I'm denying anything. I feel very comfortable with this particular language—displaying faith without truly having faith. I'm OK with that.

When Vince was acting as a visiting parish priest, he concentrated on making his sermons relevant to his surroundings.

> Well, mostly, when I would give a homily it would be basically stories of Jesus and the Scriptures. I would try to think, depending on where I was going, in terms of what possible elements might be applicable to these people. When I was in seminary, I was preaching in a lot of declining industrial towns, where I thought about what I could say to help them deal with their lives. It was different when I was in a more urban situation. I kind of enjoyed it. It was a bit of a challenge to find something that would be relevant.

He became open to other ideas about the meaning of the Eucharist.

> My involvement in sacramental theology [turning bread and wine into the body and blood of Christ] evolved into concepts that this was sharing a meal, just as you'd share a meal with friends and family, and this would create the bond of union. This was the purpose of it.
>
> I saw it as just a symbolic act, and I no longer took it to be literally true, but I knew that many of the people I was distributing Communion to still held the more traditional beliefs. That was fine with me. I didn't discuss the issue much.

He recalls just two parishioners expressing doubts about Communion, both in the confessional.

> In both cases, they confessed it almost as a sin: "You know, I don't really—I just can't understand—I don't believe it could be the body of Christ." We didn't talk about it too much. I tried to explain that it was essentially symbolic—the communion that should exist between all members of the Church. Of course, you didn't want to take too much time in the confessional to get into a long explanation. You had to keep people moving.

After a while, he was hearing and seeing things that ultimately led to his decision to leave.

> Bit by bit, any idealism I had was just shredded.
>
> Some priests, at least by reputation, were not real vigorous in observing their vows of celibacy. In some cases, we knew, or at least the

> report was, that they were caught doing something with altar boys. If it was two priests, they would be separated and reassigned. The attitude seemed to be, "Well, we'll just cover this up." But if you were having an affair with a woman, that could be dangerous. It might end up with a child-support suit and things like that, so that was not tolerated. They would be disciplined, and very severely.
>
> I was assigned to help out for two weeks at a parish that was in a neighborhood that wasn't exactly affluent but where the pastor lived very comfortably. We dined out every night I was there, and that jarred me. Where was this money coming from? It was coming from those people. After that experience, I said, "No, I can't go on with this. It's not part of my life anymore. I've got to find something else." And I knew it wouldn't be easy. I had no money. But I just couldn't see going back and continuing now. At this point, it was a pure charade. I just didn't want to do that anymore.

His family did not question his decision to leave the priesthood or pressure him to stay.

> They said, "If you feel that's what you've got to do, that's what you've got to do." That made it a lot easier.

And he did not share with them his reasons for leaving.

> I suppose I still had some part of the feeling that if they still believed in it, I didn't want to rattle their cage. On the other stuff [sexual improprieties], you don't tell tales.

From Diligent to Disenchanted

For Michael, it was the reading and thinking he did since his days in Seventh-day Adventist seminary that destroyed his fundamentalist beliefs. When he was interviewed, he was planning to leave the Adventists after a lifetime in the church and more than twenty years in the clergy. In recent years, he had also occasionally attended regional and local freethought and atheist meetings. He is grateful for the security and love that the Adventists provided him, but he can no longer pretend that he holds their beliefs.

> It's like everything I've learned recently has been totally eye-opening to

> me. I didn't learn about a lot of different divergences of Christianity—the Gnostics, the Manicheans. It was just brief touches on them as heretics, and that was about it. You know, not a lot of in-depth stuff.
>
> When I look back on my early years of pastoring, I can remember Bible studies with people and talking about creation and making a statement such as, "The concept of evolution is like an explosion in a junkyard and a 747 appears." That's all I knew about evolution, and that's what I would say. Of course, that's stupid.

Harry, when he became a Lutheran minister, initially reveled in the preaching and teaching he did from the pulpit:

> I have absolutely always loved preaching and public speaking. I love the sense of being up there, connecting with the crowd. If you can play the educational role, it's fun, because if you know your congregation, if you know the context of their daily life, you can really address their struggles. I always tried to make the message very contextual to what they were experiencing—not imposing my own agenda, necessarily—because I saw it as a means to try to help people deal with life, help strengthen their faith, help them know that God isn't a mean old guy up there throwing lightning bolts.

However, in the process of presenting his positive view of God, he ran into some communication difficulties with his congregation:

> I wanted to present a gracious, loving God. More than anything else, I wanted people to know that—to banish the conception of a threatening, judgmental God. That was a real thrust of my preaching. The hard part of preaching, for me has been— It actually got worse over the years, because you find yourself as a preacher, and I bet most preachers would say this, self-censoring all the time. You can't be completely and totally honest up there. If you're starting to have doubts, for example, you can't share that. People don't want to hear that, and you want to keep your paycheck and keep your congregation growing. But even beyond that, there were times when I shied away from maybe the prophetic role—saying things I really believed in—because it would just cause too much discord.

He started to feel uneasy about biblical teachings and elements of the liturgy that he hadn't examined closely while in seminary.

We were not taught that Paul never mentions any of Jesus' teachings, or miracles, or birth narrative. Paul doesn't quote Jesus, except one time. We did learn that Paul's letters came way before the Gospels were written. So there are many times, reading through Paul's letters, where he's making a point, and you think he could really buttress his point here by quoting something Jesus said, but somehow he doesn't know about it. So there's something fishy going on here. And there are sections here, like Romans 13, where Paul says a lot of things that sound a whole lot like what Jesus said but he doesn't attribute them to Jesus. Then you go back to the Sermon on the Mount and think, "Wow, this sounds a lot like what Paul said in Romans 13, except this was written down way later." Then you begin to see that there's something hugely amiss here. And I don't know how much you want to get into this, but it's those types of things that really started to bother me a whole lot.

I'd have to lead the congregation in the Apostles' Creed: Jesus Christ, God's only begotten son, born of the Virgin Mary. I never believed he was born of a virgin, ever. Or maybe I did a long time ago, but not in the past twenty years. There were things I had to say in the Creed every week that I would have to interpret in the most symbolic way possible, but I finally reached the point where I couldn't even say this anymore, in any way that's meaningful.

He explained how he handled tricky situations by obfuscating.

You can play a lot of word games with yourself when you say things you don't really believe, and find a way to say it with some type of integrity. For example, you could say, "I believe that Jesus is the savior of the world," meaning that you believe in the actual, literal atonement—that because he died, he somehow paid for the sins of every person on Earth. And because he justified God's wrath, he atoned for these sins, and now you could get to Heaven through him. But you could also say the same words with fingers crossed behind your back—because I believe if people really got onboard with the Sermon on the Mount and tried to live a little more lovingly and nonviolently, *this* could be the salvation of the world. See what I mean? You play these kinds of tricks with yourself, where you can say the formula in a way that's going to satisfy the person listening, and you're thinking internally, "Well, I mean something different by it."

After teaching a few Bible study classes, Harry became frustrated with people's reaction to the Bible and with the Bible itself:

> No one asks you anything. If anyone were to sit down and actually read the Bible as any kind of a narrative, you would see that this stuff does not hang together. Inconsistencies and fabrications. And they're glaring—you don't have to dig hard. I mean, in Mark 2, Jesus references a story in the Old Testament, First Samuel 21. Jesus and the disciples are being criticized for gleaning from a field on the Sabbath, and he references a time where there was an analogous story involving David, and he says it was at the time that Abiathar was high priest. Well, if you've read First Samuel 21, you know in that story it's not Abiathar but his father, Ahimelech, who is high priest. Now, Jesus, according to the Christian notion, is supposed to be God, or divine, and even if he wasn't completely perfect in his earthly manifestation you would have expected him to at least know the Bible well enough not to make that mistake. So the possibilities are either (a) Jesus was mistaken, or (b) the author of Mark was mistaken. And if he [the author of Mark] was mistaken there, what else did he get wrong? That's in the second chapter of Mark. Nobody asks about that kind of stuff at all.

Over the years, he noticed that people had very narrow concerns about religion.

> People want to typically ask you, as a pastor, issues of theodicy—issues of God and human suffering. "If there's a loving God, why did this bad thing happen to me?" or to so-and-so? The second most common question is about who's going to Heaven? You know, everybody's worried about my Buddhist friend going to Heaven—or my husband, who doesn't go to church, going to Hell. Those are the two questions people fixate on. . . . Either people don't want to deal with the inconsistencies of the Bible or they just see them and they gloss over them. But it doesn't seem to be an issue for a lot of people.

He thought back to a time when he sincerely taught things that he no longer believes.

> When teaching Bible studies years ago, when I was more orthodox, I'd tell people that the emergence of Christianity came about because of a series of unique geopolitical factors. I did this to show that Jesus had to

> be born when he was born. If he was born any earlier, the infrastructure wouldn't have been there at all, so it was like a tinder box waiting for a match to light it: "See? God's hand is in history all along, preparing the way for Jesus." But it's bogus. You don't need to say that. There were these unique geopolitical circumstances that provided a fertile field for the emergence of a movement like this. But people just loved my explanation, because they wanted to be reassured that the hand of God is at work, seriously influencing the events in history and making things happen.

When asked the follow-up question, "And you believed that at the time, is that correct?" he responded:

> Ummm, maybe. I'm trying to figure that out. At what point did I really believe it? At what point was I saying things that I knew would please the crowd? There's always that element, too. I guess I'm still trying to figure that out—how my own evolution progressed. Maybe it was happening when I was teaching these things.

His beliefs were evolving as he prepared sermons, looking for "interesting things about the world to share with people." It was during this process that he discovered evolutionary psychology.

> I was reading books on happiness, like Jonathan Haidt's book, *The Happiness Hypothesis*,[23] which isn't specifically about evolutionary psychology, but he references it, and I just started looking in his bibliography and then reading some of the books that he had referenced, which led me to things like Steven Pinker's *The Blank Slate*[24] and Robert Wright's *The Moral Animal*.[25] Then I read some of David Sloan Wilson's work, like *Evolution for Everyone*,[26] and, of course, Dan Dennett's book. I haven't read *Darwin's Dangerous Idea* yet, but I did read *Breaking the Spell*. And one thing led to another. I'd pick up a book, and when that book referenced others, I'd go read those books, too. I found it fascinating, and I'm still finding it fascinating.

After moving to a nondenominational church, where he was less constrained by dogma, Harry eventually left to start a humanist congregation. He hopes to use his new pulpit to help people gain a clearer understanding of the world and to make it a better place.

> I'd like to help people to see that what we're dealing with here is nothing supernatural. It's very much the result of the geophysical facts on the ground in human history. This wasn't anything divine that happened; it happened in very ordinary human lives. And it's not based on truth in any way, shape, or form. Archeology has not corroborated any of the most important events in the Old Testament.
>
> Religion has been such a source of oppression—from the theodicy issue to sexuality issues. You name it. Even in other social issues as well. And I'd like to play a small role in ending the oppression.

Burnout and Depression

Linda LaScola

Merriam-Webster defines "burnout" as "exhaustion of physical or emotional strength or motivation usually as a result of prolonged stress or frustration," and "depression" as "a state of feeling sad; a psychoneurotic or psychotic disorder marked especially by sadness, inactivity, difficulty in thinking and concentration, a significant increase or decrease in appetite and time spent sleeping, feelings of dejection and hopelessness, and sometimes suicidal tendencies."

Rick, a United Church of Christ campus chaplain who participated in our 2010 pilot study, often e-mails articles about religion, and when he sent information about "clergy burnout," it spurred us to think about whether burnout was a factor in our participants' nonbelief. In the interviews, some of them had discussed their depression, sometimes severe depression, but burnout was apparently not much of an issue. Or had we overlooked it? We decided to investigate the prevalence of these phenomena and check the interview transcripts for references to them.

Burnout

ReligionLink describes itself as "the ultimate source for journalists reporting on religion" and "a non-partisan service of Religion Newswriters Association and Religion News LLC . . . created by journalists, for journalists."[27] The ReligionLink page of resources on burnout does not mention loss of belief as a contributing factor.[28] Substance abuse, marital infidelity, and an undefined "spiritual emptiness" are mentioned, but not loss of belief in God. A word-check on "burn" in the interview transcripts confirmed our recollection that burnout was hardly ever mentioned. (The word "burn" usually came up in association with the word "Hell.") As for "burnout" or "burned out," only a few participants used those terms and in only one case was it in direct reference to a participant's church work. Most such references were related to pre- or post-clergy jobs. For instance, Jack, a Southern Baptist minister who participated in the pilot study, mentioned burnout in the context of leaving a dead-end job to study for the ministry: "Traveling all across the U.S. in different towns for six years, I just really got burned out. I didn't feel it was going anywhere career-wise." A life in the ministry offered him more stability and fulfillment.

Adam, a Church of Christ minister who also participated in the pilot study and who values the long-term friendships he has formed at church and the outlet that ministry has provided for his skills and talents, mentioned burnout to a prospective employer as a plausible reason for wanting to leave the ministry.

> When I interviewed with the general manager, the only thing I said about leaving the ministry was that I was pretty much burned out on church work and that I needed to make more money than the church could afford to pay.

The presumption is that employers would easily understand and accept burnout and low pay as good reasons for wanting to leave the ministry. The real reason was that Adam no longer believed in God. But he knew that this would be an inappropriate statement to make to a prospective employer, so he was deceptive, even as he sought to escape the deceit of being a nonbelieving pastor.

Pete, a youth pastor-in-training, was the only participant who mentioned burnout as a direct result of his work in the church:

> Yeah, I was definitely burned out by the Assemblies of God at that point. Mostly over being free labor for three years. They were addicted to free labor to mulch the church property and run their small groups and stuff. So they're able to keep this thousand-person youth group running on a staff of five full-time adults and an army of college kids. So, I was just a slow burnout, because I was working like sixty to eighty hours a week for zero dollars. So, yeah, by that point I was done.

Burnout, however, was not Pete's only reason for leaving. As his religious studies progressed, he found himself becoming an agnostic when his superiors brushed off his questions about inconsistencies in the Bible. The only people available to discuss his questions were other trainees. Pete first joined the Assemblies of God as a young teenager, when accepting Jesus helped to shield him from serious family and legal troubles. Since leaving the church, he has married one of his former church friends, also now agnostic, and they are both in college, majoring in fields unrelated to religion. They hope to raise their future children in an emotionally and financially stable home environment that will make them less susceptible to religious claims.

Matthew, one of our three seminary professors, wondered whether clergy who said they no longer believed in God were simply burned out.

> I think that often what happens is not a collapse of faith, in the fundamental sense that one stops believing in God, but that one no longer cares—that burnout creates a kind of apathy. . . . If you don't have the energy, the skill, the brilliance to communicate effectively and get people excited and enthusiastic, then, my God, you burn out quickly. And if you're the only intellectual, and nobody else is helping you get excited, you die of intellectual loneliness.

Perhaps Matthew was being defensive and myopic, but he could be pointing out a key difference between how seminary professors and clergy handle the same information. The professors don't have to preach their tenets to laypeople, who are generally less theologically educated and may be seeking only solace and comfort. Professors don't counsel or perform funerals and baptisms—pastoral duties that require repeating the creedal elements that professors teach their students to look at with the eyes of a scholar rather than a believer. According to some of our participants, their discomfort with Bible stories or parts of the liturgy didn't start until they had repeated them many times or tried to explain them to parishioners.

None of the clergy in the study described themselves as burned out as a result of moving from belief to nonbelief. They had been troubled, anxious, depressed along the way; however, from their descriptions of what they gained or lost when their beliefs changed, we gather that they also felt liberated, even thrilled, to be out of the bind of belief. Despite all the problems nonbelief has caused them, it also invigorates them, making burnout a nonissue. Carl the Lutheran and Bill the Episcopalian are examples; both are in liberal congregations and both have decided to stay put until retirement. They like their jobs (except for hiding their nonbelief) and are respected by their parishioners and the community. Andy, an agnostic United Church of Christ pastor, and Wes, a Methodist minister in our pilot study, also in liberal congregations, see themselves as guiding their congregants into a non-faith-centered future. Here there's no burnout either; Wes and Andy both have a strong sense of mission.

So perhaps the studies on clergy burnout are correct not to include lack of belief as a cause. Our findings uncovered no such connection. Then again, our participants are self-selected; they volunteered to discuss their nonbelief. There may well be many clergy so settled into to their routine or resigned to their situation that they have lost their initial fervor and sense of mission. Think of officiants at weddings and funerals who are disengaged, insensitive, or even downright rude. Perhaps it's not boredom but burnout due to lack of belief that has robbed them of empathy for people in their moments of greatest joy or sorrow.

Depression

When a loved one dies, the natural, healthy response is mourning, a kind of depression. Anyone remaining happy and upbeat in the face of such a radical change in life circumstances would be regarded as psychopathic. Estrangement from the creed to which one has devoted one's life is a similarly dire blow to one's psyche, so depression in such circumstances seems normal, not pathological. It is possible, of course, that clinical, organic depression is in rare cases the *cause* of abandoned belief, but that must be shown, not assumed, since it is a predictable effect in any event.

Depression was a much more common topic of conversation during the interviews. Although participants were not systematically asked about depression, the subject was raised when it seemed pertinent or when participants mentioned it, which eleven of them did. Depression came up in various contexts, sometimes related to the journey away from religious belief and sometimes not. Unlike many people in other occupations, clergy are not reluctant to discuss their personal mental-health issues. Moreover, dealing with these issues among members of their congregation is part of their everyday life. Most clergy have training in pastoral counseling and routinely refer their parishioners to mental-health professionals.

Caitlin, the nonbelieving Episcopal priest, mentioned depression not as her personal problem but as afflicting the Church itself.

> In the late nineties, I was angry because that Church I loved was diminishing and disintegrating and in a depressed state and shrinking and getting old. I see in terms of process and vision. I know how to fix things, and I know that the process I and others developed for embracing young families and children in the worship life of the community could stem the bleeding.

Two pastors—Tammie, the Methodist, and Winnie, the Presbyterian—described personal depression caused by, respectively, illness and childhood trauma and unrelated to their changes in religious belief.

Michael, the Seventh-day Adventist, although he has a family history of depression, ascribed his own long-term, low-level depression in part to his move from belief to nonbelief.

> I've been on medication since some controversial Adventist books came into my life twenty years ago and got me started seeing Scripture differently.

George, a former Greek Orthodox monk, has experienced depression, sometimes severe depression, since early adolescence. Medication never worked well for him. His own diagnosis, once he came to terms with his nonbelief, was "existential crisis."

> I didn't know how to live. I'd lost my sense of meaning, and I had no alternative sense of meaning with which to replace it. That was what was going on.

The therapist he saw for a few months after leaving the monastery diagnosed post-traumatic stress disorder—a diagnosis that George thinks fits. Though it was difficult for him to contemplate a life outside the monastery, he ultimately felt it was intellectually honest and necessary to his mental well-being.

> I had reached the point where it seemed that all the data was in, and the data was overwhelmingly negative, both in terms of the bookish stuff and in terms of how I was being treated by others—all the lying I had to be involved in by the dictates of the authorities. And I just thought, "I don't believe the truth claims any longer, and I don't feel that the men in black are in fact virtuous people at all." There was just no doubt that I had married my life to a fraud, that I just couldn't honestly continue pursuing this—and that if I continued in the Church it was going to destroy me psychologically. If I wanted to find any kind of psychological health, any kind of spiritual rest, it could only be through taking my life in my own hands, not allowing my life to be dictated by authority and . . . blind obedience.

Both of our Mormon participants became seriously depressed as their beliefs disintegrated. Joe, the active bishop, was mourning the loss not only of his beliefs but also of a culture that encompassed his whole family and community:

> I'm crushed. I'm crushed. I mean, this has been one of the worst experiences of my life, going through a crisis of faith. It's horrible. It's absolutely horrendous. I had to go on antidepressants; I was waking up in the middle of the night with panic attacks. I never had those in my life. My crisis of faith triggered this depression; I have no doubt about that. I'm not the same person I was before all this happened.
>
> I think it's a shock at first, you know. You sit there and you say, "Oh my gosh, I don't know if I totally believe the literalness of everything anymore." It's like things collapse. It's like an earthquake, you know. It's like an internal Armageddon. Eventually Armageddon will be over and there will be peace—that's how I'm viewing it.

Walt, a former bishop who left the Mormon fold, described becoming suicidal upon realizing that there was no God.

> When it became clear that there was no one looking out for me, I got really angry—at nothing and everything and just life itself. I'd never been suicidal before, but there are a lot of places in the mountains where I could be running and easily fall off the cliff. People would say, "He had an accident—it's sad." I felt there was absolutely no point in living. I know that sounds ridiculous, because I love my family, but I had based everything on the eternal perspective of life, and it was gone.

> If I don't know why I'm here, what purpose do I have being here? It was fortunately a short-lived experience when it was really severe.

Some of our participants became deeply depressed when their beliefs were changing. By contrast, others were released from depression when they first became deeply religious, in adolescence. Dave, the Baptist missionary, was a flailing teenager before he accepted Jesus as his savior.

> So I'm working at the fast-food restaurant, I'm depressed, I don't know what my life is going to be. I don't have any girlfriends and I'm seriously, seriously thinking about suicide—for the first time. Earlier on in my life it was more for attention. Now it was the real deal. I didn't have any hope in my life, any purpose in my life, any goals in my life; I'm just floating debris.

Dave, who had been neglected and abused as a child, was strongly attracted to the message of Jesus' love and protection that he heard from a coworker. Then one night, he got saved while listening to Christian Radio.

> The radio preacher said, "Do you know this Jesus? Do you believe in this Jesus?" And I said to myself, "No." And he said, "If you have not believed in this Jesus, then pray this prayer after me." So I prayed the prayer. And he said, "If you prayed this prayer, now you're saved. You're Christian, and you're a child of the King and you're going to Heaven." And I said, "Wow!"

He was impressed with the warmth he felt in his new church family.

> I became a member of a church and, for the first time, people were asking how my week went. People were talking to me. For the first time in my life, I had a semblance of a family, which meant a lot to me. And I noticed that a preacher sort of got more attention, so I set out to preach—or I was "called to preach," is the actual terminology.

Although his faith did not last, he is grateful for the early positive effect it had on his life.

> Looking back on it all, in some ways Christianity saved my life—and for that reason only, I am thankful for it.

Pete, the Assemblies of God trainee, also felt saved as a teenager. Here's how he describes his born-again experience:

> Oh, monumental! Oh, like the greatest day of my life! I had been in a lonely and depressing place, and I couldn't continue with the path I had been on, with the drinking and the drugs and the partying. I was already kicked out of my mother's house; I didn't want to get kicked out of my father's, too. Then what would I do? So it felt like this is what I needed, this is how I was going to turn my life around.

Tony, the former Catholic priest, described himself as a depressed college student who was unsure of his future direction and questioning his commitment to Catholicism. An experience at church changed that and led him on his path to the priesthood.

> I was thinking about killing myself, and I prayed for help. I went back to church over the summer and started reading the Bible. I was like, "If I'm going to leave this stuff, I want to understand it before I leave it, since it's part of my family and my history." Then about a month into the school year, I was at Mass and heard this homily where the priest talked about being vulnerable, being open, being passionate. It was the healing of the deaf mute, where Jesus says, "Ephphatha, be opened!" And I understood that about compassion, because I was always a very compassionate kid, or—What do they call you?—"sensitive." You know, a code word for gay. So I thought, "OK, God, what do you want me to do with my life?" And it was like there was this openness in me that suddenly was like, "Oh gosh, I wonder if I'm supposed to be a priest?" Then it all went pretty quickly from there. I really wanted to help people.

Tony's beliefs eroded gradually, affected by his experiences with clerical sex abuse and dishonesty. He ultimately realized that his desire to help people could not thrive within the Church. Years later, another depressive episode drove Tony away from the priesthood.

Jim, an Episcopal priest and one of two Episcopal clergy who were interviewed as believers, described a catharsis he had during an especially beautiful Episcopal service as he contemplated the Resurrection of

Christ. This experience made it possible for him to resume his seminary studies following a period of feeling distanced from Christianity.

> Because of the Resurrection, there is hope that I don't have to worry about dying. I'm not talking about physical death, I'm not talking about going to Hell. I'm talking about the soul in me dying. The pain that I felt inside was no longer my pain, it was God's pain—so that allowed me to get some distance on it, to disown it in a way. I can identify now with the God part of my soul, rather than the pain part of my soul. It's very hard to describe. But it felt like there's this golden egg at the core of my being, the pearl of great price, this indestructible, pure essence of being through which life flows. The source of my life, the source of my soul, is in there, and that is the Christ within me. And that will never die. . . . That whole depression, all of that self-pity, all of that yearning, just vanished in that church service. And that's when I knew I could go back to seminary and go into the ministry. It was the missing piece I didn't have before.

Low-level depression has come and gone throughout Jim's life, but his commitment to his faith has remained intact.

There is no clear sense, at least from our research, that burnout or depression will routinely occur when clergy move from belief to nonbelief. Burnout seems unrelated to changing beliefs. As for depression, it appears to be a by-product of the mental turmoil involved when one examines one's beliefs in the context of a troubled life. In our examples, depression lifted immediately when religion was accepted and slowly when it was rejected. In both situations, the depression lifted when a resolution was reached, irrespective of whether the resolution was for or against religious belief.

V. EMERGING THEMES

Daniel C. Dennett and Linda LaScola

The Plight of Liberal Clergy: Metaphors, Myths, Truths, and Facts
Linda LaScola

As a former liberal Christian, I was particularly eager to understand liberal clergy. I was bothered by the negative response from some of them after our pilot study was published. They complained that we didn't get it—that we saw things in black and white, just as fundamentalist Christians do, that we were missing the nuances of the liberals' sophisticated, evolved faith, which thrives on myth and mystery, tradition and reason.

Liberal clergy don't accept the Bible's miracles. They don't believe in the supernatural, and they are open to science. They realize that atheists would therefore not consider them believers, but they do believe, and several wrote to tell us so. As one correspondent put it, "According to your definition of God [as a supernatural being], I am more an atheist than you are, and yet I adore God!" They say there are many clergy like them. But we found them inexplicit about their beliefs.

In our efforts to get a better understanding of the liberals, we interviewed two "believing" Episcopal priests (classified as "others" in appendix A). Their beliefs, or lack of beliefs, were not unlike those of the sixteen liberal clergy who characterized themselves as agnostic or atheist, but they still think of themselves as believers.

Charles, an Episcopalian hospital chaplain who began his ministry as a conservative Christian, describes what he believes this way:

> I have a priest friend who says, 'There's living in the myth, and there's living outside the myth." For me, when I'm in the myth, I totally believe the themes of the Resurrection and Ascension, and those mean a lot to me. And outside the myth, I don't think they're literally true. It's just not possible, based on what I know about science. . . . And the point of this life—well, there is no point to this life, but you have to find *some* meaning, because we're meaning-making creatures. So we do a lot of things to make this a meaningful existence. Hopefully, that existence lasts beyond us to some degree, but probably not. That's really what I believe. And at the same time, the Christian mythology speaks to me at a cultural level—more [on that level] now than at a real belief kind of level.

Charles recognizes the finiteness of life and the limits of his beliefs, while finding solace and meaning in the myths that the Episcopal Church espouses. He also acknowledges the pragmatism in this stance.

> The problem is that I'm a leader in the Church, and there are lots of problems that go along with that. I've got a pension program with the Episcopal Church, so in some ways it would be a luxury, at this point, to decide that I believe something different, or that I will renounce my vows as an ordained person, or whatever. Because now my family's future, in many ways, depends on my participation in the pension program. So it's a very practical reality. And I'm like 3 percent ashamed to mention that to you, but that's just the fact of the matter.

In contrast, Jim, a cradle Episcopalian and the rector of a thriving suburban Episcopal church, is much more at ease with myth. Unlike Charles, he doesn't rationalize his acceptance of myth or apologize for it. Jim's appreciation of myth comes naturally to him.

> The information about the Divine is contained in the medium of myth and prayer. And the engagement of that realm is the nonrational realm, where the experience of the Divine occurs, and then it's left to the brain to figure what the hell that was. That's why mythology, for me, is so important.
>
> There's a reason why we have mythological imaginations. It's a path to transformation—personal transformation, emotional healing, spiritual growth—in my opinion. So I don't mind using mythological language—I think it's great. I think there's a difference between the

> ecstatic language we use in church and in worship and the descriptive language we might use outside of the worship context. When we enter a church, we enter a mythological world. I think everybody does. The people in my church are very intelligent. They believe in evolution. They also understand that what happens to us as we engage in prayer and worship and mythological imagination is fundamental to what it means to be human, and speaks deeply to the soul, and carries us into becoming better human beings. Then they ask, "Well, what am I supposed to do with the Nicene Creed? I don't know if I believe it." I talk about mythology; I tell them to sing it, consider it a poem, consider it an object of art or great literature.

Jim is particularly bothered by the New Atheists who, in his opinion, talk about Christians as if they are all evolution deniers.

> I picked up *The God Delusion* [by Richard Dawkins] at the used-book store the other day, and it was the most insufferable reading I've ever had to endure. It's incredibly disingenuous, if not equally as bigoted as the right-wingers. The arguments are laughable to me, and yet he's earnest and sincere and he really believes he's pursuing this ethical agenda. But I think he's willfully obtuse, and it bothers me, because both sides in this debate are yelling past each other. Meanwhile, a way of life that is life-giving to me and to millions of others is completely misunderstood, mischaracterized, and ignored.

From interviews with liberal pastors like Jim and Charles, and from reading the viewpoints of others like them, it seems obvious that liberal clergy think fundamentalism is horrendous for all the reasons atheists do. They also claim that atheists unfairly attack them because of a false assumption that liberal and fundamentalist clergy are one and the same adversary. Liberal clergy think atheists are dense, and atheists think liberal clergy are dense. When it comes to religion it seems that atheists lead with their heads and liberal clergy with their hearts. Where the liberals hear poetry and myth, atheists hear mumbo-jumbo and lies. The liberals may well be as intelligent, educated, and science-oriented as most atheists, but they recognize a spiritual dimension that atheists dismiss as nonsense; whereas liberals consider atheists blind to the mysterious, the divine, the sacred aspects of life that they find so meaningful—and so hard to explain to the satisfaction of nonbelievers.

Until recently, mainline liberal churches—for instance, the United Methodist, Presbyterian, Episcopalian, and United Church of Christ—were the dominant religious force in American society, and as such, they didn't have to explain much of anything to anyone in order to command respect. Obfuscation, rationalization, denial, worked just fine and served to protect their way of life. Now they're feeling boxed in: bounded on one side by fundamentalists and on the other by the New Atheists.

Compare their situation to that of men during the women's movement of the 1960s. Intelligent, well-meaning, respectful, socially conscious males were caught off guard, put on the defensive, made to feel they had a lot to lose. They could see that society was unfair to women, and some of them had had a sense of that all along, but little motivation or ability to change things. The system, after all, favored men, and the prospect of reorganizing it was scary. Scary for women, too, but women were highly motivated, as the atheists are today. Ultimately, the system would have stayed the same if a lot of men hadn't come onboard, which happened in large part because many of these men and women depended on and loved each other. We can't say that about liberal clergy and atheist leaders—at least, not yet—but they do have a similar worldview and a common enemy: religious fundamentalism.

Unlike their conservative counterparts, liberal denominations have made huge, socially conscious changes—performing same-sex marriages, accepting gay and women clergy, and (quietly) accepting the Bible as mythical, not factual truth. And what is their reward? They are losing membership, while the numbers of atheists and people with no religious affiliation are growing.[29]

Some of the liberal, nonbelieving participants in our study accept and even embrace the changes, seeing themselves as playing an important role in the societal transition away from traditional religion. Wes, the Methodist minister in our pilot study, put it this way:

> I'm interested in community, relationships. And I believe the argument could be made that that's what Jesus was interested in anyway. So I can do that at the local church level. And I'm also there for people who are recovering Christians. There are a lot of people out there who have been damaged by Christianity. And they feel guilty that they're not a Christian—or that they're not practicing or whatever. I'm their ideal

> pastor, because they can come to me and be told that they don't need to feel guilty.

He conflated Christianity with liberalism:

> I will be the first to admit that I see Christianity as a means to an end, not as an end unto itself. And the end is, very basically, a kind of liberal, democratic values. So I will use Christianity sometimes against itself to try to lead people to that point. But there's so much within the Christian tradition that itself influenced the development of those liberal values, you know. They didn't arise through secular means. They came out of some religious stuff. . . . I could couch all that in very secular language. If we were in a college setting, I would. But we're in a religious setting, so I use the religious language.

Although Wes did not speak for all liberal clergy, he provided a deeper understanding of liberal clergy's use of metaphor in sermons and in dialogue with members of their congregations—although we wonder, and frankly doubt, whether the people in the pews are as aware of their pastors' use of metaphorical language as the pastors think they are.

Andy, the agnostic United Church of Christ pastor, sees Jesus as a necessary transitional figure that will lead to a more openly secular society.

> Focusing on Jesus—not even worshiping him, but just focusing on Jesus, I would say—is an accommodation that's going to be necessary for the church to transition into something of value to our society. People aren't going to automatically jump; they're going to need a transition. And for my generation and probably several following, it's going to have to dawn slowly on people. The best way to do that is to use the historical Jesus as a bridge. I'm comfortable with the idea now, as long as we don't worship him as God—because we know he's not God. One Trinity Sunday, I preached that the Trinity was just an idea invented by humans. They found Jesus to be particularly insightful, so they called him God. He was invented to be a god—he never was. We know that.

Andy, who himself transitioned from conservative (Southern Baptist) to liberal, is as honest as he feels he can be with his congregation. He is truthful, "with one exception": He feels unable to say he doesn't believe in God.

> One of the values that helps me justify so-called lying to people, or not being forthcoming, is that I feel like I am blunting the negative impact of at least one religious community on the world. I think religion, especially Christianity, has been a very damaging force, and continues to be in national politics, so you can imagine my viewpoint on separation of church and state. I have taken one church out of that orbit. I have shielded the citizens of this country from the negative impact of one religious group, blunted that force, and helped to turn it into a choice for good, and charity, and works of justice.

Jared, a humanist and seminary graduate who was raised in the United Church of Christ, seems to agree with Andy's take on his childhood church. Jared also thinks there may be a reason that some UCC churches aren't more openly humanistic.

> The way it works is that in a lot of these UCC churches, the vast, vast, vast majority of members are liberal and probably closer to humanists than they are to any kind of Christianity—or Christian that's worth calling Christian. But the reality is that there's a third, or a quarter, of their membership—usually the oldest folks in the church and also usually the most moneyed interest in the church—who are the conservative folks. So there is often the appearance of religiosity to appease them.

Bill, the Episcopal priest whose doubts were sown in seminary and who referred to himself as an atheist during the interviews, is a pastor in a college town in a conservative state. His church is a liberal oasis for people affiliated with the university. Because he is a nonbeliever, he doesn't press belief on others. Instead, he listens empathically, and he considers himself especially able to comfort people who have doubts.

> People tell me all the time about former pastors telling them in no uncertain terms that doubting was part of their problem: "Oh ye of little faith!" Of course, having doubts and being a nonbeliever, an atheist, are two very, very different things. Well, believe it or not, a lot of people don't believe, at some point. I don't think I've ever felt like I

> needed to talk someone into being an atheist. Recently a parishioner came up to me and said, "I cannot say the Nicene Creed anymore." I said, "Really? You know, I can't either. I do say it, but I don't believe it." I was able to tell her that.

At the same time, he doesn't interfere with people's strong religious beliefs and at some level even envies them.

> Now, I've got to be just as honest with you in saying that for those who have a strong traditional faith, I cannot, I have not, I will not take that away. For many, many people, belief and faith and conviction and a personal relationship with God can be apparently very helpful. I personally feel that perhaps one is not completely and fully human as long as one embraces fantasies and myths about a theistic God who's personally involved in every aspect of one's life. But sometimes I've found myself perhaps a little bit envious of those who have that certainty and unmistakable peace and joy about death and life and just manage to get through it.

As conflicted as Bill is, he feels he is doing good work and counts himself privileged to be "invited into the most intimate aspects of a person's life—birth, dying, divorce, losing a child." His experience in these encounters is that "every person I've ever known is an unbeliever some of the time."

It is undoubtedly easier for liberal nonbelieving clergy to stay in their positions, because they are not expected to be perfect examples of living out the faith. Despite experiencing cognitive dissonance because of their loss of belief, they can fulfill a useful function in churches where parishioners with similar perspectives also see value in continuing in the Christian community.

The liberal cleric in our study who is most satisfied with his position is not a Christian. He is a Humanist rabbi. Jacob was bar mitzvahed in a Reform synagogue, and like so many of our participants, slowly became more and more liberal. Lucky for Jacob, he had somewhere to go, besides in the closet or out the door. There is a small but vibrant humanist movement within Judaism that provides a welcome respite for people like Jacob. While he appreciates the value of myth, just as liberal Christians do, he also loves being able to speak freely about Bible stories to other humanist Jews.

> They're attracted to the [humanist] movement because it seems to fit their worldview. They never believed in God. Or they don't believe in God. They're certainly not theistic. But they like being Jewish, they love the holidays, they love that affect component. And when I teach—and I do very clearly and accurately and forcefully teach about this history—they like it. They like it a lot. They come up to me and say, "Where can I read more? Where can I learn more?" And I would emphasize that this is the literature, and this is how people dealt with the literature. But here are some other things that are being uncovered, and you guys are going to have to take the evidence and weigh it. I can tell you how it weighs out for me. The way it weighs out for me is very clear: There are things in the Torah that are substantiated, that happened. And there are things that are literature.

Jacob is relieved to claim certain central elements of Judaism as myth and frustrated when others are equivocal about it.

> In my opinion, it's time for us to let go of childish things—and God language, to me, is a childish thing. The way we try to pretend that the Torah is true, even though we also know that it's not true, is a childish thing. We're trying to speak both ways. A good example is [Conservative rabbi] David Wolpe. He aroused a lot of controversy ten or eleven years ago when he got up, on Passover, of all times, and declared—as we all know and every archeologist knows—that the Exodus from Egypt was a fictional story. There may be true elements, but essentially it's a fictional story. This is the same David Wolpe who years later posted to his Facebook page: "Even though the stories of the Torah may not be true, the Torah is true." What does that mean? I don't know what that means. Something is either true or it's not true. Something is either factual or it's not factual. I know what he's trying to say, but it's a childish thing to tell people in the 21st century.

A more recent example of a well-known rabbi equivocating was in a letter to the editor of the *New York Times* on July 26, 2013, in response to an article about Mormon doubters.[30] Harold Kushner, a Conservative rabbi and author of *When Bad Things Happen to Good People,* offered this tip for Mormon leaders:

> Might I suggest that they use the tactic used by many modern Jews

> dealing with biblical narratives that defy credulity, from a six-day story of creation to Jonah living inside a large fish. We distinguish between left-brain narratives (meant to convey factual truth) and right-brain narratives (meant to make a point through a story; the message will be true even if the story isn't factually defensible).

What seems childish to Jacob but acceptable to Rabbi Kushner is also acceptable and common in Christian circles—the words "factual" and "true" are often used to mean different things. The Christian theologian Marcus Borg, in a *Washington Post* "On Faith" column about explaining Bible stories to children, instructs his readers on how to distinguish between the concepts of "fact" and "truth":

> If and when they ask, "Is that a true story?" they may be asking, "Did that really happen?" But you don't have to answer that question. You can say, "I don't know if it happened that way or not, but I know this is an important and truthful story." . . . Of course, the Bible and other sacred scriptures are not fairy tales—but we make a mistake when we think that stories must be factually true in order to be true and truthful.[31]

The conservative clergy's take on this semantic issue is quite different, as we shall see in the next section.

The Plight of the Literals: Dealing with the Challenges

Daniel C. Dennett

Many commentators have noted a telling symmetry. Fundamentalists and other defenders of the literal truth of the Bible agree with the New Atheists on one thing: Truth claims need to be taken seriously—which means they must be evaluated as true or false, not merely interpreted as metaphors and symbols. Liberal clergy, as Linda has noted, are squeezed between these two opposing adherents of the "put up or shut up" school of interpretation. The liberals think both extremes are simplistic; it's complicated, they say. The New Atheists have shrugged off this charge, accusing the liberal apologists of creating a pseudointellectual smokescreen to cover their retreat, and here the symmetry is extended, since that is also the opinion of many fundamentalists and other conservatives. One nonbeliever (Hugh, a Seventh-day Adventist student in his twenties) calls liberal Christianity "pseudo–Christianity" and adds:

> One of the things that frustrates me in debate with [liberal] Christians is that they are willing to adjust and remold their religion just to preserve its existence, not really its integrity. And that's basically because they want the assurance that they're going to Heaven someday.

He must be wrong about the "basic motive" of many of the liberals. Whatever solace they may get from their allegiance, it isn't the hope of reuniting with loved ones or meeting Jesus in Heaven, since they consider Heaven as much a myth as Christ's Resurrection or walking on water. But his opinion that the "remolding" of their religion jeopardizes its integrity is widely shared. His version is particularly demanding.

> I don't think you can just make the Bible say whatever you want it to say. I don't think that's an intellectually honest thing. And that's why I have left the Christian religion. I think I've done the intellectually honest thing.

Michael, the lapsed Seventh-day Adventist, thinks the motive of the liberals is "using the word 'God' to reach people."

> If I wanted to use the word "God" . . . I can say, "Well, to me, God is like a concept of what's ultimate reality." But to me, that's not God, that's ultimate reality. To me, it's a little bit underhanded to use God in that way.

Linda challenges him:

> *Linda:* What makes it underhanded, in your estimation?
>
> *Michael:* Again, it's how I was raised. I was raised [to believe] that God is a being—a supernatural being who is creator of the universe.
>
> *Linda:* It seems wrong to you even though you don't accept it anymore?
>
> *Michael:* Yeah. To me, that's God, and that's why I don't believe there *is* a God, because I don't see enough evidence to back that up.

Linda asks Dave, the nonbelieving Baptist missionary, whether he could imagine switching to a more liberal church.

> *Dave:* It would not be appealing to me at all. Many of the stories I'm referring to are not just Old Testament fables. Jesus quoted Jonah and the whale. I don't believe for a second that Jesus said that.[32]
>
> *Linda:* It sounds like, for you, it's really all or nothing.
>
> *Dave:* Yes. To me, and as I think Sam Harris has said, liberal theology is a lack of understanding of the Scriptures. People who are liberals are bringing modernism into their own understanding of the Scriptures and picking and choosing. I don't think that's a valid way of looking at the Scriptures.
>
> *Linda:* OK, let's say Jesus existed. He was a real person, and let's say he dies on the cross, but he didn't die for our sins. He didn't die and rise again. He wasn't born of a virgin. But he's this guy from antiquity who has had a huge effect on our lives, and he said a lot of good things. Can't we have a religion based around that guy?
>
> *Dave:* I guess you could. I wouldn't be part of it [laughing].

Then he softens his view of ecclesiastical liberalism somewhat: "If that works for them, fine. As long as they're not out there beating on doors and condemning people to Hell for not believing like them."

Candice, the nonbelieving Roman Catholic seminary graduate, has little patience with liberal theologians:

> That phrase, "I choose to call this 'God,'" I heard time and time and time again from theologians. It's their emerging concept of God—that God is kind of a different thing for every different group. I don't think most people would appreciate it. We're talking about an emerging polytheism. That's really what they're speaking of—of God continuously being manufactured for the individual. It's very self-centered.

She finds the liberal position she encountered in seminary frustrating and comes up with a devastating metaphor for the way the liberals adjust their positions.

> People start talking about God not in terms of this anthropomorphized deity from the Old and New Testaments but . . . as a transcendent, loving being that doesn't have a physical body—that's this creative force in the universe. When I listen to liberals talk like that now, it really frustrates me, because it's a cop-out. It's like you're constantly rearranging. It's like God is a Rubik's Cube, and they're constantly trying to get it into the perfect vision of this deity. And it's never going to happen. So in their desperation they're peeling the stickers off to rearrange it.

To Candice, liberal theology is too easy to count as a serious creed, and this opinion is echoed by those literals who recall the triumph of confronting the glaring problems of their creeds and defiantly endorsing them—in effect doubling down on Pascal's Wager. It's *supposed* to be hard.

Brian, the Lutheran seminary dropout, puts it this way:

> The difficult facts are treated as a challenge: Can your faith withstand this? Let me rephrase it: The truth of the religion is never allowed to be questioned, so inconvenient facts fit into the category of almost a dare. The platitude is, "Well, here is a fact that you might consider problematic, but if you can't integrate this and keep your religious worldview, it's a failure of faith."

There is a "creedal athleticism" that is an appealing feature of some religions.[33] It provides a costly signaling system—like the peacock's tail, or the giant antlers of the extinct Irish elk—for the literals to use in advertising their devotion, and also gives them a sense of community differing from that of the liberals. The liberals are a community whose members are bound together by their ceremonies, whereas the literals are an army, their loins girded by their faith. To many of them, liberal Christians are self-indulgent aesthetes, not really committed to their religion. In less diplomatic moments, they dismiss liberal Christians as atheists in disguise.

This moral disapproval of sophisticated theology is not new. The creed of the early 20th century Catholic/agnostic philosopher George Santayana was caricatured as "There is no God, and Mary is His Mother," and his combination of allegiance to Catholic themes and rituals with near-atheism was regarded with deep disapproval not only by conservative Christians but also by his generally open-minded Harvard mentor, William James.

As we saw in the section on seminary professors, liberals recognize the suspicion their clever circumlocutions often arouse, and they doubtless envy the bluff candor with which the literals can present their beliefs to potential converts. As Stan, the military chaplain, put it:

> My colleagues and clergy friends would ridicule fundamentalists, but at some point I came to realize they are preaching and teaching what they believe. If you read the Bible, they are actually being consistent in what they're teaching or they're believing. We're the ones who are sugarcoating it and trying to contextualize it and put it in other language, and we don't really mean what we say. And at some point, that just felt kind of mentally weak.

At the same time, liberals are relieved of the literals' burden of having to assert, with straight faces, belief in all the miracles in the Bible, and having to deny flat-out the obvious scientific truths of evolution in the face of mounting supporting evidence. The more literal your beliefs in the powers of an all-loving God, the more frequent the occasions for disillusionment. Dave, the Baptist missionary, trying to console a convert who wants children but can't get his wife pregnant, notes that disbelief ". . . begins to make sense to me. Why would a loving God give children to people who are going to abuse them, or might kill them, but not to people who would love them and nurture them?" Once he had accepted his disbelief, he could confess what had long been bothering him: "Just not having to defend all that crazy stuff is a great blessing."

Which project would you prefer to take on? Getting people to believe that the Bible stories are literally true, or getting people to understand the sophisticated idea that legends can be factually false but nevertheless carry an important moral message? George, the former Greek Orthodox monk, says:

> The appeal of [Greek] Orthodoxy to me—and I think this is the appeal of any kind of traditional religion—is that it gives you a set of authoritative answers to everything. Everything! And once you reject that, or once you distance yourself from that, then how do you make sense of anything? And then if you come to any of the big contentious

> questions of modern life, how do you deal with those?

Even the Orthodox are tempted to fudge their answers.

> It seems like the obvious question: "Well, did evolution happen, and if it did, how does it square with the account in Genesis?" It seems to me that that's the elephant in the room. And what Orthodox intellectuals would do would be to consider the question so abstractly that the question was left unanswered. When I was teaching Genesis myself in seminary, I was able to perform the same kind of magic trick—a sort of distraction: "Well, I'm going to talk over here, and it's all going to sound very smart, but it's not actually addressing the question." In fact, the only students I ever had that did insist [on the question of evolution being addressed] was in a Sunday school class, because the kids would want an answer, and they would not allow me to get all abstract.

One of the forces maintaining the ironclad literalism of some conservative denominations is the fact that any relaxation of it within the denomination can have the opposite effect from the one intended. Instead of making it easier for doubters in the flock to accommodate to the creed, it can ignite the fuse of doubt and trigger an avalanche of disbelief. One of the eye-opening moments for Joe, the Mormon, was reading an article in a liberal Mormon magazine that broached the idea of there being only metaphorical truth in some point of LDS doctrine. This led Joe to a liberal Mormon online chat room (*not* one of the many anti-Mormon and ex-Mormon Web sites), which strengthened and elaborated his doubts. Similarly, it was an article in a liberal Adventist magazine that shook Michael from his innocence. So conservatives are perhaps more vulnerable to well-meaning attempts from within their own denominations than to skeptical assaults from outside the faith.

Jerry DeWitt ("Johnny" in the study), a lapsed Pentecostal pastor who gave us permission to use his real name, described his vain attempts to integrate his new secular learning with his understanding of God.

> Now, at the same time that I'm trying to hold on to God, I'm still watching Professor Dennett, I'm still watching Professor Dawkins. All these other things are still going on at the same time, chiseling away, pestering me like flies around my head. So, I got to the point where I

> said, "Well, maybe it just is that God is in everybody." Then, recalling things that I had studied several years ago with Joseph Campbell, about mythology and comparative religion, I finally made that last little *click*. I finally said, "Well, the reason that we feel like God is in everyone is because really God is an internal dialogue that cultures have, that human beings naturally have, that we've evolved to have."

After he left his church and went public with his disbelief,[34] he illustrated his exodus from fundamentalist Christianity using his own self-administered five-step program. His journey began with his difficulty in accepting that God, supposedly all-loving, could deny Heaven to so many people. Starting with that apparently flagrantly contradictory premise, he softened it, softened it again, and again, and again—arriving at Richard Dawkins' frank atheism.

1. God loves everybody.
2. God saves everybody.
3. God is *in* everybody.
4. God is everyone's internal dialogue.
5. God is a delusion.

Notice that this transposition depends on beginning with a literal, unmetaphorical interpretation of God's love. It is easy enough to maintain premise #1 if you get to declare it a symbolic utterance that doesn't literally mean that God loves every human being the way a parent loves a child. But if you are a literalist, something else has to give, and this leads down the ladder to proposition #5.

Liberals and literals alike find it increasingly difficult to execute the strategies that have heretofore sufficed to keep their institutions viable for centuries, and unsurprisingly they are not eager to try altogether new approaches. Their predicament can be illuminated by comparison with another institution hard-pressed to maintain itself.

Plimoth Plantation is a living museum in Plymouth, Massachusetts, that has educated and delighted visitors for more than half a century with its meticulous re-creation and reenactment of the original Pilgrim colony. The calendar is set at 1627 and costumed actors assume specific identities drawn from the records of the time, occupying the houses, tilling the fields, tending the gardens, spinning and baking and blacksmithing. (Of course, when the museum closes they drive home to their 21st-century air-conditioned houses and televisions.) The lives of the identities they adopt have been extensively researched and internalized, so that museumgoers can adopt the perspective of a time-machine visitor and engage any inhabitants in a friendly discussion of their lives, their families, where they came from in England, what they wear and eat, how they garden, fish, and build their houses, and every other detail of 17th century life. The inhabitants will not respond to questions about modern times, modern technology, or the Red Sox, but they have a lot to say about their dreams for the "future," their gripes, their illnesses, their remedies, and their religious beliefs and practices. It is an enchanting experience for all, and, of course, nobody believes that we have really been whisked back to 1627. It's all make-believe of the highest caliber, and Plimoth Plantation is so obviously a good institution with worthy goals and high standards that it would be the equivalent of stupid vandalism to disrupt the museumgoing experience by chanting, "Not true! It's all fantasy! Hey, Miles Standish, where do you keep your cell phone while you're performing?"

Will Plimoth Plantation—a nonprofit educational institution that would welcome your support—survive for another century or more? Will there continue to be enough people to take on all the roles, preserve the traditions, repair the exhibits, and enough visitors to support the institution with their entry fees? We can all hope so.

Many churchgoers have a similar attitude toward their churches, and so do many former churchgoers who have changed their habits but not their allegiances. They see their denominations as worthy institutions that deserve our support for the good they do. As for the fact that it's all make-believe—well so what? Many good things are all make-believe. Church is morally uplifting theater, with rich traditions of music and ceremony, at least as socially valuable as grand opera or Shakespeare. Yelling "Lies!" in a crowded theater is almost as indefensible an act of free speech as yelling "Fire!"

Why doesn't everybody see it this way? We can answer that by imagining, thought-experimentally, some alterations to Plimoth Plantation. What if some of the actors playing roles fell in love, decided to have children, and then to raise their children in ersatz 1627 within the walls of Plimoth Plantation, twenty-four hours a day? No vaccinations;

no learning twenty-first-century history, science, music; no playing baseball or tennis—just to mention a few obvious deprivations. This would clearly be child abuse and utterly indefensible. Plimoth Plantation's make-believe is informed, voluntary, and enforced only during visiting hours, and these are not optional features when it comes to our approval of the institution.[35] If churches could adopt the same features, they would be as unproblematically benign as Plimoth Plantation, but few if any apologists for churches are prepared to acknowledge that their ceremonies and creeds are really just a kind of participatory theater. There is a powerful reason for this reluctance. Any such acknowledgment, if it became common knowledge, would instantly diminish the well-nigh hypnotic power of the rituals by framing them as make-believe, trading in real-life moral adventure for theme-park thrills and chills.

This threatened diminishment creates a quandary for thoughtful people who come to see their churches in this light. As our interviews show, some liberal clergy just can't say out loud, in public, what seems to loom in their reflections: that "God does not exist." Recall what one correspondent remarked: "According to your definition of God [as a supernatural being], I am more an atheist than you are. And yet I adore God!" What can this mean? Perhaps it's like the dedicated Baker Street Irregular who adores Sherlock Holmes without ever succumbing to the illusion that Holmes was a real person. Perhaps it means that the *concept* of God is adorable.[36] Then there is former Roman Catholic nun Karen Armstrong's perplexing pronouncement: "Some theologians call this [divine personality] the God beyond God. And this God isn't just a being like you or me, or the microphone in front of me, or even the atom, an unseen being that we can find in our laboratories. What we mean by God is, some theologians have said, is being itself that is in everything that is around us and cannot be tied down to one single instance of being."[37] Perhaps the most charitable interpretation of these curious circumlocutions is that they are valiant temporizing moves, designed to postpone the day when the fatal verdict must be delivered and acknowledged by all. If churches can't be effective without this liberal obfuscation or the literal deception that rivals the stagecraft of the theater, then they are unlikely to fare well in the transparent age in which we now live.

What Our Participants Gained and Lost as Their Beliefs Changed

Linda LaScola

Twenty-six participants in the present study were asked what they had gained and what they had lost as a result of changing their religious beliefs. These questions came toward the end of the interviews and in a few cases afterward, in writing or over the phone. Our participants responded quickly and easily to this exercise, in contrast to their demeanor at other points during the interview process, where they struggled to articulate their thoughts or feelings. They seemed to welcome the opportunity to talk about the changes in their religious beliefs in terms of gains and losses, and they expressed themselves clearly and without reservation.

Much of the discussion preceding these questions pertained to the difficulties and pain that these nonbelievers had experienced along the way. Those who were still in the clergy were still facing these issues, but their reflections on what they had gained indicated that they felt freed from pretending to themselves, even though they continued to pretend to others.

What they typically gained was intellectual honesty, a concomitant sense of relief that they were not fighting reality, and joy at being free from the constraints of beliefs that no longer made sense to them. They could celebrate life and explore the intriguing mysteries of the world around them. What they typically lost was a certain comfort and closeness with colleagues and family, a sense of being eternally cared for. Those who had already left the clergy also lost the status afforded by their former role as authority figures and sources of wisdom. In some cases, this loss sounded more like a gain, as they described the limitations imposed by that role which they no longer had to endure.

When we gathered their responses together, we decided that they were so heartfelt and articulate that they should be presented in their entirety. The individual responses are herewith recorded in the following order: liberal Protestant, fundamentalist Protestant, Mormon, Seventh-day Adventist, Roman Catholic, Orthodox, Jewish.

§

Harry, the former Lutheran and nondenominational pastor who left the ministry, shortly after being interviewed, to become a secular activist:

I only have everything to gain and nothing to lose, really. It feels so liberating to be able publicly to get up and say I don't think this works and that life can be so much better without God. I think life is going to be better without religion.

The closest I have come to having a religious experience in many years has been reading about natural selection, and I never expected it to happen. To just be sitting there, reading books and articles, having your eyes opened, and realizing, "Yes, this is the way everything around us emerged!" I hate to use the word "miracle," but to me there can be no greater miracle than how natural selection has created our world. And how it's created not just the physical structure but even in terms of how it's impacted our mind, our psyches, who we are as people. It's been absolutely thrilling, and I can't wait to read more about it.

The theodicy issue no longer torments me. I don't have to reconcile an all-loving God with the suffering in the world, because there's nothing to reconcile anymore, and that's been liberating. I'm not tormented by the silence of God in the face of any pain, because it's just not a factor. I really don't miss the mindless ritual that was enacted each week in my previous denomination. I don't miss the sense that even in denominations where there's an emphasis on the loving, gracious God, there's still a nagging feeling that you cannot measure up no matter what. It's always there. You open the service with something they call the Brief Order of Confession: "I confess that I am by nature sinful. I sinned against you in thought, word, and deed." That's how you begin worship every week, even in the liturgies of some of the more progressive mainline churches. And that's very oppressive, to think that in some way, shape, or form you are unacceptable to this supposedly loving deity . . . and you can't really measure up, no matter what. It's nice to be free of that.

And what he has lost:

There will be some relationships that I will lose—some former colleagues I'm still in contact with, who might not be onboard with this. But my really good friends will be with me. And my family and my mom—even if she doesn't understand, she's really good in the unconditional love department.

§

Carl, the "womb-to-tomb" Lutheran:

> I gained new understandings, new horizons, the freedom to say, "Nothing is off-limits"—that if I find it helpful to read Harris, or Dawkins, or Borg, and so on, that there's something exciting about the journey in that. I gained a sense of personal integrity, but it's tough—tough to maintain that, just kind of staying the course. I've gained some humility, I think, realizing how big this is, so much bigger than me, so much bigger than the tradition I've been a part of.
>
> I've lost naïveté. I lost unbridled enthusiasm for the tradition, for the teachings, just head-over-heels joy in being a part of this—a kind of simple joy. I lost, I think, associations with other clergy. I've chosen to distance myself a bit when I've tested things and have sort of felt rebuffed. So I feel lonelier in this by far than I would have ten, twelve, fifteen years ago. I lost peace of mind—you know, "This is what I'm going to do." It's good, although I think I've always been somewhat restless.

§

Brian, the Lutheran who left the seminary on his first day there and never looked back:

> [A life in the ministry] seemed to be a bullet that I was really lucky to have dodged, and I didn't know how lucky I was at the time to have avoided it.

§

Winnie, the Presbyterian pastor who left many years ago to pursue a doctorate in another field:

> I gained my sanity. I feel I gained more integrity. I've gained a sense that there is no one organizing principle, and that's kind of a loss, because I'd like to think that I've gained some certainty in my life where I am now, some stability. I think I have stability.

§

Stan, the Disciples of Christ military chaplain, who left the ministry and entered graduate school to train for another career:

> I've gained, I feel, this radical independence to think for myself, to make my own choices. The world is fascinating and beautiful and wonderful in itself. I've gained an appreciation for the natural order, for us as a species. In fact, it makes me feel more connected to people and want to do more good for people. I have more compassion for people, and also, being in a war zone, more contempt for . . . forces that would try to enslave people's bodies or their gender or their mind. There's a sense of a greater clarity of right and wrong, and being accountable and responsible not only to the natural world but to my fellow humans and the animal world. Trying to be more responsible about that, and more appreciative. It almost feels like I've been out in the sun and I walk into a room and I can't see. And then all of a sudden my eyes adjust to the light and reality, and I feel like the blinders are off.
>
> So, yes, there's sadness about what's been left behind, but I'm thinking I'm still young, and I've got the rest of my life to do something positive. I think that's what I've gained.
>
> I feel liberated, and I also feel some grief. Because the temptation is to say, "Well, I just wasted the last eighteen years of my life." But I don't want to look at it that way. Yes, I feel like I have missed out on some things, in terms of education—what I could have perhaps done earlier. Thinking or reading or other pursuits that may have come my way if I had chosen to leave seminary and gone to another field, things maybe I could have written or contributed to society, to the world. I feel that I have wasted some of that time. There is a sadness.
>
> I could quote Christopher Hitchens. He was in some debate and he said he's glad, he's happy, that there is no God. And looking back, I genuinely wanted there to be a God. Because God for me was not this punisher who sent people to Hell but this loving parent figure that cared for you. I can understand, based on my background, why that was so attractive. So I think there's the loss of that, which is a grief. I've lost the idea that there's something out there, that there's someone out there in control of the universe but also very, very personally concerned for my life.

§

Andy, the former Southern Baptist turned United Church of Christ pastor, who hopes that Jesus can become a "bridge" leading to a liberalization of religion, and who plans to stay in the clergy until retirement:

> I've gained a lot more than I've lost. . . . Well, I think the clear gain is that I feel good about the educational process I've had, which is to take the mind as far as it will go. I don't imagine I'll ever go back to believing—but I'm still developing. It could be that there'd be a time when I become just a flat-out atheist.
>
> I prize the academic world; I prize being honest with myself about where my research and my thought is taking me. That's been a very warming thing. I have, I think, gained an appreciation through this, oddly enough, for conservatives and fundamentalists, to the point where I will fight for their inclusion in the body [of faith traditions], if they're not aggressive and if they don't want to change everybody. Oddly enough, I think I stand more for an inclusive Church than many of my UCC brothers and sisters in the pulpit. And maybe that's because of my coming out of that [fundamentalism]. It has helped me appreciate that. But with limits. I don't want somebody telling me I'm going to Hell and threatening me that way. But your voice will be heard there, and you'll be allowed to be a part of the discussion. I don't see that going on with liberal UCC clergy. So I've gained that appreciation for my former home, theologically.
>
> I've certainly gained materially [switching to UCC], which is not a primary thing for me, but I have gained. The Baptist Church doesn't pay much.
>
> I've lost a little bit of innocence, and by that I mean I can say without guilt that I lie. And to me, that suggests that I've got used to it [lying], so I'm hardened to it. I don't remember, but at first, I would imagine, I felt guilty about that. However, I've gotten so used to it that I don't feel guilty about it. I almost feel guilty about not feeling guilty, if that makes any sense. And that, to me, even presents somewhat of a loss of the childlike innocence of, "Wow, look at this world! And I'm here, I'm here, and this is what I see." Just the innocence of being childlike and totally honest and truthful.
>
> What else have I lost? Part of that loss of innocence is that I've lost the fear of being discovered and found out. I guess that comes with age. I have several more years—but oh, well. It's not that I want to broadcast and get caught. I think some people want to get caught, but I'm not at that point. But I've lost the fear of losing my job or my career, because I feel pretty safe in my lies and the careful footing I have established.

§

Caitlin, an Episcopal pastor in her sixties:

> What I've gained is freedom to speak uncensored. That's the case, however, only because I have retired from all parochial work, but for an occasional talk to the Unitarian Universalist Church, where I get to try out all my new material.
>
> I've gained a certain congruence. To know the sacredness of all life without having to attribute it to divine agency is a relief.
>
> I have my Sunday mornings back, and a release from a pretty pervasive anxiety about everything I wasn't managing to accomplish.
>
> I have lost a collegiality among fellow clergy. It's not that they don't like me or want to be in my company, but I am uncomfortable with church talk, God talk, General Conventions, and so on. I have lost the capacity to go to the rail for Communion, which cuts me out of quite a few church services. As clergy, I was/am expected to process with clergy, to take Communion with clergy, and so on, and I don't really want to draw attention to myself by not vesting, or by vesting and not receiving.
>
> My colleagues don't really know my current thinking, because I haven't shared it, and no one has asked.

§

Bill, the Episcopal pastor in a college town, now in his fifties and planning to remain a pastor until retirement:

> There's a kind of joy I have experienced in . . . being more and more human, fully human. And if I could put it negatively, I would say that religious faith, religion, robs the human spirit, the human being, from realizing the fullness of humanity. That is, it does the exact opposite of what it claims to do. It's easier to talk about that kind of religion robbing the person of fullness when you're using the fundamentalists as an example. But the real challenge, of course, is to get to the place where I am, and where many are, where there is really joy and happiness and the absence of fear, of living and dying.
>
> It's hard for me to talk about the losses now. I think they were incremental losses. The losses were a sense of a certain identity, a solid identity. The loss of security, even security blankets; the loss of that

safety net that protects one from the deep anxiety about living and dying. Those were significant losses, and I think probably there was pain and grief involved in all of that—particularly the loss of certainty. That happened pretty early on in my life. But there was always a searching. Like any human being, I missed that security, and I desired that, and I wanted that very deeply. And every time I returned to that security, I would realize it was a façade. It was not real. I believe eventually that helped me with others.

§

Jim, one of the two Episcopal priests interviewed as a believer:

[If I became a nonbeliever], I'd probably gain an easier life, in some ways. The life I lead right now is very challenging. I don't know of many jobs that are as difficult as the job I have, and I've had it a long time. I might gain income ultimately, once I made the transition. Who knows, maybe I'd find a more satisfying vocation, because there are times when I'm like, "Why am I doing this?" I really think I'd be happier in another field. But that ship has sailed. I mean, happier in the sense that it would be a better fit for my collective skills and interests.

[As for what he would lose:] Ha! I'd lose my income. I would lose a sense of purpose that has been with me since I was seventeen. I would lose a lot of freedom that I currently enjoy as a priest, because I'd have to go work in a cubicle somewhere, which is horrifying to me. I suppose I would lose my prayer life, and that would not be good.

§

Charles, the Episcopal hospital chaplain who moved from fundamentalism to liberal Christianity; the other Episcopal cleric interviewed as a believer:

I think what I've gained [since changing from a fundamentalist to a liberal] is a greater appreciation for the ambiguity and messiness of life, and hopefully a more compassionate approach to people of different beliefs, knowing that people are on a life's journey regarding their beliefs and that at any one moment in time they may believe this, as I did at one time, and then later they may not believe it. I hope that I can have a greater sense of compassion for them and recognize that I'm only seeing a snapshot of their life right now and that this is not the final story. Recently I was playing a game called "Fact or Crap" with some friends, and I kept thinking, "Are those my only two options?" The nondualistic approach to life gives me a greater sense of comfort. It can be both right and wrong at the same time, all at once. It makes things murkier.

What I've lost is a binary approach to believing, to theology—meaning choosing that it's this way or the other way—and in that, I've lost some certainty.

§

Tammie, a Methodist pastor who left the ministry shortly after being interviewed:

It's funny to think that I have gained peace, because that's what Christianity promises—"Now my peace I give unto you," and all the things that Christ ever said about peace—but that's the first thing I've gained. Even in the middle of all the conflict of my emotions about integrity, I still feel very peaceful. I feel like finally the pieces fit, that things make sense and I don't have to ignore certain things or rationalize them.

I feel like I've lost a lot of time, a lot of money, education, and so on. I've potentially lost friendships.

Experiences, especially in a sense of childhood experiences. I spent most of my time passionately studying the Bible and wanting to fit in this mold for a long, long time—from the time I was very young. So I didn't enjoy a lot of things that kids enjoy; I grew up way too fast, took things too seriously, and a lot of that is because of the faith. It was a serious time, and people were dying without Jesus, and they were going to suffer eternally, and it was my mission as a Christian to keep that from happening at all costs.

We've done so many things—and we've stepped out on faith to do them—that have been financially negative for our family, believing that God will take care of us. So I feel guilt that I've robbed my kids of certain things.

I've lost people and relationships that I know are going to be gone. I'll lose a sense of community, a sense of belonging, a sense of identity—something that I don't know how to exist apart from, really.

§

Jeb, the former Southern Baptist pastor who left the church four decades ago; he is now a secular activist:

> What I gained is a normal life, full of *joie de vivre*, and the ability to explore and weigh evidence on a multitude of subjects without being shackled by an unwarranted assumption that all the important things in life had already been "revealed" by an inaccurate bit of writing from millennia ago. I have also been able to use my inherent therapeutic orientation and platform skills to reach a much wider audience than in the pastorate.
>
> Leaving the ministry was at once the most challenging decision I've ever made—and the most rewarding.
>
> What I lost was my marriage, a lot of my former friends, and a guilt-ridden lifestyle into which I was born and in which I was raised. Plus a forum in which my natural skills found easy expression.

§

Dave, the Baptist missionary. He left the ministry shortly after being interviewed and now has a secular job.

> What I've gained is absolute freedom, outside of the fact that I'm still in the closet [about lack of belief]. But I just can't begin to tell you, looking at a person here in the mission field and knowing that they are not going to die and go to Hell, that's just the best thing. The gain is myself again, which I never had before.
>
> What I have lost is the feeling that I'm not alone, because right now I feel really alone. . . . The Clergy Project will help in some aspects of that.
>
> Just being able to tell your thoughts and feelings [to God] without any judgment was a nice thing, and knowing someone truly loved me was a nice thing, and I do miss that. But I try now to apply that to myself, because it was all in my head anyway. And so, without talking to myself, I try to do it in my thought processes—that I am somebody and I have things to contribute.

§

Pete, the Pentecostal student who left pastoral training in his early twenties. Now a part-time college student in an unrelated field:

I gained an appreciation for life in the here and now. Perhaps I've become slightly hedonistic, since I believe this is the one and only life I have. So I enjoy food more, and strong drinks, and dinner with my wife. I've taken my career plans much more seriously, for better or for worse. Since I'm not concerned about the afterlife and pleasing a god, I've been able to hone my craft and become somewhat successful at my work. I didn't have the time or concern for that when I was all religious. It was too worldly.

I've gained a deeper richness in the friendships I've maintained. Many of us came out of religion together, or around the same time, and so we have a shared bond and acceptance in that. I've gained more empathy for others, because I don't see them as souls to be converted but, rather, as human beings struggling to get by in a life that is often very hard. There's definitely a newfound urgency to life that wasn't there [before]. It's as if I can feel the clock ticking, so I frequently think about the end of my days. I'm almost daily trying to make sure that what I'm doing now will align with a life of no regrets seventy years from now. In many ways, I skipped over my life before, when I was religious; seventy years was nothing, compared to an eternity with God, so why trouble myself with the here and now? I'm glad to have the newfound appreciation for today and the people I'm with.

I've lost a lot of things Alain de Botton discusses in his book *Religion for Atheists*. Things that aren't particular to religion intrinsically but, rather, areas that have gone unaddressed by secular society because they've been within the purview of religion. I don't have a place to really discuss morality or ethics. I also don't have anyone exhorting me to be more moral. Not that I view the concerns of the church as aligning with morality, but I just mean the general impetus. I'm less reflective and meditative, since I don't set aside quiet time anymore. I've lost *a lot* of friends. They weren't good friends, so it's been OK. But church provides an avenue to meet a lot of new people and form relationships pretty quickly and organically. I don't really have a venue for forming new relationships anymore, besides maybe the workplace.

I've lost a lot of self-righteousness, certainty, and pretension. I've lost a sense of moral superiority. I've also lost most absolutes and very binary thinking. I've lost superstition and guilt.

§

Johnny [Jerry DeWitt], a Pentecostal pastor who left the ministry shortly after being interviewed; now a secular activist:

> I feel like I've gained myself. I actually wrote a little letter to Professor Dawkins—knowing he probably would never see it but throwing it out there anyway—and basically told him that all of his videos, all of his media, all of his books . . . really redeemed my family's life. I think it brought back what we had before we got messed up, or what we could have had before we got distracted.
>
> Once we're no longer obligated—and we're closer now then we've ever been—to follow this cultural pattern, then the door is wide open to make our own direction, to go our own direction. You know, there's a lot of emotional misery inside religion that people don't emphasize, which you don't have when you're out of it. So I feel like listening to the logic, the reasoning. Whether it's Professor Dennett or Professor Dawkins, listening to that forced me to come to conclusions, forced me to be honest. You know, it's almost like Professor Dawkins is saying, "Here it is; now what are you going to do with it? Now what will you say? Will you go back and lie to yourself, lie to other people, or will you admit that this is true?" And in admitting it, it really did redeem our lives.
>
> I've lost that invisible friend. I've lost eternal life, living forever. I've lost control—a belief in control, of being able to manipulate situations. I was young and naïve enough to believe I could manipulate the weather if I could just pray fast and hard enough. I've lost all of that. I'm now at the whim of nature and reality, just like everybody else. The tornado may or may not kill me; there's nothing I can do about it other than get underground. I've really lost a sense of control, a sense of empowerment. And the social side of it: I've lost the prestige; I've lost being able to run for mayor; I've lost the chance to pastor that thousand-member church that I was in line for; I've lost possibilities; I've lost income; I've lost a lot by not believing.
>
> I feel like I'm coming back to when I was about fifteen years old, and I'm starting to figure out who I am again. And I'm starting to plan a future based on my likes, my motivation, my personality, where that's not what I've done for the last twenty years.

§

Joe, the Mormon bishop halfway through his five-year commitment, who will remain a Mormon but does not intend to accept other Church positions when his term ends:

> I've gained more freedom in how I choose to act and what I believe. I've gained a more nuanced view of faith and all religious experience. I've gained new respect for atheists, agnostics, intellectuals, LGBT individuals, liberals, and feminists. Instead of seeing them as misguided, or even as enemies, I now see them as people just like me. They are my neighbors now, and I can more honestly say that I love them and accept them for who they are. I have gained many new friendships with people—friendships that I otherwise would not have had. My life is much richer and vibrant. I see a full spectrum of colors rather than just everything and everyone in black and white. I am more relaxed and happier than I have ever been. I'm able to filter what is beautiful about my faith from what is harmful and in some cases destructive. I've gained more comfort, patience, and acceptance of myself. I've gained more confidence to just be me and not worry so much about what others think. I have found new purpose and meaning and mission in my life.
>
> I lost mental health and wellness, for a while. I developed an anxiety disorder that lasted a little over a year and had to go on medication. It affected me physically. I was drained. Couldn't eat. Couldn't sleep. I lost some stability in my relationship with my wife. She believed that now we had "nothing in common," which really hurt. Our relationship was damaged but, thankfully, not beyond repair. . . . So some of the things I lost were just temporary. On the whole I have gained so much more than I have lost. It was hell for a while, but now I am doing much better.
>
> I lost a romanticized and idealized view of my faith—almost a loss-of-innocence archetype. I lost my political ideological bearings. I've lost commitment to religious ritual; I don't feel as much of a need for it. . . . I've lost the safety of believing I had all the answers.

§

Walt, a former Mormon bishop who left his bishopric and the Mormon Church before his five-year commitment ended:

> Appreciating the Now. The relationship with my family members. The ability to trust myself more, to do things and realize I'm the one doing

> it, it's not God doing it for me. I'm more capable than I thought I was, and more willing to take a few business risks that I wouldn't have done otherwise. A lot better self-confidence.
>
> Less guilt. Lack of fear for the next life. I'm pretty sure that it's going to be nothing, and I'm OK with that, too. No one's standing on the other side who's going to chastise me for anything.

§

Michael, the Seventh-day Adventist pastor who took a leave of absence and does not plan to return to the ministry:

> I think I've gained a lot more freedom. I think I've gained a better understanding of who I am as an individual. . . . A lot more freedom to pursue what I choose to pursue, and it's hard for me to do that, because I've always been told, or had the mindset, that God's will is what I'm supposed to do, and that I need to find what God's will is and then just do it. To have the total freedom to pursue what I want to pursue is hard for me to get my head around. . . . I'll probably know more once I get more ducks in a row and I get figured out where I'm going. There's a lot of uncertainty right now.
>
> There's a loss of ignorance. That sounds egotistical, but I think that's true. There's loss of—I don't know if "understanding" is the word—but kind of a compassion for people who are still stuck in it. It bothers me that intelligent people don't keep searching, that they're content to say, "Well, I don't know—you know, God did it, and we'll understand by and by." That bothers me. I've lost freedom and openness with my social group, with the group that raised me, with my parents, with my friends. I cannot be myself; I've lost that.

§

Hugh, a Seventh-day Adventist religion student in his twenties who decided not to pursue the ministry:

> I gained my freedom back, and I have to say that, very honestly, I feel like my life is back in my hands now and that I can make the decisions I want to make and I don't have to appeal to the Bible. I don't have to look to God for permission. I really feel like I actually have my free will back, which is great. . . . I'm able to navigate these problems on my

own now and not have to look to some kind of authoritative Scripture.

Drinking beer.

I've lost a lot of the answers to life's biggest questions: Where did we come from? Why are we here? Where are we going, and how should we act in the meantime? Those questions were all answered for me by religion. But now I actually have to think about them myself and try to draw my own conclusions. And they're big questions. So I've lost that, and in some ways I do feel like it's a loss, because I don't have a firm framework always to make my decisions and a way to view the world. But in some ways it's almost better, because my view of the world and my answers to those questions are constantly changing and adapting and evolving and getting better

I've lost some employment prospects that I otherwise would have had studying theology.

Romantic prospects: All of my close girlfriends believe things that I find absurd, so in my view they're not really on the table.

§

Glen, the gay Roman Catholic parish priest on a leave of absence, with no plans to return to the Church:

I've lost community. I've lost the comfort of those immediate relationships that are formed just because you're clergy and people know you're clergy, so you know where you stand with people. I've lost respect. I've gained so much more. I've gained a freedom to be myself.

I've gained a freedom to be authentic. For the first time in my life, I've actually come out to some people as a gay man. I've really gained the authenticity, the freedom. I've gained—this may sound strange—but I've gained in self-esteem.

I realize I don't need to wear a collar to feel good about myself. I don't need to be a Catholic priest, or a Catholic, to feel good about myself. I don't need to think of myself as loved by some mysterious supernatural being to be a person of value. I don't need to seek a super-logical Daddy figure to make up for my own absent Daddy figure. I haven't really replaced it with another figure, I just realize I don't need it.

§

Tony, another Roman Catholic parish priest, also gay, who left the priesthood several years ago:

> I gained myself. I really did! I gained my integrity. I've always been somebody who seeks the truth—that's what sent me into the Church. I said, "I've got to understand what's true about this Church before I leave it completely, because I was raised in it." I just went to the extreme of becoming a priest in the process.
>
> I gained my mental health. I gained my peace with who I am. I gained my ability to love and be loved—the very thing religion says it's about. It didn't give that to me, as a gay man; it gave me the opposite—it taught me to loathe and be loathed. I gained this incredible relationship that I have with my partner. I gained a family, in that sense. I gained my self-respect. I gained a whole new career possibility. Who knows what will happen with it? I gained this great relationship with another friend of mine from seminary, who has left, who was one of my best friends there, who has also come through pretty much all the same things I have, in terms of leaving the priesthood. I gained the ability to help people like him. When he was suicidal, I flew to see him, and I nursed him to health for a week and made sure that he realized there were options. Just like a few priests had done for me on the phone, people who are still priests, but they nonetheless talked me down. So I gained the ability to help people like me, which I didn't have before. I thought I was doing it, but I wasn't. I was actually poisoning them, as people had poisoned me before—people like me within the Church, these priests who kept passing on these generations of ways that they have been taught to control, to be in control, then remain celibate in the Church, and voiceless and ball-less.
>
> I gained my balls; I gained my manhood. I gained the respect of not only myself but of my family, these people who have stood by me. They're like, "You know, this all makes sense. You've made some hard choices in your life." I gained the ability to communicate. I mean, I was always a communicator but I didn't really communicate about these things. I regained and regained my happiness and my joy.
>
> I lost a lot of my distortions about myself, about the universe. I lost financial security when I left. I lost that immediate praise of having that ready-made community or family. I lost my depression; I lost my self-loathing; I lost my . . . relationship with one of my siblings. And I lost relationship with my two best friends from college, and . . . a handful of other people from college that were friends as well. I lost—and I don't know if this is because I came out as gay or as an atheist—I

lost a friend that I was friends with since kindergarten. It's very hard.

I guess you could say I lost my prayer life. But to me it was just another form of masturbation. It was just self-centered. I mean, what's more self-centered than praying to an imaginary friend about what you need?

§

Vince, the former Roman Catholic teaching monk, who left the order a few years after Vatican II:

What did I gain? Just the feeling that I'm really dealing with reality now. Existence—not the way I'd like it, or imagine it, but just the way it is. So it's more important than ever to try to make it something I can enjoy and can get as much as I can out of the life I'm living now, because there is nothing more coming, and when it's over, it's over.

I guess it's probably easier to think back about what I feel I lost. Certainly, for many years, I felt the promise of believing that there was something beyond this existence. It was more than just living our lives on Earth, there was something to look forward to beyond the present existence. That's definitely gone now. That would probably be the main thing I lost. And a certain sense that I had an understanding of what life and existence was about and where it was all leading to.

§

Candice, the Roman Catholic seminary graduate who did not pursue a career in religion; now a secular activist:

I'll start with the positive. I have gained a firmer sense of reality. I've gained an understanding of what the world is, and I recognize that as beautiful.

Gone are the mysteries, but that's been replaced with new mysteries, and I think specifically of things like physics, and the nature of the universe, and physics as a cosmology instead of theology.

I feel happy about the knowledge that I gained and the opening of my mind. It hasn't frightened me. It's made me feel more thankful that I'm alive and have an opportunity to be alive and experience my own little corner of the universe vis-à-vis my own physical body and the family I have and the community I live in and the friends I engage with.

> I find it wonderful and pretty much transcendent—I have to use that word, I guess; it's the one most easily available. And it makes me feel a sense of happiness for humanity, but also sadness for people who are still trapped by faith.
>
> When it comes to the things I've lost, they are mostly tied to music, and some with writing, because a lot of my writing prior to leaving religion was deeply intertwined with religious imagery and allegory. And when I decided I didn't believe anymore, I also lost the language and methods that I used to articulate my experience in my writing. Everything linked to my faith seemed artificial and out of place.
>
> So there are certain things I feel a longing for. When I was reading Mary Johnson's book *An Unquenchable Thirst* [the memoir of a former nun in the order founded by Mother Teresa], I found myself weeping at certain parts where she would detail her prayer life, because I realized that in some ways I missed that prayerfulness. Because that process, that way of discerning and introspection, was very enriching for me. It gave me a way of scrutinizing and decision making that I still utilize but not in such an engaged way.

§

George, the Greek Orthodox monk who left the monastery shortly before being interviewed:

> For the first time in my life, everything I do is my own accomplishment, like getting this jacket. Before, if I needed clothes I'd simply tell the monk doing the shopping that I needed some underwear, I needed a T-shirt, I needed a new pair of shoes, and as long as it wasn't anything that was considered a luxury, I'd get it when they went shopping next time. And I was always grateful that it was that easy, but at the same time it meant that I didn't own it. And now, having left the monastery with two shirts, some underwear and the jeans I was wearing, every piece of clothing I acquire is my own acquisition, and I really feel that it belongs to me, and I'm grateful for the fact that the Salvation Army does sell clothes dirt cheap. That's a very prosaic, pedestrian example, but everything I've done for the past three months has been my own doing. And I've gotten pretty far—I mean, just from being completely homeless to being in a place that's not ideal but I'm doing all right. There's a very good chance I'll be accepted into a doctoral program a year from now; I'm getting a fellowship.

As odd as this sounds, I've gained a clean conscience—the sense that I may very well be making big mistakes but they're my own mistakes and they're coming about honestly, in the sense that I am, for the first time in my life, autonomous. I'm not simply the puppet of the Church, forced to dance the dance I don't really believe in and mouth words I don't fully embrace. And the fact that I could be completely wrong is almost exciting. It's like the scientific process: As long as you're honestly pursuing a worthy goal, every mistake you come along in the process can be used to advantage. So I've gained a clear conscience, I've gained autonomy, I've gained a sense of accomplishment, and for the first time I've gained the sense that I can be responsible for my own life and my own thoughts and my own mistakes. There's no need to be obedient to authorities I do not recognize, or to teach dogmas I don't believe in, or to recognize Scripture that is man-made. All of that is really fairly liberating.

I've lost 99 percent of my material possessions, and 99 percent of my social network—essentially everything. Everything that I'm wearing is from thrift shops.

§

Sherm, the Orthodox rabbi:

I'll start with what I've gained. I've gained a perspective on the world that I appreciate more. I appreciate the fact that everything is nature and that there is a natural reason for things. I think this is where I will agree with Richard Dawkins: The magic of reality is certainly much greater and grander when you view it in terms of nature than in terms of a God who just snapped his fingers. To me, it's much more majestic. It's something that I appreciate.

Ultimately I am very, very joyful. We were talking about the feelings. I don't know if "relief" would be a feeling, but I do think I did feel relief knowing that if I did something wrong in my life, it's over and now I'm moving on—it doesn't have eternal repercussions. It's nice to know that—I don't know—watching a movie is just watching a movie, it's not doing something forbidden. Very simple. I know, you're probably thinking: "You're not allowed to watch movies?" Well, in the community I grew up in, you are not allowed to own a TV and you're not allowed to watch movies.

I've gained a sense of community—that I'm joining a community, although it's going to be in a very inactive fashion. It's nice to be part of something where it's almost impossible to question, because the answer "I don't know" doesn't do anything, doesn't cause any problems. When an atheist doesn't know anything, we'll have to wait until we figure it out. It's the absence of belief. You're not believing something, so if you don't know something, . . . that doesn't take a toll on your way of life. If I don't know the answer to why God does evil things, that should theoretically take a toll on my religious observance, and it should affect my religious belief. But there's nothing that can affect your nonbelief.

The gain of intellectual freedom, for sure. And the gain of perspective, I guess, is something that's changed for me, which I enjoy.

I certainly feel a lot more lonely. I feel a lot more secluded. These interviews have not been easy on my wife, and I'm hoping that doesn't, you know, tailspin. But it's been difficult.

I feel that one can have many purposes in life, and as a believer you are given additional purpose. I am not sure if losing that purpose is a net gain or net loss—perhaps both.

§

Jacob, the Humanist rabbi, formerly Reform, plans to continue in the rabbinate:

The loss has been more than compensated by living in the real world. Religious people, both liberal and conservative, do not really understand human nature. That is to say, they may understand or even be experts at human behavior and relationships, but it is always wrapped in a mythology of one kind or another. Even the most neutral or liberal mythological interpretations of life are bound to mischaracterize human nature because, ultimately, they're always posing the wrong questions—usually phrased, for better or worse, as "What does God want from me?"

Once I abandoned the vestiges of those ideas, I was free to understand human nature in a way that connects us profoundly to all of the other life on this planet. In a twist of irony, this has given me a much greater sense of gratitude for my own life and for our human journey here on Earth. This is not gratitude to anyone in particular. How could it be? It is, rather, an appreciation of the chain of fortunate events, from our point of view, that led to our presence here. I think it was Richard Dawkins who compared being born a human being to winning a kind of lottery. Given the numbers, it was quite unlikely, but yet it happened.

My humanism, or atheism, actually gives me so much more inspiration to be a better person. I've shed useless feelings of guilt about so many things, including sexual feelings, and replaced them with a realistic appreciation for all of the things I love about being alive. I also have gained a sense of mission to help make life better for everyone else, including our fellow animals. I am now enormously aware that there is no one else who can do that. This creates a sense of responsibility that is both more serious and liberating all at the same time.

As a rabbi, I have lost the authority that I am in some ways speaking for God. Of course I still possess all of my knowledge about Jewish history and culture, and this is why I remain a rabbi—a teacher. But it would be dishonest for me not to acknowledge it as a loss of some kind.

VI. WHERE ARE THEY NOW?

Linda LaScola

Checking in with Four Pilot Study Participants: An Interim Report

We decided to conduct follow-up interviews in 2012 with the original five Protestant pastors from our 2010 pilot study, to see how they were doing. Because of the many media requests we had fielded after the study was published, there had been e-mail and phone contact with all of them at one time or another, but there had been no in-depth conversation about their lives since the original interviews.

At the time of these follow-up interviews in 2012, all five participants were still in their positions: Adam and Jack, the two fundamentalist ministers in the South, were still hoping to get out of the ministry; Darryl, the Presbyterian, had looked unsuccessfully for other work and had considered Unitarianism; and Wes, the Methodist, and Rick, the UCC campus chaplain, were contentedly continuing their work. Of the five, only Wes declined the invitation to do a follow-up interview at that point.

Rick, the Post-Supernaturalist Jesus Follower and Atheist Friend

When the pilot study first came out, Rick, whose real name is Mark Rutledge, let his friends and colleagues know that he was the United Church of Christ chaplain who had been interviewed. There was also a story about his part in the study in his local newspaper, the Raleigh-based *News & Observer:*

> Rutledge, identified in the study as "Rick," was comfortable enough to come forward to a reporter with his real name. Unlike the other men—a

> Southern Baptist, a Methodist, a Presbyterian and a minister in the independent Church of Christ—Rutledge fears no retribution. At 76, he says he has never concealed his views from his denomination, the liberal-leaning United Church of Christ, or from Duke [University], which pays him a $55-a-month stipend for his part-time duties. Moreover, Rutledge is proud of his views and wants to share them with the world. He is frustrated that Dennett and co-author Linda LaScola, both atheists, hold what he considers such restrictive views of God.[38]

Of his "outing" in the *News & Observer*, Mark noted:

> I do go to these monthly lunch meetings of all the UCC clergy in the area, and the articles [various reports on the study] were kind of a nonissue. Right after the local article [about me] appeared, I went to a luncheon. There wasn't much said about it, but several people came up and said things like "Good article" and "Thanks for being out there." It was kind of a nonevent.

Mark was now semi-retired as a UCC chaplain at Duke. He had always been open about his beliefs to colleagues and laypeople. Since participating in the pilot study, he had begun describing himself as a "post-supernaturalist, non-theist humanist who tries to follow the original [historical] Jesus—the first-century peasant Jewish wisdom teacher."

This was his effort at being more explicit about his beliefs. Like all the original participants except for Wes, he joined The Clergy Project, where he could converse privately online with other nonbelieving clergy. Though he had not experienced the pain others did when their beliefs changed, he sympathized with their plight. He was an advisor to the local Secular Student Alliance and was teaching adult-education classes that foster communication and understanding between believers and nonbelievers. He was still active and accepted in the traditional church, where, as he put it,

> I think I am more liberal than most of the pastors around. In fact, even the pastor of my own church said, "I might have a little more orthodox beliefs than you do, but so what? We can tolerate the diversity." But I think I am to the left, theologically, of even most of the ministers in my denomination. It's kind of a nonissue with them.

Mark was also tolerant of his religious colleagues' differing beliefs.

> It's not my job to talk a supernaturalist out of believing what they believe. It would be my job to say, "Here's an alternative," and to those who want to continue to believe in the supernatural God, fine. I would say we have many who do and many who don't in our Church family. It's like a family argument. You don't leave the family because you have an argument like that. And I would say, "We are a family here, and we have diverse views. Let's love each other and get on with it."

Within his church community, he saw himself as a useful source of information about supernaturalism, not an advocate for a particular point of view.

> It's kind of an unending conversation in the Church, and I'm not trying to talk anybody out of holding supernatural beliefs. I'm saying, "I don't; here's why; here's the resources to think differently."

He was also keeping up with the secular community. He had dinner with Richard Dawkins and another member of The Clergy Project when Dawkins came to the Raleigh area for a speaking engagement. Mark later made a point of visiting several former clergy at a conference they were attending in another city.

Darryl, the Presbyterian: Still Playing the Game

Our account of Darryl in the pilot study opened with an excerpt from an e-mail he sent expressing his interest in participating:

> I am interested in this study because I have regular contact in my circle of colleagues—both ecumenical and Presbyterian—who are also more progressive-minded than the "party line" of the denomination. We are not "unbelievers" in our own minds—but would not withstand a strict "litmus test" should we be subjected to one. I want to see this new movement within the church given validity in some way.

While still considering himself a "Jesus follower," he felt it was

> arguable whether I am also a Christian. . . . I reject the Virgin Birth. I reject substitutionary atonement. I reject the divinity of Jesus. I reject

> heaven and hell in the traditional sense, and I am not alone.

In the follow-up interview, Darryl declared himself disappointed that the pilot study was not having more of an effect within the Church. Without disclosing that he had been a participant, he presented the study to a clergy group he meets with regularly.

> We talked about it, and they weren't surprised at all that there would be people you found to talk to. No one else pointed the study out to me in any dimension, in any conversations that I've been privy to in the Presbytery . . . or in the General Assembly. No one said, "Hey, what about that Presbyterian in there?"

While he did not speak openly about his nonbelief with mid-career clergy, he was finding some comfort in confiding in older or retired ministers who shared his views and did not hesitate to express them.

> I've encountered a lot of other Presbyterian clergy, a number of whom are retired, who are more able to articulate things similar to what I talked about in my interviews with you. And they have no problem calling themselves Presbyterians, and they don't feel it's a conflict of interest. That's been a real eye-opener for me. It's made me feel much more comfortable about my profession, and I'm able to understand that it is a flavor of Christianity that I fit into, even if it's more of a philosophy-of-life kind of thing. The faith language may be allegorical, but the values are good values.

He had applied for several secular jobs but had been turned down or declined offers that did not meet his salary requirements. If he ever managed to leave the ministry, he thought he and his family would likely join a more open religious community.

> I think we might become Unitarians or we might join a Quaker congregation. Those groups would provide that ritual and that community that helps to give meaning and structure to life in ways we still value.

In the meantime, he found some satisfaction in helping parishioners who were questioning religion, by demonstrating how Bible stories and

Christian doctrine can have meaning without being literally true.

> I talk about the Tower of Babel and the Genesis stories and the Noah story as being fables, and I use that word in the pulpit. And we can talk about the Resurrection as valuable doctrine if it's as a metaphorical thing, if it allows us to understand ways that we can be resurrected in our own lives, or transform our lives, or be good people.
>
> When working on my Communion notes and script for Christmas Eve, I was modifying the prayers—taking out things that didn't need to be said, or changing language, taking out some of the Christology. I'm sure I still play the game to some degree. I guess I'm couching, or I'm softening.
>
> I can compromise and feel like I'm providing a middle ground for the people who are out there who would feel the same way that I do. I think I'm throwing them a lifeline.

He recognized the difficulty of his situation and was trying to make the best of his investment in Christian ministry.

> I've been doing it for a long time, years now, and it's something that I'm able to do, that I was trained to do. What else was I trained to do? How am I going to make use of all that money I spent on my education? And that's one of the things that you and Dan Dennett have identified as an issue. I have years of practice. It's a lifestyle that I'm familiar with. It's a language that I can speak, even though I'm trying to alter it. And there have been pastors who have found very welcoming churches that are very progressive and open, and there's not enough of them to go around. But if I find one of those, I think I would be very, very content.

He had definite ideas about how he would like religion to change:

> I'd like to see fundamentalist Christianity, or fundamentalist religious faith, severely curtailed. I'd like to see a Unitarian flavor of faith. I'd like there to be a voice for people like me out in the pews, or for people who are avoiding the pews.

Jack, the Southern Baptist: Hanging on and Looking to Leave

Jack, a Baptist worship minister in the South, lost his faith by reading the Bible over a period of ten years. As he recounted in the pilot study:

> I've just this autumn started saying to myself, out loud, "I don't believe in God anymore." It's not like, "I don't want to believe in God." I *don't* believe in God. And it's because of all my pursuits of Christianity. I want to understand Christianity, and that's what I've tried to do. And I've wanted to be a Christian. I've tried to be a Christian, and all the ways they say to do it. It just didn't add up.
>
> I didn't plan to become an atheist. I didn't even want to become an atheist. It's just that I had no choice. If I'm being honest with myself.

Jack, who had unsuccessfully sought work outside the ministry, was still unhappy in his ministerial role and beginning to resign himself to staying for another few years until he could retire—if his church let him stay.

> I think I could take it for a few more years. I mean, I'm just being blunt; that's what I told my wife. She kind of doesn't want me to do it, because she knows I'm unhappy. And I said, "Where else will I find a job paying this much that I could do so well?"

He sensed that there were people pushing for him to leave, but not because they found out that he no longer believes. He thought it was related to money and church politics.

> Some of them kind of resent that I make a good salary. It's like "How come you pay him that much?"
>
> The politics of church is like no other. People can make your life miserable if they want you out. And they will. And they have.

At the time of the follow-up interview, he had still not told his wife about his lack of belief.

> I've talked about my unhappiness with my job many times, but I've never told her I just don't believe in God anymore.

While his wife was supportive in the difficulties he was having with his Church, Jack frequented The Clergy Project's private Web site for the peer support he felt he needed.

> It's the only place I have to go to talk about this, so that's been a wonderful resource for me. I go on it two or three times a day.
>
> I just connect with someone in a similar position and get to share my thoughts and my concerns and my frustrations and get a different sense from people. That always helps. We're social creatures who need that reassurance from other people, and that's the only place I get it now.

He wanted to stay in his job as long as he could, for practical reasons.

> I've worked myself through this personal crisis of faith, realizing that I'm not that person anymore, but I have myself in this situation and I've just got to be practical about how I'm dealing with it. It still frustrates me, but at the same time, you know, I can't be foolish and just walk out the door.

He had found ways to speak to members of his congregation without being openly dishonest.

> You can always say, "The Bible says this and that," and that would be true. I wouldn't say, "Well, I believe that the Bible is true." I could always say, "Well, in the Bible, the story of Noah goes this way." And that's true, I don't have to say I believe it.
>
> I see politicians do it all the time. They have pre-set answers. Somebody will ask them a question, and they'll answer with something that had nothing to do with the question. That's the way I'm going to do it—because the truth is, I can do my job and do what they're asking whether I believe it or not.

Jack felt he had little choice about the ways his life has changed since he accepted the reality of his unbelief.

> This has been a very difficult thing for me to do. I've changed my whole life, my whole belief system, and the way I work. It's not because I wanted to, but because I felt I had no option. Because it's like, "How can I keep telling myself I believe this, when I don't?"

Adam, the Church of Christ Minister: Secret Secular Activist

Since the pilot study was published, Adam had become an engaged but clandestine activist in the atheist, freethought, and humanist community.

He helped found The Clergy Project and moderated its private online Web site for nonbelieving clergy. He was also the first recipient of its outplacement services, provided by a grant from the Stiefel Freethought Foundation.[39] He has written and recorded humanist songs, which he cannot distribute publicly for fear that his voice would be recognized. Along with Jack, he appeared on a November 9, 2010, segment about nonbelieving pastors on *ABC World News Tonight* with his voice and appearance disguised.[40] He also appeared twice, with his voice disguised, on Canadian Broadcasting Company (CBC) Radio.[41] Though a few of his Clergy Project colleagues know his real name, they call him "Adam" to avoid any slips that may inadvertently out him.

As reported in the pilot study, Adam's religious beliefs changed as the result of intense study, which he originally pursued to learn how to be a better defender of Christianity. Instead, his investigation led him away from faith.

> If God is God, he's big enough; he can handle any questions I've got. Well, he didn't. He didn't measure up! And that sounds, you know, so funny, because if I heard somebody else saying that a year ago, I'd have thought, "You are such a sacrilegious person. God's going to strike you dead by lightning or something!" I've actually thought and tried to pinpoint, but I can honestly say that intellectually, from within the first few weeks of my studies, I thought, "Wow! Could this be true?" So almost from that point on, it's almost been downhill if you're Christian; uphill if you're a nonbeliever. Coming to the truth—and I always thought there was absolute truth out there. Now I'm a lot more relativistic.

Three years and many job applications later, he was still trying to leave his position in the Church. He considered many options, including academic religion. He rejected that idea, because it did not seem like a clean break from the deception he found in religion.

> It seems like there is some dishonesty with those academic people I spoke with. They would admit that, "Yeah, we felt that we could not believe in the literal Genesis. We also doubt the historicity of Moses and the Exodus and all that." But they kind of liberalize it and say, "But either way, we believe that God sent us the story." Yet they don't tell that to the churches that support their seminaries; the churches are more literal.

> I've decided that for the rest of my life I can't hide in my environment. I just can't do that. So I was looking for secular work. What can I do? I've applied for probably fifty to sixty to seventy jobs—positions in any kind of field.

Although he considered "coming out" in dramatic fashion as some other nonbelieving clergy have done,[42] he thought that for him a better option would be "oozing out," by quietly taking a secular job in his community. He is determined not to harm his family's lives in pursuit of his own need to leave the ministry. His changed attitude continued to be particularly hard on his wife, who remains a devoted Christian.

> It's like trying to mix oil and water together. You can shake it up as hard as you can, and sometimes you're kind of together. But the natural tendency is polarization, because my view is so at odds, at least with literal, fundamental, evangelical-type Christianity.
>
> My wife's in a very tough situation, because she's been almost as trapped as I have been, but for different reasons. She couldn't share with anybody because of her fear that I'd lose my job.
>
> I've told her that I've just got to get out of ministry, because I don't believe. I cannot keep pretending for the rest of my life. And that's been very point-blank. She knows that.

Broaching the subject with his children was easier. They were older now, and it seemed to Adam that they were more open to other ways of thinking about religion.

> A big change in the last year for me is that my older child knows. It was shocking at first, but now [my older child] completely understands, and we have a kind of a secret bond.

While Adam had not yet approached his younger child, who was still at home, he anticipated that the conversation would go well.

> I think my younger one would love Julia Sweeney's DVD.[43] I thought that when some questions come up, maybe I'd just say, "This is really interesting. It made me think about a lot of stuff. Go watch it. Don't tell your momma about it." That might start the conversation, I don't know. I don't want to mess my kid's life up—it has such promise right now.

> But I honestly think that when I do tell the younger one, a lot of things will click, because there's already a little bit of a bad taste there toward the Church, just because of the hours I'm putting in, with no benefits.

As eager as he was to get out, he knew it would be a big change.

> I have over twenty years in full-time ministry. That's been my life completely for twenty-four hours a day, seven days a week. And of course, all my friends and acquaintances, social contacts, business contacts, are all around that. So I'll be losing part of that—the congregation that I'm serving, wonderful people.

He was looking forward to the day when he could express himself freely.

> I keep dreaming about being openly involved in this freethought movement. It might involve music. It might involve speaking or making presentations on behalf of a group or organization. It could mean running for something—I don't know.
>
> I'd be so much more comfortable sharing what I think is the really good news about humanism and freethought. I'll be so much more a better advocate for that than I ever was for God, because that is tangible. God was not.

Checking in with Our Study Participants from 2008–2012: An Update

Much has happened in the lives of many participants since 2008, when the study began, and 2012, when it ended. Some of them have left religious life and gone on to secular careers. Some have moved from pastoral work to administrative work, or vice versa, and a few who left religious employment altogether have reentered it, either part-time or full time.

Much has also happened in the world at large. According to a respected and widely publicized Pew Research Center poll, between 2008 and 2012 (which happens to coincide with the period of our study), the number of people who describe themselves as "religiously unaffiliated" has increased from 15 percent of the U. S. adult population to just under 20 percent. This includes nearly 6 percent (more than 13 million) who describe themselves as atheist or agnostic and 14 percent (nearly 33 million) who report having no particular religious affiliation. This study also reports a decline in religious affiliation in all age groups and a larger decline among young people (aged 18–22) than in the past.[44]

The continued growth of The Clergy Project, from 52 to over 600 in three years, is also suggestive of the decline of formal religion. In 2014, the blog *Rational Doubt, with Voices from The Clergy Project*, which I edit, debuted on www.Patheos.com, an Internet site that hosts eleven "faith channels," representing eight major religious groups along with "atheist," "pagan," and "spirituality."[45] While The Clergy Project is a private online community limited to clergy who no longer believe, *Rational Doubt*, one of twenty-eight blogs on the Patheos atheist channel, is the first Internet venue aimed at clergy who are reluctant to discuss their growing religious doubts with colleagues or family. *Rational Doubt,* which features blog posts written by members and founders of The Clergy Project and includes an "Ask an Atheist Ex-Pastor" column, addresses an audience of religious doubters that was unidentified and unassisted until just a few years ago. This is not to say that clergy doubt was an unknown phenomenon. Rather, the conventional way to handle doubt has been to live with it, or surmount it and return to faith; pursuing doubt as it leads away from faith was not a subject openly discussed among clergy. Another new development is the growth of humanist communities in the U.S. and other countries.[46] Some of these new communities are headed by nonbelieving clergy who have left their pulpits.

In this chapter, we'll catch up with more of the study participants, particularly those whose lives have changed since the study (and in some cases as a result of the study). Other participants were unreachable or declined to be included in an update. I'll talk in detail about the few who wanted to share the changes in their lives, and more broadly about those who chose to continue to protect their privacy.

Changing Perceptions about "Coming Out"

In the course of conducting this study, I've noticed that concern about confidentiality and "coming out" is an individual matter and something that can change over time. All of the study participants wished they could be more open about their beliefs, and some have remained fearful of exposure. Others seemed to be getting more comfortable with their nonsupernatural perspective and more confident about expressing it.

I'm occasionally approached by journalists who want to interview the "atheist clergy" I've found who are willing to talk with journalists confidentially. When that happened back in March of 2012, for example, the only person who immediately agreed to be interviewed also eventually decided to "come out" on national TV, on the MSNBC Sunday morning *Up with Chris Hayes* show.[47] That was Mike Aus, "Harry, the Lutheran" in the study. Mike has given me permission to use his real name, as have several others who have gone public with their change in beliefs. When he learned that the show he would be on would also feature cognitive psychologist Steven Pinker and Richard Dawkins, author of *The God Delusion*, Mike wanted to be able to talk with them freely, instead of being interviewed with his identity protected, as originally planned. He was also financially and psychologically prepared to move on to start a humanist community.

That March I also approached Bill, the Episcopal priest who wants to stay in his parish until retirement, about the same opportunity to be interviewed under cover, but he declined, preferring to keep his low profile. Fast-forward two years later with a similar request from a CNN producer. This time, Bill agreed to a background interview. He ultimately decided not to appear on the show itself, but the fact that he had even considered it was a huge change from his past behavior.

Another pastor who plans to stay in the pulpit until retirement also volunteered for the CNN background interview. This was Andy, the former Southern Baptist and current United Church of Christ minister. After a long background interview, Andy gave the producer a tentative "yes," in the event that another atheist pastor did not volunteer. (Someone did—a recent Clergy Project member who was not in our study.) While Andy strongly supports further public understanding of clergy who have abandoned supernatural beliefs and greatly appreciates UCC liberalism, he acknowledges that he has not shaken the strong sense of sin and the fear of retribution inculcated in his Southern Baptist youth. And despite his new denomination's tolerance, he also fears being asked to leave his post if his lack of supernatural beliefs became known. Andy has used the *Rational Doubt* blog as an outlet, writing anonymously about his feelings of being a fraud and his hope that his social justice work is paving the way for a more open church in the near future.[48] Although he called himself an agnostic during our study interviews, he now refers to himself as an atheist. I asked him about this change. "I would say I became more comfortable with the term 'atheist' as I participated in the

Rational Doubt blog," he said. "Conversing with others helped to clarify things. I think it always does, if we aren't reactionary and truly listen to what others are saying."

The "Out" Humanists

Several of the study participants have become engaged in humanist activities and communities that have blossomed since the study ended.

Three of them, who were all "in the closet" when first interviewed for the study, are now "out" and active humanists. Probably the most well known is Jerry DeWitt ("Johnny" in the study), who has written a book, *Hope After Faith: An Ex-Pastor's Journey from Belief to Atheism*, and has been interviewed numerous times on radio and national television. He has also spoken at national and regional conferences, been featured in documentaries, and in 2011 started his own humanist community, the Community Mission Chapel, in Lake Charles, Louisiana, about fifty miles from his home in the small city of DeRidder. Jerry and I held our interviews in Lake Charles, because Jerry was afraid that in DeRidder somebody he knew would see us and wonder what he was doing meeting with a Yankee lady several days in a row. At the time, he thought being a part of our research might be his only chance to be "immortal"—that is, the only way his journey away from faith would ever be recorded.

Mike Aus, at the time of our interviews, had already left his Lutheran denomination for the increased flexibility of a nondenominational church. A short time later, when his nonbelief became publicly known, he started a humanist congregation called the Houston Oasis, which includes some parishioners from his two previous congregations. Its core values are the following:

1. People are more important than beliefs.
2. Human hands solve human problems.
3. Reality is known through reason.
4. Meaning comes from making a difference.
5. Labels are unimportant.
6. Unity in our values, charity in our differences.
7. Be accepting and be accepted in return.

There is also now a sister group, the Kansas City Oasis, which held its first meeting in April 2014.

Catherine Dunphy ("Candice" in the study) did not continue a career in religion after becoming an atheist during (and as a result of) her graduate seminary studies (see chapter IV). Still, she hid her nonbelief for several years after completing her education. Her activism began shortly after our interviews when she joined The Clergy Project in March 2011, as one of the fifty-two original members. Catherine became active in the group, serving for a while on the board and as executive director. With a supportive husband and an eagerness to become involved in the growing humanist movement in her native Canada, she soon became a speaker at conferences and on radio talk shows. She has written a book about The Clergy Project, *From Apostle to Apostate,* and conducts wedding ceremonies as a secular officiant with the Ontario Humanist Society.

John Figdor ("Jared") was a recent Harvard Divinity School graduate, training to be a leader at the Humanist Community at Harvard when I interviewed him in 2011. He is now the first "professional leader" for the Humanist Connection at Stanford University. He is coauthor (with Lex Bayer) of *Atheist Mind, Humanist Heart: Rewriting the Ten Commandments for the Twenty-first Century,* a book about "positive atheism."

"Jeb" is John Compere, humanist speaker, author of *Towards the Light,* and retired clinical psychologist, who left the Baptist ministry decades before participating in the study. He, too, is one of the first members of The Clergy Project and quickly became its head screener. He trains and supervises members who screen new applicants to the group, determining their status as current or former religious professionals who do not hold supernatural beliefs.

Mark Rutledge ("Rick"), the UCC campus chaplain in our pilot study, continues in his role as an ambassador for understanding between liberal Christians and the atheist/humanist communities established after the pilot study was published. He, too, has contributed to the *Rational Doubt* blog trying to explain his nonsupernatural concept of God and Christianity:

> I think that once you remove supernatural elements from the Bible, Jesus, creeds, doctrines, concepts of God, and theologies, there is something left worth calling "Christian."[49]

Also, to his great delight, while visiting the United Kingdom, his exchange with Richard Dawkins was mentioned in a British newspaper.[50] They both describe themselves as "secular Christians," while Dawkins leans decidedly more toward the secular side.

Jeff Falick ("Jacob," the Humanist rabbi) is ecstatic at having acquired, as of July 2013, his own congregation at the Birmingham Temple Congregation for Humanistic Judaism in Milwaukee, Wisconsin. He described his work in a post he wrote for *Rational Doubt*:

> Today I have the privilege of functioning as a rabbi in all of the ways that matter. I visit the sick. I preside over life cycle ceremonies. I teach. I speak about a wide range of Jewish and Humanistic topics. I do it all in the context of a community of committed Humanistic believers. I do not carry out my duties in the name of any kind of authority. My sole authority as a member of the "clergy" is educational. I represent no ancient wisdom and certainly no god.[51]

One study participant who became an open humanist had difficulties along the way. "Tammie," a Methodist minister whose real name is Teresa MacBain, came out to much fanfare during the 2012 American Atheists National Convention. She worked for a while for American Atheists and the Humanists of Florida Association. She also served as executive director of The Clergy Project. Later, shortly after being appointed director of the Humanist Community Project at the Humanist Community at Harvard, it was revealed in the *New York Times* that she had falsified some of her credentials, so her affiliation with HCH was terminated.[52] Now she is living with her family in Alabama, where she tells me she is reflecting on her childhood as well as the events of the recent past. In September 2014, she made her first public appearance at a national humanist/atheist event since leaving HCH a year earlier. She is now a writer for a Patheos blog, *Ex-Comunications,* and is media coordinator for The Clergy Project.

One Vacillating Humanist/Progressive Mormon

Joe, the self-defined "hopeful agnostic" first interviewed in 2011, was released as a Mormon bishop in 2013 after serving a standard five-year term. While he is still involved in his local Mormon community, he no longer accepts requests to take on formal leadership roles. Instead, he is active in progressive causes both inside and outside the Mormon Church, while celebrating aspects of his Church that, as he put it, are "positive and useful." However, when he found himself mourning the excommunication of Kate Kelly, a prominent Mormon feminist, he wondered whether he could continue his association with the Church. He tells me that even if he does ultimately move away from formal Church membership, he "will always consider [himself] a Mormon, although now on the most progressive end of the spectrum." When I asked him if he would still call himself a hopeful agnostic, he expressed his ongoing vacillation about his beliefs and his feeling about his Church, saying, "I suppose I like the freedom and flexibility of not fully defining myself" and "I am open to there being a God and I am open to there not being a God." He also called himself a "hopeful truth seeker" and acknowledged that he might be "wired to be slightly more on the faith side."

Finally Out of the Pulpit

Darryl, the Presbyterian pastor from our pilot study, has finally found his way out of parish ministry after six years of searching for other options. He and his family are moving away to be closer to his parents, to a city where Darryl has a temporary secular job and his wife can continue in the career she left after starting a family. In an e-mail, Darryl told me that he does not plan to "come out," and that although he is not "making a full escape" he's "making progress in that direction." One thing he's sure of is that he does not want to "continue to be in hiding" in his new city. He "needs to feel out in the culture there."

Adam, the Church of Christ minister in our pilot study, finally found a good secular job with help from The Clergy Project's outplacement program. His new job uses his administrative and organizational talents, offers health benefits not available at his former church, and is close to home. He has become less active in The Clergy Project, while continuing to appreciate the help and camaraderie it has offered him. He left its board of directors, dropped his administrative responsibilities, and participates less frequently on the private online forum, preferring to concentrate for the time being on his new job. Adam has received numerous requests over the years from the media and atheist/humanist groups to come out publicly, but even now that he's no longer in the ministry he resists going public with his beliefs. Here is his response to a query he received from a freethought organization after a few months in his new job:

> I would not foresee any problems arising from [my employer], but life would be very difficult even there as most of the people I work with have some religious affiliation. Coming out would change my world dramatically. Not sure I can even calculate all the implications. I think it would only be a quick flash of news and then I would be quickly forgotten and left with a life in shambles and perhaps regret. At the same time I relish the thought of being completely honest with everyone. Oh what a tangled web circumstances have woven for me.

His wife is still very religious; his children, now grown, are not, although they maintain a casual affiliation with their father's former church. Unlike his wife, they are aware of and supportive of his involvement in The Clergy Project and *Caught in the Pulpit*.

Stan, the military chaplain who was about to return to civilian life to study for a career in social work when I interviewed him in the summer of 2011, is even happier now than he was during our final in-person interview. He reports that "life has been just great since going back to social work graduate school and now working in a secular setting. I consider myself very fortunate!"

He especially wants young people considering ministry to know that there are other helping professions they can enter that don't require a belief in God. He laughed, recounting how people he counsels are "more real" with him now, not hesitating to use curse words or talk about their sex lives. While Stan has "come out" with good results to his close friends, and finally to his mother, he does not mention his religious transformation to new friends and colleagues in civilian life. He is grateful that the topic of religion doesn't come up much, and he certainly doesn't bring it up. Although he is interested in hearing about the new humanist communities started by some other study participants, he is not at all interested in organizing one himself, instead relishing his free Sunday mornings and not being the leader of a community that meets regularly. He was, however, intrigued by the idea of being a humanist officiant. He always enjoyed the "hatch, match, and dispatch" aspects of ministry and contemplates combining his new clinical skills with his ministerial background to create an interesting sideline presiding at naming ceremonies, weddings, and funerals.

Still in the Closet

Bill and Andy are still active in their congregations and plan to remain until retirement.

Sherm, the Orthodox rabbi, has found a level of comfort with his situation as an atheist who intends to continue presiding over the rituals of his faith. In a telephone conversation, he enthusiastically described the joy he finds in his close-knit religious community, which is liberal and relaxed compared with many other Orthodox communities. He has an outlet for airing most of his views with a few members of the congregation who know they can discuss their true thoughts only with one another. He says he's "a little trapped but not that trapped" in his community. Having weighed the pros and cons, he has concluded that staying is an attractive and satisfying option. His wife's views are crucial in that determination. She accepts the idea that he does not believe in God, as long as he continues in the rituals of the faith. Sherm and his wife have remarkably similar Orthodox attitudes, except that she believes in God and he does not.

Of his situation in general, Sherm says that he "sometimes daydreams" about expressing what he feels and "not being judged," but that he's "OK with it." He is optimistic about the demise of religion, sure that it's coming faster than he expected. He thinks the reason is simple: an abundance of information about evolution and accurate biblical history available on the Internet. Orthodox Jews are not as isolated as they once were, nor will they ever be again.

Complex/Shaky Transitions

Michael, the Seventh-day Adventist, was on a health-related leave of absence from the ministry when I interviewed him in 2012. Since then, he has filed for, received, or been denied various forms of insurance or financial assistance and has applied for numerous secular jobs without success. Though he does not participate in any Church-related activities, chance encounters with old Adventist friends and colleagues are always warm and friendly. He occasionally attends the local atheist/freethinker group but has told no one in his former Church community about his changed beliefs.

For four other study participants who left the ministry, the transition has not been smooth either. Three have returned to full- or part-time ministry and the fourth is considering it, depending on his luck finding full-time secular work. He thinks he could function as a hospice chaplain or wedding officiant without compromising himself or the people he would be serving. Of the three who have returned, one has accepted a part-time position as a church musician in a liberal denomination as a way of earning extra cash. Coming from a conservative denomination, he was impressed that during the new denomination's hiring process, he was never asked to join in prayer or asked about his beliefs. He was relieved and amused when I told him that I knew of lay church musicians who became nonbelievers after performing in the ceremonies of several different Christian denominations. Religious beliefs weren't relevant to the job description and the musicians noticed that churches didn't ask or seem to care about their beliefs.

Another study participant did not expect to return to religious life, but ultimately did when his secular job did not work out. Because he had not revealed his lack of beliefs when he left his denomination, it was not administratively difficult for him to return to ministry.

The fourth study participant contacted me on his own to let me know that he had left his position. He provided details of his departure, including information about his new job and his feelings about leaving parish ministry. However, he asked me not to mention any of that, even in a veiled way, because he is fearful that the smallest detail could make him the object of suspicion among people in his former church community. While he thinks it's unlikely that anyone from his former life would try to out him, he feels less anxious knowing that no one has enough information to make a connection. We both felt that simply commenting on his fear and anxiety would help people understand the range of reactions pastors have when leaving the pulpit.

Happily Preaching; Not an "Atheist-in-Secret"

While some might classify Wes, the Methodist pastor interviewed for the pilot study, as still "in the closet," he does not think of himself as an "atheist-in-secret." After talking with him for the first time in five years, I would say that he doesn't come across to me that way either. His pastoral message focuses on what's important in this life and not at all on preparation for the afterlife. He continues to preach his liberal message to his congregation, which I confirmed by visiting his church's Web site and listening to several of his sermons. Except for the designation of a Bible verse for the day, they were completely secular, focusing on living responsibly within the larger human community. His strong sense of mission was evident; he told me that he was "still fighting the good fight, helping people break the ties that bind them." He is proud of his ongoing work using "the appeal of the gospel to help people make sense of this life," and he has encouraged people who no longer feel a need for organized religion to leave the faith without fear of eternal damnation.

He has heard nothing from his colleagues or his congregation about humanist communities or The Clergy Project (which he declined to join). When I told him that several study participants were now leading humanist communities, he was interested, thinking that working in that capacity would be a way to "increase [my] repertoire" beyond the Christian gospel. However, he is happy continuing in his current situation. His main concern with his denomination is not about its beliefs, but about its propensity to hire lay leaders instead of seminary-trained clergy, which he fears will lower the quality of church leadership.

After talking with Wes, I wondered how many other Christian clergy there were who, like him, do not perceive themselves as atheists-in-secret but have abandoned any supernatural beliefs. While they may avoid admitting this to the people in the pews, they may also preach a humanist message that tacitly encourages their congregations to grow into a future without supernatural religion.

Participants' Differing Motivations and Reactions

Everyone I interviewed was happy to talk with me initially (they were volunteers, after all), and many were eager to catch up with me later on as well. Talking with study participants again—in many cases, several years after the original series of interviews—helped me to understand them better and to see how their thinking evolved. I noticed some key differences among them regarding their motivations for participating and their reactions to the study's outcome.

Closeted Seekers of a Confidant. All the participants enjoyed talking privately about their changing beliefs. However, a few seemed to have agreed to the interviews solely because they wanted a confidant with whom they could express and explore their unconventional religious views without personal or professional repercussions. While they understood and supported the research process, their primary motivation was personal. They were more interested in understanding themselves and speaking freely in a protected environment than in contributing to a body of knowledge on nonbelieving clergy.

Flirters with Self-Revelation. Some of the study participants seemed, at times, as if they were trying to get caught—or at least trying to drop clues. For instance, they would arrive for an interview dressed in clerical garb, sometimes stopping at the hotel's front desk to announce themselves even though I had given them a room number in advance. In follow-up conversations, they might provide details about changes in their lives that I felt would give them away, and I would be the one to encourage them to reconsider including a possibly revealing detail in the follow-up report. And in some cases, I would be the one to decide not to take the chance. The most flagrant "flirter" was Jerry DeWitt, who said during our interviews that he thought it might be easier just to change his "religious views" status on Facebook. He proceeded to do just that a few months later—along with posting a photo of himself and Richard Dawkins taken at a freethought conference. While this was an extreme case, and indeed constituted Jerry's "outing," perhaps the other pastors were consciously or unconsciously testing the waters instead of (or before) making a complete break.

Behind-the-Scenes Agents of Change. Some participants were eager for societal change in religious thinking and hopeful that our study and their part in it would help get things moving. But their preference was to stay in the background. They savored their secret catalytic role in the process, yet they themselves planned either to leave the clergy quietly without revealing their nonbelief or to stay, as quiet agents of change, teaching and preaching as liberal a message as their denomination allowed.

Active Agents of Change. Besides those who have written books and given talks about their experiences as nonbelieving clergy, several of our study participants, as noted, have started humanist communities or work for humanist or atheist organizations. This activism is mirrored by a trend we have noted taking place outside our study. For instance, Gretta Vosper, pastor of the West Hill United Church of Canada, in Toronto, revealed her lack of belief several years ago during a Sunday sermon; her church now sponsors workshops on how congregations can "transition" to a nonsupernatural framework. Another Canadian, David Galston, ecumenical chaplain of Ontario's Brock University, is a fellow of the Jesus Seminar, an international group of more than two hundred scholars dedicated to the study of the historical, human Jesus. Humanist campus chaplaincies are starting up with increasing frequency. Bart Campolo, son of the well-known evangelical writer and minister Tony Campolo, is the first humanist chaplain at the University of Southern California. He served in numerous Christian ministries before becoming an agnostic and switching to humanist ministry. Tufts University has hired its first humanist in residence, Walker Bristol, who previously worked at the Humanist Community at Harvard and continues to study at Harvard Divinity School for his Master of Divinity degree.

It is too soon to know how this nascent trend will develop or to what degree it will thrive in the current environment, in which church attendance is dropping and more and more young people assert their religious nonaffiliation. What we can say with some confidence is that the nonbelieving clergy we have identified and studied are not an anomaly, and that many of them are adapting their skills to serve a society that has a diminishing focus on religious belief.

VII. THE INNER SHELL—ISOLATING PASTORS FROM THEIR PARISHIONERS AND FROM THEMSELVES

Daniel C. Dennett

> *But it's sort of a pet issue of mine that clergy have very, very few places where they can be honest with anyone.*
>
> —Jim, Episcopal priest

More interesting, in many ways, than the membrane protecting the church from the outside environment are the policies and practices composing the additional membranes that typically function to protect the clergy, insulating them from subversive forces and temptations inside the church while maintaining the inner balance that seems to be necessary for proper functioning. Once again, these are designed policies without a designer. For the most part, they are the product of long ages of trial-and-error from which have emerged traditions—"best practices," in effect—that have stood the test of time. Although they have served their functions well in the past, some of them are beginning to do more harm than good. Most of them have familiar counterparts in other contexts.

One is well-known by the name Bill Clinton gave it in another application: *Don't ask, don't tell.* There is a long-standing and unspoken taboo in many churches to the effect that inquiring pointedly about the religious beliefs of any church member—or, indeed, of any pastor or other leader in the church—is not just bad form but altogether too aggressive and rude. This is a godsend (if I may put it thus) to many of our nonbelieving clergy participants, since they don't have to worry overmuch about being put on the spot and forced to lie or confess. Except in private confessional conversations, and even then it is rare, this is just not done, one gathers—even in the case of interviews by a church search committee for a new pastor.

This policy is part of a larger pattern that our pastors often comment on, the clerical versions of *Go along to get along* and *Don't rock the boat.* The need to "fit in" looms large in church settings. Confrontation is of course frowned upon, and the manners and habits installed in pastors as part of their training in pastoral care tend to carry over into all their interactions. The tenure of a pastor is almost always somewhat precarious in any case, and you never can tell whose feathers you dare not ruffle, at least early in your appointment, before you get to know the lay of the land. This discourages bold experiments, so even though some pastors occasionally dream of trying some risky venture in hopes of opening the minds of their congregations, few can bring themselves to carry out such an undertaking. It would be too likely to violate the tradition that is the clerical variation on the physician's maxim *First, do no harm*: *First, do not undermine anybody's faith.* Pastors are thus encouraged to spin different messages to different congregations, or parts of congregations. As Marcus Borg candidly put it in commenting on our pilot study in the *Washington Post's* "On Faith" Forum:

> If their congregation is mostly elderly and unlikely to survive beyond the death of its members, and if their elderly flock is not using "common Christianity" to judge and beat up on other people, then there may be no need to try to change them. Clergy in situations like this might see themselves as chaplains in an old folks home.
>
> But if clergy are in intergenerational churches with a potential future, then I encourage a different approach. Seek to bring your understanding of Christianity into your congregation. This can be done in sermons, but especially in adult theological re-education.[53]

Can it really be done in sermons? Most of our pastors find this too risky. They have to fall back on "adult theological re-education." What can't be said from the pulpit—since it would upset the old guard, who cling to the literalist understanding of their youth—can be discussed in a book-discussion group or an informal study group focused on some issue. The book chosen, or the topic announced, can telegraph an approach of open-minded, freewheeling discussion in which possibly heretical views can be broached in a spirit of inquiry, not inquisition. Our pastors are familiar with this move and some of them use it to good effect, but it has its risks. The pastor can hide behind the book's author ("Well, Bart Ehrman/Rob Bell/Marcus Borg/Bishop Spong certainly has some challenging ideas! What do you folks think of them?"), remaining neutral while introducing the ideas to those in the congregation who might be ready—indeed, yearning—for them. A daring pastor might even start a group that read through the New Atheist books, in the spirit of "know thy enemy." But once this tactic becomes an open secret, it will no longer be taken at face value by those in the congregation it is meant to bypass. The fact that the pastor wants members of the congregation to read these dangerous books will be taken as a telltale sign of a lapse in faith.

This illustrates a big problem facing the clergy today: the distressing way that diplomacy tends to erode into hypocrisy. We are all familiar with the delicate question of where on the sliding scale called-for diplomacy leaves off and becomes uncalled-for lying. When do white lies turn evil? When does politeness morph into manipulation? When is silence golden, and when is it culpable reticence? We tell fibs and withhold truths to protect people at risk of suffering from a surfeit of troubling facts, and then also to protect our own ability to do that very thing, and then also to protect our reputations as candid and sincere truth-tellers, and so we become accomplished liars. Nobody is unfamiliar with this slippery slope, which can complicate our relations with friends and family, but pastors never get off it. They are always onstage, always confronted with the problem of self-presentation.

Just as a rhyme scheme imposes constraints on a poet and may thus be a spur to creativity, this predicament forces pastors to find ingenious ways of speaking. Consider the subtly evasive language resorted to by liberal pastors. They are adept at talking to two (or more) audiences at once, speaking in literal language about "what God wants," "when God listens to your prayers," and the "Risen Christ" and other miracles (*calling* them miracles, to reassure the old-timers), while leaving plenty of room for the sophisticated members of the congregation to interpret everything they say as metaphor and poetry, not literal truth. (Hey, if sports broadcasters can speak with impunity of "miracle catches" and "miraculous" comebacks, pastors can just as insouciantly speak of the biblical miracles without thereby suggesting that they believe in miracles when in their hearts they don't.)

This talent for articulating double meanings from the pulpit might be compared to the talent of the best children's-book authors, who provide an extra layer of meaning for the delectation of parents engaged in reading bedtime stories to their youngsters. Paternalism is, of course, in order when dealing with one's children—that's precisely when paternalism is called for, after all—but some of our pastors were uneasy about the paternalism they were indulging in with segments of their adult congregation. At the very least, they felt obliged to adopt this double-speak without ever mentioning it. No church will thrive if it mounts a neon sign over the pulpit reading, "Understand all this as metaphor if you don't want to understand it as literal."

Another useful tradition is epistemological modesty: "Think twice before you challenge what the elders say. What do you know?" A nice feature of this ambient attitude is that it can be iterated in a pinch. Pastors can hold off skeptical challenges by subtly impugning the comprehension, the experience, the sophistication of a lay challenger—or, if that doesn't do the trick, confessing their own abject incomprehension in the face of Mystery. Not "Who are *you* to question these sacred and difficult truths?" but "Who are *we* to question these sacred and difficult truths?"

One of the troublesome aspects of the books by the Four Horsemen of the New Atheism (Dawkins, Harris, Hitchens, and me) is that none of us bother to wrestle with the intricate arguments and analyses of theologians, and none of us back off. We don't accept the modest role that self-styled religious sophisticates try to impose on us. This "arrogance" of the New Atheists is often criticized, but, as I never tire of responding, we, like scientists and philosophers generally, are forever asking ourselves, "But what if I'm wrong?"—a reflection that is not just rare but positively discouraged among religious spokespeople. There are some famously arrogant Nobel laureates in the scientific community, but I have never encountered one who can hold a candle to the overweening confidence and smug certainty of the typical defender of the faith, whose disdain for evidence-seeking and careful argumentation is often breathtaking. Those who view it as immoral to entertain alternatives or even objections to their faith place themselves outside the marketplace of ideas. They are incompetent to participate in the serious political conversations we ought to be engaging in today.

I have been asking defenders of sophisticated theology for a reading list of works they are prepared to defend as intellectually bracing and honest, but I have yet to have my challenge met. I am tempted to conclude that they have realized, on closer examination, that they, too, have adopted a double standard, letting pass as deep thought work that is actually just obscure—and often apparently deliberately obscure. Such works serve only to buttress the adopters of epistemological modesty, who can reason as follows: "These professors are professional thinkers about religion. They are still in the church, so they must have gone way beyond me in thinking these issues through. I don't get it, but they do, so I should accept their authority." These high-flown ruminations may well be incomprehensible, but they are nevertheless deemed inspiring and authoritative. "Go read the meticulous arguments of this thinker; they should sweep away your doubts." (And if they don't, it must be your fault.)

A natural accompaniment to epistemological modesty is the habit of turning away from too much reflection. This is not easy for clergy, since their professional lives are inundated with the very contents that they don't want to dwell on too intently. But somehow they manage to stay oblivious of many issues. One of the surprising patterns in Linda's interviews was how often she posed issues that struck the interviewees as novel. Again and again she was told, "I've never thought of that before." Andy, the Southern Baptist turned UCC pastor, says to her at one point,

> I've learned a lot about myself just by sitting here. No one's ever asked me these questions, and I love this. It's very clarifying, very clarifying.

And see what happens when Linda closes out her first interview with Glen, the Catholic priest on leave of absence:

> *Linda:* If you think about our conversation tonight and think you left something out or want to expand on something, be sure to bring that in tomorrow.
>
> *Glen:* OK. I'm sure I will, because a lot of this I've never thought about

> before. It's interesting that . . . for the first time there is a kind of depth, because to me . . . the struggles that I had that . . . I just wanted to scream to that self, ten years ago in seminary, and say "Don't you understand? You can't—Why are you not facing these doubts? Why are you not challenging your professor?"
>
> *Linda:* Do you have an answer for that?
>
> *Glen:* I will. Not yet.
>
> *Linda:* OK, I have an answer. It might not be the right answer, but I have an answer. Because you wanted that structure, you wanted to complete the degree so you could be that person that you had in your mind that you wanted to be.
>
> *Glen:* Maybe you're right. There was such a fear in seminary, by all of us, of being dismissed or being one of the ones who chose to leave, because we didn't want to be one of them.

Poignantly, opening up a novel perspective did not always make our participants' problems seem worse; as often as not, it eased their minds in one way or another, clarifying their predicament or pointing to a saving grace that hadn't occurred to them. Might they have benefited personally from rather more reflection? It's hard to say. It is reflection, typically, that plants the seeds of doubt. They hear themselves saying something to a parishioner that doesn't pass muster with their conscience, or they discover that they no longer enjoy some aspect of their duties—or, even more upsetting, they discover that they enjoy some aspect of their duties too much and for the wrong reasons (it's the limelight, or the ceremony, the stagecraft, that they relish, not the message they're expressing). Glen notes that he reads while he's supposed to be contemplating the Blessed Sacrament, in the practice known as Eucharistic adoration: "Would I be reading a book, trying to kill time, if I were in the presence of God?"

Jerry DeWitt, the Pentecostal preacher, also questioned his own sincerity.

> From the beginning, I've been conflicted. I've always had these aching doubts about the supernatural side of things. I would push the doubts aside, and try to get as involved in it as I could. I would speak in

> tongues, but I always, always knew that it wasn't what everybody was making it out to be. Because I was the guy doing it.
>
> I'll give you a good for instance: I would be in a service where I would give a message in tongues and interpretation of encouragement to someone. And the whole time that I'm speaking, "Thus sayeth the Lord: Fear not, I'll walk with thee, blah, blah, blah," there's this other part in my head that just knew it was coming out of me, not from the Lord. I fasted, I prayed, I sought in every way that I knew to try to get so immersed in the spirit that there was no longer that other voice in my head.

We realize that any clergy reading this book may well become, as a result, more self-conscious about any self-deceptions they have mastered to get them through the difficult parts of their days. And that, once again, is the problem all religions face today: They cannot easily withstand the attention the world is beginning to focus on them, now that the spell is broken, and there is no defensible, respectable way of putting that genie back in the bottle.

Some commentators have urged that the best response to the new transparency would be to switch away from dogma and endorsement of a set of dubious propositions and toward commitment to a tradition more like loyalty to one's community. One of the most thoughtful of these is the British philosopher Philip Kitcher. In an essay titled "Militant Modern Atheism," he argues for preserving religion's proven role in providing meaningful lives for many whose circumstances prevent them from being, in Kitcher's good phrase, "important participants" in the world they were born into.[54] He sees no future for any religion based on what he calls the *belief model*, and he recommends instead what he calls the *orientation model*. This, he claims, would likely reverse the otherwise standard dependence of religious commitments and aspirations on grounded beliefs. That is, the orientation-type religionists put commitments to community and tradition first, as the fundamental landmarks of their lives, and let the expression of the (dubious) grounds for these commitments wander somewhat opportunistically between "mythically self-conscious" metaphor at one pole and "doctrinal entanglement" (flirting with the belief model) at the other, with convenient vagueness ("doctrinal indefiniteness") in the middle. (The "doctrinally indefinite" folks "take refuge in language that is resonant and opaque, metaphorical and poetic, and deny that they can do any better at explaining the beliefs they profess.") Whatever floats your boat, as one says. And indeed, if maintaining a religious orientation is the only way for you to have a meaningful life, you *should* rely on whatever floats your boat. But then it will just make matters harder for you if you have to confront Kitcher's trio. "Tell me, sir, have you decided to go with mythic self-consciousness, doctrinal entanglement, or doctrinal indefiniteness?" Don't ask! Don't tell!

Kitcher is at pains to express his defense of these delicate options sympathetically:

> I'll suggest that doctrinal indefiniteness can be a reasonable expression of epistemic modesty, and that even doctrinal entanglement can be justified when it is the only way of preserving, in the sociocultural environment available, a reflectively stable orientation.

But a somewhat less diplomatic version hovers in the background: Kid yourself if you have to. I am happy to say that Kitcher firmly draws the line at letting any of these options abrogate a commitment to reason when deciding ethical matters.

> Someone who makes decisions affecting the lives of others is ethically required to rely on those propositions best supported by the evidence.

In a felicitous phrase, he notes that "there ought to be no 'teleological suspension of the ethical,'" but then his attempt to make the harrowing story of Abraham and his son safe for posterity runs afoul of his own requirement. Just what is the *positive* role of Abraham as a "knight of faith" supposed to be, when he so clearly violates this principle? Kitcher says that Abraham's "sort of trust is not legitimate"—you can't put it much plainer than that—but how, then, does Kitcher find a way of endorsing Abraham's (mythical) story as any sort of talisman for a meaningful life?

As Kitcher's well-intentioned, imaginative attempt to avoid hypocrisy shows all too vividly, there is no stable stopping point on the slippery slope between being patronizing, on the one hand, and uneasy complicity with unacceptable nonsense on the other.

Are these reflections on religion offensive? They concern topics that many people would rather leave unexamined, but unlike most earlier criticisms of religion they do not point a finger of blame. It doesn't take conniving priests to invent these cultural contraptions, any more than it took a devious social engineer to create the Japanese tea ceremony or debutante cotillions, no matter how resentful and trapped some of the participants in those superannuated traditions may feel. Just as there is no Intelligent Designer to be the proper recipient of our gratitude for the magnificent biosphere we live in, there need be no intelligent designers to be the proper targets of our anger when we find ourselves victimized by "social cells,"[55] like the church. There are, to be sure, plenty of greedy and deceitful people who tend to rise to power in any of these organizations, but if we concentrate on hunting the villains down, we misdirect our energies. The structures themselves can arise innocently, out of good intentions, and gradually evolve into social mechanisms that perpetuate themselves quite independently of the intentions and values of their constituent parts, the agents who bustle about inside them executing the tasks that keep the institution going. Some of those agents, the clergy who must confront the deluge of information and attendant curiosity on a daily basis, are showing signs of strain, suggesting that the task facing religions everywhere is only going to become more difficult.

VIII. WHAT'S NEXT? A RESPONSE TO REQUESTS FOR OUR STUDY'S "CONCLUSIONS"

Daniel C. Dennett

Linda and I found some striking patterns in the ways our interviewees dealt with their circumstances. We suspect that the people interviewed are unusual only in the sense that they were eager to talk with us.

Our encounters with clergy outside of the study suggest that our participants are not alone. Linda has had several casual discussions with clergy since the research was first published, in which they "confess" to her, saying things like "I could be one of those people in that book." Others seem to apologize, saying that they've softened their message or that they are careful not to say anything to people in the pews that they themselves don't believe or that could be misconstrued. (In no case did she challenge or solicit their views; she simply mentioned our research.) Others scurry when they see her coming (she doesn't pursue). Two clergy who signed up for a luncheon where she would be discussing our book canceled at the last minute.[56]

I have had good interactions—and no confrontations, except in e-mail or print—with clergy since our pilot study was published in 2010, including several university chaplains, and Reform rabbis, and my sister, Cynthia, a hospice chaplain in Vermont until her recent retirement. It may be that less liberal clergy avoid me, and I certainly don't seek them out. A few clergy have sent me angry e-mail messages and a few more have let me know they are praying for me to come to my senses, but most of my e-mail from clergy confirms the veracity of our interviewees and welcomes our efforts to inform the public.

Some of these writers venture to say that they think "most" clergy are in the same predicament, but we doubt that they have any way of gauging this "from the inside," since in general clergy are systematically isolated from one another by the prevailing traditions. To a surprising degree, they are outsiders in their own worlds. Perhaps our book will provide an entering wedge for more candid internal discussions among clergy when they meet to discuss the many problems faced by all their churches. They might begin with the acknowledgment that candor is one human virtue they are enjoined to forgo. They cannot be candid with the general public, or with their parishioners; they cannot be candid with their colleagues and superiors, or even with themselves. In spite of their professional obligation to immerse themselves in the social world, or maybe because of it, they strike us as the loneliest people we have ever encountered.

Our pilot study provoked a vigorous response from spokespeople for the various denominations (and religion in general): The literals condemned as "atheists" all the liberals we had found, and implied that they always knew they were there, corrupting the faith; liberals offered bromides on how our clergy should improve their methods of coping with doubt—or get out of the ministry. The anger of both literals and liberals was directed not at us for conducting our inquiry but at the clergy who had broken ranks and participated in it. Since the advent of The Clergy Project in 2011, the religious establishment has gone largely quiet. Now, with church attendance and religious affiliation continuing to drop, they do not defend their institutions as much. It couldn't be because they no longer see changing clerical beliefs as a threat. It is as least as much a threat as laypeople leaving the church. To us it seems more likely that they have recognized that condemning our work is a losing strategy, drawing attention to an issue they wish everyone would forget, and no other effective defenses have occurred to them. It seems to us that those in positions of power now are just riding it out until retirement, hesitant to make changes that would affect the status quo without the promise of improving the future. They have given up.

There is an alternative hypothesis worth considering. They have taken the good advice they give the parishioners who come to them for counseling: First, don't try to hide the facts from yourself; articulate them in private and confront them with ruthless honesty. Maybe we have been misled to our impression that they cannot be candid among themselves; maybe their silence is a sign that they are busy exploring, in strictest confidence, the implications of the patterns we have found. One would think they would want to know—and mutually acknowledge—these patterns, the better to find an informed way to deal with them.

For instance, they would do well to discover how many of their colleagues, while not dissuaded from completing their studies and going into the ministry, were shocked—or at least seriously unsettled—by the facts of religious history introduced to them in seminary. Are they afraid that if they included this history in their youth education programs the pipeline of recruits into the ministry would dry up altogether? We wonder whether clergy should be more worried about repelling the worthy, intelligent, idealistic young people who would seriously consider a career in the church if it weren't for all the nonsense they would be obliged to pretend to take seriously. The clergy will learn—if they don't already know—that their colleagues have mastered the art of compartmentalizing, and then rationalizing the awkward information that cannot be easily concealed in some mental cupboard. The first step for some of today's clergy was private and personal: finding a way to overcome the cognitive dissonance they felt, a way that could quell the inner voice of doubt at least temporarily.

In making this momentous decision to enter a life of hypocrisy, they were aided by the tacit approval of their professors and classmates—and some of them hardly realized what a pivotal step they were taking. In a new and challenging setting, it is usually prudent to blend in as invisibly as possible until you learn your way around. When in Rome, do as the Romans do, and in seminary, seminarians often keep their doubts to themselves.

Later, they are aided by their parishioners, who don't seem to want the facts. (Don't ask, don't tell.) They learn that if they shine in their pastoral duties—or are successful fund-raisers—the church governing body will be loath to confront them. And, to be sure, this tactic of reticence is also dictated by narrow self-interest: If they are too straightforward, they will likely lose their jobs, and—the Concorde Fallacy—they have invested so much in preparing for this vocation that they decide this is no time to abandon it. Besides, they tell themselves, they can see much good in the gospel message they are teaching. All of this adds up: Accentuate the positive and don't dwell on the negative aspects of lying—telling only white lies, of course—to their congregations. Finally they don't see it so much as *lying* or even *obfuscating*; they see it as *comforting*—the best thing a pastor can do.

Clergy are taught to "meet people where they are." So are psychotherapists. The difference is that professionals trained to care for people's psychological health have a central responsibility to help people grow, and in particular to grow more independent of their counselors. In contrast, the central responsibility of clergy has been to comfort people, which fosters an increasing dependence on counselors and on the community of the church. This may be called inculcating "spiritual growth," but it can amount to encouraging addiction to the comforts to be found in the arms of the faithful, the surest way of keeping one's parishioners where they are—needy and trusting and obedient. So if, as many clergy tell us, their congregations are not ready for the truth, not strong enough for the truth, their own practices are in part responsible for this frailty.

And meanwhile the storehouse of knowledge about the world continues to grow, overpowering the ancient myths of Scripture with new ways of understanding. In response to this, liberal clergy give the Bible a new role: It is no longer an unquestioned source of truth that must be consulted as the final authority; it has been transformed into a familiar, beloved, and bountiful source of *stories*—and who cares whether or not they're true? These stories can be interpreted, shaded, twisted, shoehorned into Good Examples illustrating universal truths that needn't be found explicitly enunciated in the text. Moral progress is imported from secular debates and political movements and "found" in the Good Book, which can then be honored as *a* source, rather than *the* source, of the wisdom attained by the open forum of rational discourse outside the church. The Jewish tradition of *midrash* described by Sherm, the Orthodox rabbi, has many less forthright cousins in the world of Christian scriptural interpretation. To outsiders, this often appears to be spin-doctoring at its most transparent, but so well-established is the tradition within the denominations that it usually passes for constructive and imaginative exploitation of hidden riches rather than grafting borrowed insights onto dying rootstocks.

Some who decide to stay in the ministry try to use their positions to help prepare their congregations for a future that emphasizes values instead of beliefs. Philip Kitcher commends this shift from the *belief model* to the *orientation model* but the transition is a perilous one. The belief model is the more or less standard supposition that, as Kitcher puts it, "individual religions are distinguished by their different doctrines, and that to be committed to a particular religion is to believe the doctrines constitutive of that religion."[57] According to this view, co-religionists share values, aspirations, attitudes, and loyalties *because* they share belief in a set of propositions, the defining creed of their religion. The proposed orientation model inverts this dependence: The shared values and loyalties are an "orientation" definitive of a religion, with the characteristic beliefs tagging along as a typical *effect*, not the core or essence of the religion. The idea is that religious creeds are no longer the protective shields they once were, uniting the brethren in a shared litany of proprietary and unquestioned truth; they have become part of the problem, and not a small part. If religions could just find a way of quietly jettisoning their creeds while preserving their traditions, rituals, art, and music and honoring the symbolic and historic value of their holy texts, they would actually shed the source of their greatest vulnerability: the all-but-demonstrable falsehood of most of the cosmology and history they have heretofore felt obliged to profess. Some religions—some denominations or at least some congregations—already occupy this enlightened niche, so we know it is a possible stable outcome, but for other denominations the prospect of such a transformation must seem more like extinction.[58] It is hard to imagine a series of gradual steps that could loosen the white-knuckled grip on a creed that paralyzes most literal churches, and it is no easier (after learning of the efforts of Carl, Wes, Andy, and Darryl, for example) to imagine pastors in liberal traditions trying to help people grow but doing it surreptitiously, hiding the results of their own growth.

So let's consider some triage. Doubting clergy in the literalist denominations—Protestant fundamentalists, archconservative Catholics, Orthodox Jews, Islamists—will just have to fend for themselves, since they cannot expect radical communal soul-searching to arise under any circumstances. As we have seen in the case of Johnny (now a free man as Jerry DeWitt), a giant step *out* is just about the only path available. What can clergy in more liberal traditions do? They can actually help their colleagues in the literal traditions by putting more pressure on them, creating greater separation, not relaxing into bland "ecumenical" blurring of the boundaries.

It was the "militant," undiplomatic, impolite support of civil rights by some Christian churches in the South that shamed other churches into abandoning their traditional racist quietism (at best) and in some cases their ardent support for segregation. The "open and affirming" churches have played a similar role more recently in swaying opinion on same-sex marriage. The groundswell in favor of same-sex marriage has even prodded a synod of Roman Catholic bishops into an awkward two-step: First they issued a preliminary report saying that the Church ought to provide homosexuals "a welcoming home," according to Cardinal Péter Erdo of Hungary, the general reporter of the synod.[59] This was a large positive step for the Catholic Church to take, but not quite all the way to same-sex marriage: Erdo reported that the bishops want a stance of "accepting and valuing" anyone's sexual orientation "without compromising Catholic doctrine on the family and matrimony." This was still too large a step for most of the bishops in the synod, and when the final report was issued the welcoming language had been rolled back, first stumbling over the translation of the preliminary report ("welcoming" was replaced in English with "providing for," but the Italian word *accoglienza*, meaning "welcome," remained). And then the conservative bishops rolled the final report back further, to the disappointment of many Catholics and other commentators who had been hoping for a bold new stroke from the Church under the leadership of Pope Francis.

What lessons might be learned from this surprising development? First, it goes some way to demonstrating that even such a mighty fortress as the Roman Catholic Church trembles when the winds of opinion shift. Second, it shows how ineffective, or even counterproductive, hesitant half-measures can be.

By more forthrightly acknowledging the white lies of the past and risking some distress among the older, more literal members of their congregations, liberal clergy could not only salvage their personal integrity but also help others with the same task. They may well be surprised to find how many of their elder members have been quietly hoping for this day. Yes, it will be painful, but if the pain is inevitable, why not get it over with by making a grand gesture that has some hope of inspiring others instead of always playing catch-up, pressured into acknowledgment, like the synod of Catholic bishops, by the shift in public opinion? Clergy are supposed to be moral leaders, the vanguard not the rearguard, so they should pull themselves together and lead.

It would be particularly refreshing and empowering, we would think, to catch the media flat-footed once again. For decades there has been a prevailing tacit policy among journalists and commentators not to push hard on any religious issue, no matter how flagrant the offense to morality or common sense. Until independent organizations of Roman Catholics insisted on embarrassing their own church leaders with outraged demands for an end to sexual abuse and official coverup, investigative journalists were not encouraged to pursue the leads that were there to be followed. The laughable misinformation purveyed by creationist fantasies such as the Creation Museum, in Petersburg, Kentucky, is passed over in respectful silence, instead of receiving the searing exposure that the media often inflicts on nonreligious scams and hoaxes. Or consider the carefully designed Benson study that showed quite conclusively the ineffectiveness of intercessory prayer. What study? The Benson study, conducted by a Harvard Medical School professor and colleagues, and lavishly funded by the Templeton Foundation and the Baptist Memorial Health Care Corporation of Memphis. The Benson team labored for years to establish some positive effect on curing disease, or at least ameliorating suffering, among patients who were prayed for by devout Christians under carefully regulated conditions. It came up with nothing—except for one arguably significant effect in the wrong direction! (The patients who were told they were receiving prayers showed a small but measurable increase in postsurgical complications.)[60] The experimental work had been completed for months before the research team announced its results to the public, and speculation ran high that the statisticians had combed again and again through the mountain of data in hopes of finding some positive result to announce, but without success. It can hardly be doubted that if this prestigious study had found any positive result, it would have been on the front page of every newspaper and on the cover of every news magazine and featured repeatedly on the television news programs. Since the result was embarrassing to religions in general, the press duly reported it and dropped the story with scant comment, which is no doubt why so few people can remember anything about it.

Suppose a group of liberal clergy were to join hands and issue an unapologetic, frank announcement, acknowledging the flat-out falsehood of the least emotionally loaded biblical myths (such as Noah's Ark, Jonah and the whale, and some New Testament miracles. Save the Resurrection for another day). This would put literalist spokespeople in a difficult bind. Do they themselves lapse into the "symbolic, metaphorical, incomprehensible" dodge that they have heretofore despised when coming from the mouths of the liberals, or do they double down and insist that they believe that this palpable nonsense is the literal truth? The media would be in a bind, too, since the press conference announcing this acknowledgment would be a sober, respectful, serious presentation by prominent church leaders. The next time an archeological study or scientific experiment highlights the mythological status of some heretofore endorsed biblical proposition—and these discoveries are abundant—this would provide an ideal pretext for the liberal clergy to acknowledge the falsehood and add, "While we're at it, here are some more falsehoods in the Bible we'd like to recognize, belatedly, as such. In the interest of truth, we hereby abandon these claims." They would in any case only be admitting what most thoughtful people have long believed, and the refreshing spectacle of clerical candor would be likely to make up for any loss of face such a break from tradition would involve.

Without such a precedent-setting, cleansing innovation, today's closeted clergy can be sure that another generation of idealistic innocents will follow in their footsteps, repeating the same mistakes, falling into the same traps, agonizing over the same dilemmas about how to draw a line between diplomacy and dishonesty. We hope this book will convince them that they are not alone, and inspire them to break the cycle and put the knowledge they have acquired from their own private agonies to good use.

ACKNOWLEDGMENTS

We wish to thank all our study participants, whose courage in volunteering should not be underestimated. Our highest obligation is to honor the trust they put in us, by preserving their anonymity while putting their contributions to use in the service of greater understanding of these complex issues.

Our study was funded by a small group of donors who prefer not to be named, and by Stephen and Diane Uhl. We are grateful to them all, and to the Institutional Review Board of Tufts University for advising us and approving the design and execution of our study.

We could never have conducted our first study without the early and continuing help of Dan Barker of the Freedom From Religion Foundation and the late Reverend James Rowe Adams, founder of the Center for Progressive Christianity. Others who advised us include Dan's sister, Cynthia Yee, who is an ordained United Church of Christ minister, and Rabbi Robert Goldstein of the Center for the Study of Jewish-Christian-Muslim Relations at Merrimack College. Bart D. Ehrman, author and James A. Gray Distinguished Professor in the University of North Carolina's Department of Religious Studies, helped us find seminary professors, providing a short list of professors and permission to use his name when inviting their participation.

We were ably assisted throughout the project by Rosina Maiers, who provided both practical and analytic support, and Teresa Salvato, Program Coordinator at Tufts' Center for Cognitive Studies, who oversaw the budget and handled logistical details regarding both the conduct of the study and the production of the book. We are also grateful to Sara Lippincott, whose sharp-eyed editorial work did much to improve the shape, substance, and clarity of the book, and to Kurt Volkan of Pitchstone Publishing for expertly guiding the publication of this expanded edition.

Linda wants to acknowledge the continuing advice and support from her Humanist Book Club, J. Anderson Thomson, Jr., Pamela J. Blake, Carmen Vaughn, Mary Beth Favorite, the Women in Communications lunch group, and her clever and exacting husband, Art Siebens.

Dan wants to thank his wife, Susan, for a bounty of good suggestions, and John Brockman, as usual, for expert advice and encouragement.

APPENDIX A
The Participants

The information provided herein is based only on the data gathered from the study's inception in 2007 to the study's conclusion in 2012 and thus does not include more recent updates or changes in status. The one exception is that real names are provided in brackets for those participants who are today open about their participation in the study and who have given us permission to use their names.

Sample Characteristics

Thirty-five people participated in this and our 2010 pilot study. In age, they ranged from twenty-four to seventy-six, with all but seven between thirty and sixty. All were Caucasian. Twenty-six were married, including three to same-sex partners (the ages and marital status of the three seminary professors interviewed were not recorded). A total of ninety interviews were conducted, from November 2008 to June 2012.

Herewith a list of our clergy and seminary student informants:

The Mainline Protestants:

- Andy, a United Church of Christ pastor in his fifties, who plans to remain a pastor until his retirement;
- Bill, an Episcopal pastor in his fifties, who plans to remain a pastor until his retirement;
- Brian, a former Lutheran seminary student, now in his thirties, who left on the first day of seminary;

- Caitlin [Caroline Fairless], an Episcopalian pastor in her sixties, about to retire;
- Carl, a Lutheran pastor in his fifties, who plans to remain a pastor until his retirement;
- Charles, an Episcopal hospital chaplain in his thirties who is a believer;
- Darryl, a Presbyterian pastor in his thirties, who remains in the clergy *(pilot study participant)*;
- Harry [Mike Aus], a former Lutheran and nondenominational pastor in his forties, who left the ministry shortly after being interviewed and started a humanist community;
- Jared [John Figdor], a humanist, formerly UCC, recent divinity school graduate, who plans to lead humanist communities;
- Jim, an Episcopal pastor in his fifties who is a believer;
- Rick [Mark Rutledge], a United Church of Christ campus chaplain in his seventies, now semi-retired *(pilot study participant)*;
- Tammie [Teresa MacBain], a Methodist pastor in her forties who left the ministry shortly after being interviewed;
- Wes, a Methodist pastor in his forties, who intends to remain in the clergy *(pilot study participant)*;
- Winnie, a former Presbyterian pastor in her fifties who pursued a doctorate in another field.

The Mormons:

- Joe, a Mormon bishop in his forties, halfway through his five-year commitment, who does not intend to accept other Church positions when his bishopric commitment ends;
- Walt, a former Mormon bishop in his forties, who left his bishopric and the Mormon Church.

The Fundamentalists:

- Adam, a Church of Christ worship minister in his forties who remains in the clergy but is a clandestine secular activist *(pilot study participant)*;
- Dave, a Baptist missionary in Asia in his forties, who returned to the

United States, left the ministry shortly after being interviewed, and now works in an unrelated field.

- Hugh, a former Seventh-day Adventist religion student who is now planning a secular career;
- Jack, a Southern Baptist worship minister in his fifties, looking to leave *(pilot study participant)*;
- Jeb [John Compere], a former Baptist pastor who left ministry years ago to become a clinical psychologist;
- Johnny [Jerry DeWitt], a Pentecostal pastor in his forties who left the ministry shortly after being interviewed and is now a secular activist;
- Michael, a Seventh-day Adventist in his fifties on a leave of absence and planning to leave the ministry;
- Pete, a student who left Pentecostal pastoral training in his early twenties and is now a college student in an unrelated field;
- Stan, a Disciples of Christ military chaplain who left the military and the ministry to enter graduate school to train for another career.

The Roman Catholics:

- Candice [Catherine Dunphy], a seminary graduate in her thirties who did not pursue a career in religion; she is now a secular activist.
- Glen, a parish priest in his forties on a leave of absence, with no plans to return;
- Tony, a former parish priest in his forties;
- Vince, a former teaching monk in his seventies who left his order a few years after Vatican II.

An Orthodox:

- George, a former Greek Orthodox monk in his thirties.

The Jews:

- Sherm, an Orthodox rabbi in his thirties who plans to remain in the rabbinate until his retirement;
- Jacob [Jeff Falick], a Humanist (formerly Reform) rabbi in his thirties who plans to remain in the rabbinate until his retirement.

Detailed, Aggregate Information
90 total interviews, including:

- 30 new respondents (one to three interviews, 60 or 90 minutes each)
- 5 pilot-study respondents (three interviews each, 60 or 90 minutes each)
- 4 follow-up phone interviews with respondents from the pilot study (60 minutes each)
- 4 follow-up phone interviews with "active/former" respondents in the Phase Two study who "came out" during the course of the study, after first being interviewed as clergy (60 minutes each)

Demographics
Career status of all 35 respondents (clergy, students, and seminary professors):

- 27 clergy, active or former, or active/former, i.e., left the clergy during the course of the study
    - » 20 active clergy
        - 11 active throughout the course of the study
        - 5 "active/former" who left the clergy a few months after being interviewed—only one planned in advance
        - 2 on sabbatical/leave of absence
        - 2 "others"—practicing clergy who do not identify as non-believing
    - » 7 former clergy
- 5 students—2 graduates, 1 active, 1 former, 1 who left seminary on the first day
- 3 seminary professors of Old or New Testament Studies

Religion/denomination of the 32 clergy or students (27 active or former clergy and 5 students):

- 22 Protestants
    - » 4 Episcopalians—3 active (including 3 "others," i.e., believers), 1 former
    - » 1 Disciple of Christ, active/former (he planned to leave before the interviews began)

  - 2 Presbyterians—1 active, 1 former
  - 3 Lutherans—1 active/former, 1 active, 1 seminary student for one day
  - 2 United Church of Christ (UCC)—1 active, 1 retired
  - 2 Methodists—1 active, 1 active/former
  - 3 Baptists—1 missionary, active/former, 2 pastors (1 active and 1 former)
  - 2 Assemblies of God—1 active/former, 1 former student and youth pastor
  - 1 Church of Christ—active
  - 2 Adventists—1 on leave of absence, 1 student

- 4 Roman Catholics—1 on leave of absence, 2 former (1 priest, 1 monk), 1 seminary graduate
- 1 Greek Orthodox—former, just left
- 2 Jews—1 active Humanist rabbi (formerly Reform), 1 Orthodox rabbi
- 2 Mormons—1 former, 1 active bishop
- 1 Humanist—recent seminary graduate

Gender: 28 men, 4 women

Race: 32 Caucasians

Marital status: 26 married (1 separated later)—3 to same-sex partners, 5 single, 1 divorced (of the 26 married respondents, 23 had spouses who were supportive, irrespective of their own beliefs; 2 had spouses who were not aware of the change in beliefs)

Children: 15 with children, 12 without (7 married, 5 single)

Education: 6 doctoral (4 PhD, 2 DMin), 16 master's (9 MDiv, 6 other), 3 bachelor's (including 1 master's student), 3 less than bachelor's (1 bachelor's student, 1 Bible college grad, 1 technical school grad)

Ages: from 20s to 70s

- 3—20s
- 7—30s
- 10—40s
- 8—50s
- 2—60s
- 2—70s

Locations: 22 urban, 10 rural

- 6—Northeast
- 9—South
- 6—Midwest
- 2—Southwest
- 5—West
- 4—Outside of U.S. (2 Canada, 1 Near East, 1 Far East)

Liberal (e.g., Mainline Protestant, Roman Catholic) *vs. Literal* (Fundamentalist, Orthodox): 11 literal and 21 liberal (including 2 "others"), 8 of whom started out literal

- 19 original literals: 8 who switched to a liberal denomination before becoming nonbelieving, 8 who are still active clergy, and 3 who are inactive (on leave of absence or on military reserve status).
- 13 original liberals: 5 are still clergy, including 2 UCC, 1 Presbyterian, 2 humanists, 1 Lutheran, and 1 "other" (believing Episcopalian).

Clergy Project Connection

Of the 32 clergy/student study participants, 24 are Clergy Project members:

- 15 first learned about it as a result of volunteering to be interviewed in the study.
- 8 learned about the study after becoming a member of the project.
- 1 learned about the study and the project simultaneously, while searching "atheist clergy" on the Internet.

Of the 8 study participants who are not Clergy Project members:

- 2 are "others"—believing clergy, so not appropriate for membership.
- 3 are students who did not complete their studies and thus did not qualify.
- 1 did not have Internet access.
- 2 declined membership.

APPENDIX B
About Qualitative Research

Qualitative research is designed to reveal a target audience's range of behavior and the perceptions that drive it with reference to specific topics or issues.[61] It uses in-depth studies of small groups of people to guide and support the construction of hypotheses. The results of qualitative research are descriptive rather than predictive.

Qualitative research methods originated in the social and behavioral sciences: sociology, anthropology, and psychology. Today, qualitative methods in the field of marketing research include in-depth interviews with individuals, group discussions (from two to ten participants is typical); diary and journal exercises; and in-context observations. Sessions may be conducted in person, by telephone, via videoconferencing, and via the Internet.

Several unique aspects of qualitative research contribute to rich, insightful results:

- Synergy among [group] respondents, as they build on each other's comments and ideas;
- The dynamic nature of the interview or group discussion process, which engages respondents more actively than is possible in more structured survey;
- The opportunity to probe ("Help me understand why you feel that way"), enabling the researcher to reach beyond initial responses and rationales;

- The opportunity to observe, record, and interpret nonverbal communication (i.e., body language, voice intonation) as part of a respondent's feedback, which is valuable during interviews or discussions, and during analysis;
- The opportunity to engage respondents in "play" such as projective techniques and exercises, overcoming the self-consciousness that can inhibit spontaneous reactions and comments

What are the statistical limitations of qualitative research?

The results of qualitative research cannot be statistically projected across a target population. That's because the methods used to recruit participants and explore issues in qualitative research tend to be quite different, by design, from the methods that a projectable quantitative study might involve. However, when decisions must be made that require quantification, qualitative research is often used in advance to help plan effective quantitative studies, or as a follow-up method to help interpret quantitative results or explore selected topics in greater depth.

APPENDIX C
Linda's Personal Story

Before conducting this study of nonbelieving clergy, my only intense interest in religion coincided with a brief period in early adolescence when I wanted to become a nun. It was not unusual for Catholic girls to go through a phase like this. Boys seemed icky and convent life seemed romantic—a way to be respected and set apart from ordinary mortals. In my case, that phase ended quickly, supplanted by a growing interest in boys who had somehow shed their ickyness.

Aside from that episode, religion played a central but minor role while I was growing up in New Castle, Pennsylvania, a small industrial town near Pittsburgh. My family's Catholic faith was always present but was neither a burden nor a special joy. I went to church every Sunday, ate fish on Friday, went to confession once a month, made my first Holy Communion at age seven, and was confirmed at thirteen. Looking back on it, I'd say we were liberal, cultural Christians, though that's not how my family would have described ourselves. We were Italian Catholics, with the emphasis on "Italian." Christmas and Easter meant family gatherings with a focus on food, music, a good poker game, and not a word about religion that I can remember.

As a teenager, after my sister and brother were grown and gone, Sunday mornings at church were a chance to be alone with Dad and to learn Latin. I compared the Latin on one side of the Sunday Missal with the English translation on the other, while trying to ignore the dreadful sermon in which the parishioners were regularly scolded for not putting enough money in the collection basket.

After church, we went to Nonna's for percolated coffee and sweet rolls. Nonna never mentioned anything about church, and I never thought to ask whether she had gone herself. I certainly never saw her there. As for my mother, she didn't attend church except on special occasions. She had a terrible case of claustrophobia that prevented her from doing anything she didn't want to do. I credit Mom with keeping me out of the Catholic schools that were springing up in the fifties. She greatly resented the attempted intrusion of the church into our lives; I just wanted to stay with my friends in public school. Now I'm thankful for having been spared the indoctrination I heard about later from Catholic friends who attended parochial school.

As an adult, without children and married to an agnostic, I drifted away from church. I believed in God but didn't pray and didn't ponder religion very much. In retrospect, I think of myself during that period as a "lazy believer." If I were to have been asked to state my religion on a survey, I would have responded "Roman Catholic," because that was my cultural identity. But I was really a "None."

Eventually, my husband, Art, was drawn to the Unitarian Universalist Church, wanting a sense of community. I attended with him a couple of times and found the people lovely and the services completely inoffensive. I certainly didn't miss the authoritarianism of the Catholic Church, but I did miss the "smells and bells," and I couldn't imagine trading my leisurely reading of the Sunday paper for the vague spirituality of the Unitarians.

We looked around for a place we could both enjoy, finally landing in the Episcopal Church. It was like a liturgical throwback to my childhood, complete with incense and some chanting in Latin, but with no need to adhere to doctrine. Art was openly welcomed as an agnostic and even invited to sing his original "agnostic" song from the pulpit. (Its final lines: "A few simple answers would make life so concrete, / If I could phone up God on Sunday, would my search be complete?")

Everything was fine, until I started studying religious history a few years ago. Although I love to delve into subjects until they are explained to my satisfaction, I had never studied religion in a serious way; I simply hadn't cared enough to take it on. But after a trip to Italy in 2005, where I saw Christian history unfold in the many brilliant works of Christian art and architecture, my interest was piqued and my studies began.

I was fascinated. There was so much more here than what I'd learned in church or catechism classes. The Bible is long on myth and metaphor and short on facts and history. Organized religion, like any other power structure, is an exclusively human enterprise. Religious leaders can claim divine inspiration and guidance, but scholars know that no supernatural assistance is needed to compile a book of ancient stories or build a system of belief.

I was angry. Why hadn't I figured this out sooner? The information was at my fingertips: in the public library, at the bookstore, on the Internet. But I hadn't bothered to think about it, and in our society faith is the default position. Also, I suppose I had been ignoring or discounting information that didn't fit into my inchoate but comfortable belief system. I remember my response when my then fiancé learned about Transubstantiation (the literal turning of bread and wine into the body and blood of Christ) and was astounded that I believed in something I knew was biologically impossible. "It's a miracle," I blithely declared. I had never bothered to analyze Transubstantiation, because it had no impact on my daily life. The Virgin Birth and the Resurrection were ancient events. I hadn't received Communion in the Catholic Church in over a decade by then, and I had no intention of ever doing so again. Nonetheless, I had continued to accept the miracles and myths I learned about in childhood and never thought or cared about since.

I was confused as well, and it was the desire to sort out my confusion that ultimately led to this study. One of the fascinating facts I learned during my personal religious research was that seminary students are taught the same religious and biblical history I had learned on my own. Of his seminary studies, Marcus Borg has written: "The news that 'the Jesus of history' (as I learned to call him) was very different from the Jesus I had heard about growing up in the church seemed important to me. It also seemed vaguely scandalous, and something I shouldn't tell my mother about. But I was hooked."[62]

He was hooked? My reaction was to wonder how seminary students could continue their studies after learning that what they were expected to preach was different from what they were discovering in school. This disconnect clearly required further study. I'd had a long career conducting qualitative research for government agencies and nonprofit groups, and now I wanted to research *this*.

What I didn't realize at the time was that it was easy for someone like me—removed from religion and indifferent to it—to respond logically to what I was learning about religion. All I had to lose was a vague hope for an afterlife that, frankly, I could never quite imagine. For clergy, such introspection was much more difficult and complex. They had felt a calling; they had made a commitment. They had the mindset of faith, dedication to a cause, and the expectation of a lifelong vocation. I would learn that all this had a huge effect on how they processed information.

My intense curiosity prompted me to contact Dan Dennett. I had read his *Breaking the Spell,* in which he calls for treating religion as a subject for scientific study. I had also just read an essay he wrote on Mother Teresa's extended "dark night of the soul," in which she did not feel Christ's presence but continued to follow his directive to serve the poor and dying. In that essay, "The Agony of Misplaced Ecstasy,"[63] he conjectured that many other clergy experienced persistent disbelief. We soon decided to collaborate on exploratory qualitative research to investigate pastors' "cognitive dissonance"—how they squared what they had learned with what they were preaching. As we eventually found out, there was much more to it than that.

APPENDIX D
Dan's Personal Story

Some of my earliest childhood memories are of listening to the muezzin sing the prayers from the minaret that rose within a hundred yards of our house in Beirut. Some of my early playmates were Muslims or Druze, but I doubt if I knew what a Christian was until I started going to Sunday school at the First Congregational Church in Winchester, Massachusetts, at age six or so, in the late 1940s. I had been raised on the wonderful folk tales about the 13th-century Sufi sage Nasr din Hodja, and I found Bible stories to be almost equally engrossing, although seldom as amusing.

In Winchester, churchgoing was a social thing. As I recall, just about all children went to one Sunday school or another: Catholic, Baptist, Methodist, Unitarian, Episcopalian, Christian Scientist. (No Jews lived in Winchester. I was in high school before I learned that there was a secret agreement among the realtors in town to keep Jews out, a shameful legacy that was dismantled in the 1960s.) My sisters and I attended Sunday school and its teenage continuation in "Fellowship," and I learned the rituals and hymns, which I also sang at summer camp, a nondenominational camp for boys with a beautiful open-air chapel in the woods. I loved the weekly (Christian) services at camp, which were long on music and short on Scripture, with no chaplain. When puberty arrived, Fellowship became much more important to me, because all the best dances for teens were at the "Congo"—though there was something to be said for the somewhat less chaperoned sock hops at the CYO, the Catholic Youth Organization. The word on the street was that

Catholic girls were easier, because they went to confession.

I did have a brief, intense intellectual adventure with Christian Science. There was a large contingent of CS boys and counselors at my summer camp, and though they were discreet about their meetings and didn't do any proselytizing, I became intrigued and participated in their sessions, reading Mary Baker Eddy's *Science and Health with Key to the Scriptures* and sitting in on two nightlong prayer vigils to cure, without medicine, a badly sprained knee and a shockingly inflamed and swollen ingrown big toenail. (The toenail was markedly better by morning, a fact that has impressed me ever since.) My mother worried that I would join the Christian Scientists, but she needn't have; I was already too much of a skeptic to go in for that. She herself never went to church, unless it was to the Unitarian church, whose minister she adored. My grandfather, for more than half a century one of Winchester's doctors, never went to church, but my grandmother was a loyal attendee and contributor to the Congregational coffers, though I never heard her mention religion outside of church or say grace. Shakespeare Club was the target of her devotions.

I discovered atheism at about age fourteen or fifteen and knew immediately, and with no emotional turmoil, that I was an atheist, but I have maintained diplomatic relations with churches, singing in choirs, attending Easter and Christmas services and (of course) weddings and funerals. I even gave a guest student sermon at the Congregational Church in Middletown, Connecticut, where I was a freshman at Wesleyan University in 1959. My theme was to reflect on, and applaud, the fact that, as a little research had just shown me, the Congregational Church does not have a creed; individual churches may develop one if they see fit. Most don't, I gather. My kind of church. But I don't belong to any—unless it counts that I was "confirmed" at the Winchester church when I was a young teenager and have never gone to the trouble of renouncing or rescinding that.

Fortunately for us both, my wife, Susan, had an almost identical religious upbringing in Wellesley, another Boston suburb, so we knew all the same Scripture, rituals, and hymns and felt equally comfortable attending—or not attending—church. We love the music, and so, it turns out, do many of our friends. I have sung (many times, in most cases) all the great choral music of Christianity, and for over thirty years we have hosted an annual Christmas Carol sing and potluck. I curated a songbook of all the best versions of all the best carols, gleaned from choirs, glee clubs, and chorales I have sung in—from "Lo, How a Rose E'er Blooming" to "Sweet Was the Virgin's Song" to "Masters in This Hall." No "Frostie the Snowman" or "Chestnuts roasting on an open fire" for us, and yet of the three dozen or so loyal attendees I am not sure if any regularly attend church.

That tolerant neglect typified my attitudes toward religion in general, not just Congregationalism—until the early 21st century, when the theocratic stirrings of the religious right alarmed me enough to decide to do something about it. I had been appalled for years by the deliberate spreading of falsehood by churches opposed to evolution or to birth control, and by the breathtaking dishonesty of televangelists of various stripes, but I was content to support the efforts of others to redress the balance. I don't think I had bothered mentioning that I was an atheist to anyone for decades, until Richard Dawkins drew my attention to the attempt by Paul Geisert and Mynga Futrell, two retired high school science teachers, to popularize the term "bright" as a noun to cover atheists, agnostics, freethinkers, humanists, and others who have no place for the supernatural in their worldviews. On the spur of the moment, I decided to experiment with the term by announcing, to a large gathering of high-achieving high school students from around the country, that I was a bright, explaining what the term meant.

The effect was electrifying. Many of the students flocked to me after my brief talk to exclaim that they had never encountered an adult who would say such a thing and they were thrilled. They were brights, too, but had thought they were alone. After that, perhaps half of the rest of the speakers at that conference, including several Nobel laureates, casually mentioned that they, too, were brights, to loud applause. This was an effect worth amplifying, so I wrote an op-ed piece for the *New York Times*, "The Bright Stuff" (their title, not mine), in July of 2003. It was the most e-mailed *Times* piece of the month, and I was importuned by many to build on this beginning. The result was my three-year vacation from my usual topics of research (consciousness, the brain, free will, and evolution) to research and write *Breaking the Spell: Religion as a Natural Phenomenon.* That in turn led to my collaboration with Linda on this book, as she explains in her own personal story.

APPENDIX E
Pilot Study

Evolutionary Psychology

www.epjournal.net—2010. 8(1): 122–150

Original Article/Essay

Preachers Who Are Not Believers

Daniel C. Dennett, Center for Cognitive Studies, Tufts University, Medford, MA, USA. Email: Daniel.dennett@tufts.edu (Corresponding author).

Linda LaScola, LaScola Qualitative Research, 3900 Connecticut Avenue, NW 101F, Washington, DC 20008, USA.

Abstract: There are systemic features of contemporary Christianity that create an almost invisible class of non-believing clergy, ensnared in their ministries by a web of obligations, constraints, comforts, and community. Exemplars from five Protestant denominations, Southern Baptist, United Church of Christ, Presbyterian, Methodist and Church of Christ, were found and confidentially interviewed at length about their lives, religious education and indoctrination, aspirations, problems and ways of coping. The in-depth, qualitative interviews formed the basis for profiles of all five, together with general observations about their predicaments and how they got into them. The authors anticipate that the discussion generated on the Web (at On Faith, the Newsweek/Washington Post website on religion, http://newsweek.washingtonpost.com/onfaith//2010/03/disbelief_in_the_pulpit/all.html) and on other websites will facilitate a larger study that will enable the insights of this pilot study to be clarified, modified, and expanded.

Keywords: religion, clergy, disbelief, Protestantism, qualitative, interviews

Introduction

Are there clergy who don't believe in God? Certainly there are former clergy who fall in this category. Before making their life-wrenching decisions, they were secret nonbelievers. Who knows how many like-minded pastors discover that they simply cannot take this mortal leap from the pulpit and then go on to live out their ministries in secret disbelief? What is it like to be a pastor who doesn't believe in God? John Updike gave us a moving account in his brilliant novel, *In the Beauty of the Lilies* (1996), which begins with the story of Reverend Wilmot, a Lutheran minister whose life is shattered by his decision to renounce the pulpit in the face of his mounting disbelief. But that is fiction and Wilmot's period of concealment is short-lived. What is it like to be a pastor who stays the course, in spite of sharing Wilmot's disbelief?

With the help of a grant from a small foundation, administered through Tufts University, we set out to find some closeted nonbelievers who would agree to be intensively—and, of course, confidentially—interviewed. The interviews were all conducted by Linda LaScola, a clinical social worker with years of professional experience as a qualitative researcher and psychotherapist, and, until recently, a regular churchgoer. Like her co-author, philosopher Daniel Dennett, the author of *Breaking the Spell* (2006), she is an atheist who is nevertheless a sympathetic and fascinated observer of religious practices and attitudes. For this pilot study we managed to identify five brave pastors, all still actively engaged with parishes, who were prepared to trust us with their stories. All five are Protestants, with master's level seminary education. Three represented liberal denominations (the liberals) and two came from more conservative, evangelical traditions (the literals). We decided to concentrate this first project on Christians, and we would have included a Roman Catholic or Greek Orthodox priest, for instance—if we had encountered any, but we didn't. We initially had six participants, but one, a woman in the Episcopal church, had a change of heart as we were about to go to press and, at her request, all further references to her and quotations from her interviews have been removed.

Our sample is small and self-selected, and it is not surprising that all of our pastors think that they are the tip of an iceberg, but they are also utterly unable to confirm this belief. They might be deluding themselves, but in any case their isolation from others whom they suspect are in the same boat is a feature they all share, in spite of striking differences in their stories and attitudes. While we couldn't draw any reliable generalizations from such a small sample of clergy, the very variety of their stories, as well as the patterns discernible in them, suggest fascinating avenues for further research on this all but invisible phenomenon.

Materials and Methods

How on earth did we recruit them? By spreading the word discreetly. Eighteen people were contacted to participate between September 2008 and April 2009. Initial recruiting attempts were made via personal contacts (e.g., clergy and seminary acquaintances, non-believing clergy who had retired or left the profession). When approached, potential respondents were told that the intent was to "learn more about the issues that clergy face when their beliefs are not in synch with church teachings." Dennett mentioned the study at conferences he attended. Ultimately, the five participants came from two sources: two from a list of clergy who had originally contacted the Center for Progressive Christianity (TCPC) for general information, and three from people who had personally contacted Dan Barker, co-director of the Freedom from Religion Foundation. Barker is a former minister and author of two books about losing his religious beliefs. Jim Adams, a retired Episcopal priest, author and the founder of TCPC, provided a list of 28 names. Of those, nine were contacted and two of the nine participated in the study. Four people contacted Dan Barker directly. Of those, two agreed to participate. One contact who was a former clergyman, and therefore not eligible to participate, referred a colleague who then agreed to participate. Three women who expressed interest were not asked to participate: one because she was no longer in a pastoral role and two because their denominations were already represented in the study. Four men declined to participate: two did not follow up after showing initial interest; two others cited concerns about the term "non-believing." Though neither of them believed in a supernatural god, both strongly self-identified as believers.

But what do they mean by this? Are they perhaps deceiving themselves? There is no way of answering, and this is no accident. The ambiguity about who is a believer and who a nonbeliever follows inexorably from the pluralism that has been assiduously fostered by many religious leaders for a century and more: God is many different things to different people, and since we can't know if one of these conceptions is the right one, we should honor them all. This counsel of tolerance creates a gentle fog that shrouds the question of belief in God in so much indeterminacy that if asked whether they believed in God, many people could sincerely say that they don't know what they are being asked.

This is not just agnosticism, the belief that one does not (or cannot) know whether God exists, but something prior: the belief that one cannot even know which question—if any—is being asked. Many people are utterly comfortable with this curious ignorance; it just doesn't matter to them what the formulas mean that their churches encourage them to recite. Some churches are equally tolerant of the indeterminacy: as long as you "have faith" or are "one with Jesus" (whatever you think that means) your metaphysical convictions are your own business. But pastors can't afford that luxury. Their role in life often requires them to articulate, from the pulpit and elsewhere, assertions about these very issues.

A Problem of Definition

> I think my way of being a Christian has many things in common with atheists as [Sam] Harris sees them. I am not willing to abandon the symbol "God" in my understanding of the human and the universe. But my definition of God is very different from mainline Christian traditions yet it is within them. Just at the far left end of the bell shaped curve. (Rick, one of our participants)

A spectrum of available conceptions of God can be put in rough order, with frank anthropomorphism at one extreme—a God existing in time and space with eyes and hands and love and anger—through deism, a somehow still personal God who cares but is nevertheless outside time and space and does not intervene, and the still more abstract Ground of all Being, from which (almost?) all anthropomorphic features have been removed, all the way to frank atheism: nothing at all is aptly called God. To some people, deism is already atheism in disguise, but others are more flexible. Karen Armstrong (2009), for instance, dismisses both the anthropomorphic visions ("idolatry") and the various brands of atheism, while claiming, as she recently put it while speaking with Terry Gross on *Fresh Air*, that "God is not a being at all." Assuming that she meant what she said, she claims, by simple logical transposition, that no being at all is God. That would seem to be about as clear a statement of atheism as one could ask for, but not in her eyes.

There is no agreement at all, then, about where to draw a line across this spectrum, with belief in God on one side and non-belief on the other, and many people are quite content to ignore the question. But two of our pastors have felt the need to draw the line, and to recognize that, given where they draw the line, their own view has crossed it: they no longer *deserve* to be called believers, whatever others may think. The other three say that they may not believe in a supernatural god, but they believe in something. Still, they all find themselves with a secret: they don't believe what many of their parishioners think they believe and think they ought to believe.

The fact that they see it in such morally laden terms shows how powerfully the phenomenon of belief in belief figures in our lives. Most people believe in belief in God; they believe that it is a state one should aspire to, work strenuously to maintain, and foster in others—and feel guilty or dismayed if one fails to achieve it. Whether or not our pastors share that belief *in belief*—some still do and others no longer do—they recognize only too well that revealing their growing disbelief would have dire consequences for their lives. So they keep it to themselves.

Results

After introducing them, we will explore the most interesting similarities and differences we discovered. We have given them fictitious names and scrambled the inessential details of their stories that might serve to identify them, so any similarity seen between their stories and known individuals should be viewed as mere coincidence. Here are their stories.

Wes, the Methodist—Making Clergy Obsolete

Wes, age 42, has been the pastor of a liberal Methodist church in the Northwest for 10 years. He has a 10 year old son and is married to a schoolteacher who shares his views about religion. Wes and his wife are raising their son to recognize that Bible stories are not factual:

> And so when we talk to him about Bible stories, we remind him constantly that these are just stories. These are stories; think about them in no different way than you would any other stories.

Wes was raised Baptist in the South and attended a liberal Christian college and seminary before moving west. Although he rejected his family's conservative views as a young adult, he was positively involved in the life of the church in his youth:

> I felt very surrounded by people who were concerned about me. I was very comfortable in that environment. And I suppose I've always been, perhaps, most comfortable in a church environment. I flourished there. I was the one that answered all the questions. I cared about all this kind of stuff . . . Bible trivia. It made me think I knew the Bible.

From Liberal to Literal

Once in college, he was surprised by what he learned:

> I went to college thinking Adam and Eve were real people. And I can remember really wrestling with that when my Old Testament professor was pointing out the obvious myths and how they came to be. And I kind of joked at the time that I prayed my way all the way to atheism. Because in the early days, it was wrestling with God; praying to God.

Wes decided to go on to seminary because the credits he would receive there could be applied either to PhD studies in the philosophy of religion or to a career in the clergy. Looking back on it, he realizes that he also felt limited in his choices:

> If you finish your junior year, if you're going to declare a new major, now you're setting yourself back. And I'll be the first to admit that my upbringing placed limitations on what I thought was possible for me, which is something I've sworn to not do with my son. . . . Not that I

> believe in such things, but it was almost predestined that I would be a minister because of my role as a kid in church, my parents' role. . . . I'd love to be a scientist. I think that would be wonderful.

When in seminary, he noticed the differing reactions that his classmates had to the scholarly information they were receiving about biblical history:

> I would guess if there were 30 people in the archeology class, there would be 25% of them who would become very defensive and argumentative with the professor. And probably only one or two of the 30 would be open to it. The rest would just not say much.

Eventually, he decided to pursue a career in the ministry. It seemed like a natural fit:

> So I kind of thought, well, you know I really know religion; I know Christianity. It's been in my blood. And I suddenly felt like there was a certain strand of Christianity that I could identify with. And the Methodist Church—was different . . . really, it's a very progressive church. So I felt at home there.

Wes has had some qualms about his role as a non-believing minister, but overall he thinks he is being true to the very worthy mission of developing liberal, democratic values among his church members:

> My first few years of doing this were wracked with, "God, should I be doing this? Is this —? Am I being —? Am I posing? Am I being less than authentic; less than honest?" . . . And, I really wrestled with it and to some degree still. But not nearly as much.
>
> I will be the first to admit that I see Christianity as a means to an end, not as an end unto itself. And the end is very basically, a kind of liberal, democratic values. So I will use Christianity sometimes against itself to try to lead people to that point. But there's so much within the Christian tradition that itself influenced the development of those liberal values, you know. They didn't arise through secular means. They came out of some religious stuff. . . . I could couch all that in very secular language. If we were in a college setting, I would. But we're in a religious setting, so I use the religious language.

Demythologizing Religion

Wes thinks that what separates him from people who identify themselves as atheists is his openness to using the word "God":

> The difference between me and an atheist is basically this: it's not about the existence of God. It's: do we believe that there is room for the use of the word "God" in some context? And a thoroughly consistent atheist would say, "No. We just need to get over that word just like we need to get over concepts of race. We quit using that word, we'd be better off." Whereas I would say I agree with that in a great many cases, but I still think the word has some value in some contexts. So I think the word God can be used very expressively in some of my more meditative modes. I've thought of God as a kind of poetry that's written by human beings. As a way of dealing with the fact that we're finite; we're vulnerable.

He says he is happy in ministry, knowing that it provides a flexible and comfortable lifestyle and an opportunity to positively influence people's lives. Although he thinks that religion will be around a long time, he sees that part of his role is to help make his job obsolete. He thinks many of his liberal Christian colleagues have similar views, which they would express if they had a suitable opportunity:

> My colleagues here are very educated, very well read, and do not believe the significance of Christianity lies in whether it's literally true. They do believe that it is metaphorically describing something that is real. Something spiritual that we cannot get at, that is a presence in this universe. That's where they differ from me. But the way we use the language is going to be very similar, and the reason it's going to be similar is that our goals are the same. Our goals are to help people become freer than they were before, and to be transformed. So if becoming a Christian transforms a person's life for the better, I have no problem with them becoming a Christian. But I also have no problem with it if it means betraying Christianity, if that's what helps them. And I think many of my colleagues, if they were in this kind of environment [confidential interview], would admit to that. They wouldn't, though, in front of their bishops.
>
> They're very liberal. They've been de-mythologized, I'll say that. They don't believe Jesus rose from the dead literally. They don't believe Jesus was born of a virgin. They don't believe all those things that

> would cause a big stir in their churches. But that's not uncommon in mainline denominations, or even in the Catholic Church. I mean, you have a professional class of people, basically, who are working with an organization of non-professionals.

Coming Out to a Friend

Wes has confided his non-belief with one of his church members. He and Wes became close friends while working on various church projects over a period of several years:

> We kind of felt each other out over the course of time . . . just a little bit of self-revelation at a time. And we got to the point, you know, where he felt comfortable saying things to me.
>
> Perhaps he was the one that maybe kind of initiated asking questions, trying to figure out what I thought of some things. I can't remember exactly what he said, but he brought it up: "Do you think there is a being out there somewhere?" And at that point, I knew him well enough, so I said "Oh, no." He absolutely died laughing! And he said, "You know, I've really been wrestling with that myself, but I've never met anybody who just said, "Oh, of course not!" He hasn't been privy to all my years of struggle. He was just shocked that I was just so matter-of-fact.

Offering Community

Wes thinks he is especially effective at offering community to people who doubt they would fit into a Christian community:

> I'm interested in community, relationships. And I believe the argument could be made that that's what Jesus was interested in anyway. So I can do that at the local church level. And I'm also there for people who are recovering Christians. There are a lot of people out there who have been damaged by Christianity. And they feel guilty that they're not a Christian—or that they're not practicing or whatever. I'm their ideal pastor, because they can come to me and be told that they don't need to feel guilty.

Rick, the UCC Campus Minister—Social Justice Through the Church

Rick is a 72 year old United Church of Christ (UCC) minister receiving a full pension from the church and a monthly stipend for his part-time work as a campus minister at an academically top-ranked university. He has served in campus ministry throughout his long career because it has allowed him to pursue his interests in social causes. While working on various campuses across the country, he has worked in civil rights, gay rights and women's rights, including assisting women who were seeking abortions before they were legalized nationally. He specifically chose the UCC denomination because it had "no forced doctrine," offered "a lot of freedom to believe what you want to believe," and had a large and active social justice mission.

The Accidental Minister

Rick's family was not very religious, but attended a socially liberal mainline protestant church when he was growing up. While in college, he says:

> . . . like many students, I became agnostic—I didn't believe any of it. I wasn't reacting against it; I wasn't abused, as many I talk to are. But I just said, "there's nothing much there."

He majored in philosophy, political science and English and would likely have entered his father's profession of law if the Korean War hadn't intervened. He learned that he could avoid the draft by signing up for seminary. That wasn't his only motive, though. He was truly interested in learning more about Christianity:

> I didn't believe in God, but I thought, before I reject the street version of Christianity, I'll go to seminary for a year. And I'll argue with the best theologians and the best religious scholars, and then I'll get out. I'm not going to leave the church; I'm not going to leave what I was formed in until I have a chance to confront the scholars and argue and see what's going on. Is there anything in this God business? That was the way I kind of put it. Is there anything to this? So I determined to enter seminary.

It was a good move for him and he decided to see it through. He enjoyed his professors, describing them as, "people of faith who were also deeply intellectual and critical." He respected the fact that they could, "hold the life of the mind and the life of the faith together." He also realized that, unlike many of his classmates, he was not destined for parish ministry. He remembers his reaction when a professor said:

> When you get into your own churches, you've got to realize that there's these two things that are important that you've got to do: you've got to raise money, and you've got to recruit members. And I checked out.

It was not just the responsibilities of parish life that held him back, it was the beliefs:

> I knew I'm not going to make it in a conventional church. I didn't believe the conventional things, even then. I mean, sure, I'm studying theology with Paul Tillich—and Bultmann who says we can't know much about Jesus, and Paul Tillich's philosophical stuff about "God is the ground of being." I'm not going to go into a church and talk like this; I'm not going to, I'm not going to—I did not believe the traditional things even then.

Choosing the Christian Tradition

When asked about how his classmates reacted to learning the details of Christian history, he said:

> Well, they sat through the same Old Testament courses I did, and half of them were fighting against it the whole way. Because they didn't like the scholarship, they couldn't—it was a challenge to their faith. Well, I didn't have to deal with that; because I wanted to know what it was. They felt threatened; they pulled back . . . they would fight the professor about his interpretation about Old Testament passages. They were kind of literalistic about it. And when we'd talk about myth and stories, they'd say, "No, it happened!" So there was kind of a clash. They didn't like to have their literalistic interpretation of the Bible undermined by an Old Testament scholar. It was quite a thing to see!

Still, Rick identifies strongly as a Christian:

> These are my people, this is the context in which I work, these are the people that I know. These are the communities I've worked with. These are the communities where I can make a difference.

While he does not believe "all this creedal stuff" about Jesus dying for our sins, being God or being incarnate, he is attracted to Jesus as "... somebody who was concerned about social justice" and "... a compelling vision of what it means to be human, and what it means to—live life fully in the world." He acknowledges that:

> ... if I'd been born in China, I'd be a Buddhist. I wasn't. I was born here, and I was formed here. ... I do not see the passion for social justice in the Buddha. Jesus was born a poor peasant, and worked with the poor, and talked about the poor.

According to Rick, his UCC ordination does not require taking vows. He made "a statement of faith," which meant presenting a paper to clergy in his Conference (i.e., the association of local churches). His paper was on liberal scholars Paul Tillich and Rudolf Bultmann. This was adequate, he says, because:

> ... as long as ... you're talking about God and Jesus and the Bible, that's what they want to hear. You're just phrasing it in a way that makes sense to [them] ... but language is ambiguous and can be heard in different ways.

A Place to Question and Grow

Campus ministry gave him freedom within the structure of the church, allowing him to work with students who were questioning as much as he was. He could "run and be creative," making his own "exciting programs" without having too many people "in authority" over him.

He especially enjoys doing adult education and sees his goal as liberating people from "bad ideas" about Christianity, saying, "Can you imagine the pain that people suffered with? 'I'm going to hell if I don't believe this?'" He feels some of them have been "wounded, like an alcoholic" and points out that they will "invariably" ask, "Why didn't they teach us that in church? If I'd known this 25 years ago, I wouldn't have had to carry this burden around!" So he feels he's playing "a kind of a therapeutic role."

When asked his opinion of why ministers do not pass on their knowledge of Christian history to parishioners, he said:

> They don't want to rock the boat. They don't want to lose donations. They want to keep their jobs. They don't want to stir up trouble in the congregation. They've got enough trouble as it is, keeping things moving along. They don't want to make people mad at them. They don't want to lose members. What they will often do is bring in someone like me to be a lightning rod, and teach it, and they'll follow up on it.

He expressed more about his views on God after the interviews, commenting on an article he emailed that was written by atheist author Sam Harris (2006b). He felt that he'd been "educated and sensitized" by the article, saying, "If not believing in a supernatural, theistic god is what distinguishes an atheist, then I am one too." But he also said, "I don't consider myself an atheist" and, "I am not willing to abandon the symbol 'God' in my understanding of the human and the universe."

Darryl, the Presbyterian—Transcendency of the Human Spirit

Darryl is a 36 year old Presbyterian minister with a church outside of Baltimore. He is married and has three young children. After an initial phone conversation about the study, he sent an email further explaining his desire to participate. In it, he wrote:

> I am interested in this study because I have regular contact in my circle of colleagues—both ecumenical and Presbyterian—who are also more progressive-minded than the "party line" of the denomination. We are not "un-believers" in our own minds—but would not withstand a strict "litmus test" should we be subjected to one. I want to see this new movement within the church given validity in some way.
>
> I reject the virgin birth. I reject substitutionary atonement. I reject the divinity of Jesus. I reject heaven and hell in the traditional sense, and I am not alone.
>
> I am a "Jesus Follower" for sure. It is arguable whether I am also a "Christian." I can't imagine continuing in this work if I did not have a strong personal faith of some kind. My cognitive dissonance revolves around the urge to rescue others who find themselves in the same boat—and who still strongly believe in God in some sense, and find Jesus a compelling religious figure.

His Beliefs and Others'

He described himself as a believer in God, but not in the traditional Christian God:

> . . . it's not that I'm not a believer. I do believe in God. But I find that the character of my belief is much closer to that pantheist view than the typical theist.

He says he and his wife are "very similar theologically," and he doesn't think she has any problems with where he is. She's "very progressive, very liberal."

He also thinks his seminary professors and some of the members of his congregation have similar feelings:

> . . . certainly the professors I respected at seminary were very open minded people. And for the most part, with education comes a healthy skepticism, but not necessarily disbelief. I think most of the academics in my congregation would agree with me that—that God is not the literal God from the bible that the tradition has somewhat purported. I don't think that these men and women in my congregation, for the most part, believe in the virgin birth. I know that some of them don't. I had these conversations with some of them. That it's something that's just not important to them.

Following the Call

Darryl was raised in the Presbyterian Church and was drawn to the ministry as a youth after a playmate was killed in a terrorist attack while abroad on a family vacation. After experiencing frightening thoughts of suicide, he decided that:

> Whether there was a God or not, I would choose to live as if there was a God. Because I didn't like the alternative. I didn't want to kill myself. The alternative was despair.

He felt that "there was always this sense of call in my life. The process of becoming a pastor was exploring this sense of calling from God."

He enjoyed his seminary experience, saying that it "blew open" Christian doctrine, allowing him to realize that Christianity wasn't "black and white, it was plaid, polka dot—there was just such a variety of thought that went in every different kind of direction."

At some point in his studies, he gave up the idea of an afterlife that was an extension of our current consciousness. He started thinking in terms of "a transcendency of the human spirit" that he has difficulty describing, saying, "I know that it's not going to be something that I can comprehend with my mortal brain." Still, believing in something is important to him. He thinks clergy would be "really sad individuals if they just didn't believe in anything and that they're just sadly going through the motions of the job."

He likes his work and the flexibility his job offers. He'd like an opportunity to openly minister to people like himself:

> I do feel called to work with people who have the same doubts and questions. . . . I think there's room in Christianity for this. Is the Presbyterian Church willing to make that room within its own? I don't know.

Considering Other Options

He also thinks about the freedom he'd have if he left or retired from the church, specifically mentioning Jack (John Shelby) Spong, the retired Episcopal Bishop who writes and speaks openly about how Christianity needs to modernize in order to survive:

> Well that guy has a glow to him; he's just fantastic. But he can say whatever he wants because he's got his nest egg. He's not concerned about his retirement or anything like that. Liberating!

He expressed concern about the possibility of moving to a more conservative presbytery where he might not be able to honestly respond to the doctrinal questions he could be asked:

> If I had to jump through too many hoops, . . . I just have to look and see how genuine I would be, and how comfortable I would feel.

He has broached the subject of his lack of traditional beliefs with a few colleagues whom he thinks are like-minded, but has not talked as directly with them as he talked during the interviews. He did talk fairly candidly with a trusted older colleague whom he felt had similar beliefs:

> I doubt [he] believes in the virgin birth. And probably wouldn't admit that he didn't believe Jesus was God. . . . and I did tell him that I didn't think Jesus was God necessarily. . . . We talked about whether it would be a problem if at some point, I transfer.

After seeing *Religulous*, Bill Maher's (2008) comedy documentary about religion, he had good things to say about Maher:

> He's a genuine, honest guy who's acknowledging the questions in his heart, and is fed up and passionate and angry about the religious violence in the world. And there's a lot of justification for that. And I'm right there on 80–90% of the stuff, so we'd have a lot to talk about. You know, we'd go out and have a beer together. And I think we agree on a lot of stuff, and I think he would criticize me about just sticking with this right now.

And despite his many stated concerns, he also had good things to say about the role of the church in his life:

> The church has been a positive thing in my life overall. It's been a place of affirmation, it's been a place of comfort, it's been a place of ritual and wonderful mystery.

Practical Concerns

During the interviews, he often discussed his feelings toward the ministry and how his changing beliefs could affect his family. For instance, he said:

> This is not only the course of my life I've chosen to pursue, but I provide for my family this way. So if I'm having this cognitive dissonance, then sure, I've got to come to terms with how I do this in a genuine way. And at what point do I not do it any longer.
>
> So maybe there'll be a divorce between myself and the Presbyterian Church. I need to feel fulfilled, and I need to provide for myself and my family. I can go back and get new education and training, but I've got to do something. And so do I completely pitch this? Well, I don't think it's completely without value.
>
> I realize that if I come out a little more, I may be burning bridges in

> terms of my ability to earn a living this way. At some point, that may be less important. But it still would be something I would grieve, because this has been a meaningful experience in my life even though there are parts of the hierarchy of the church that I have become dissatisfied with.

He also raised the possibility of being defrocked at different points in the interviews:

> To a certain extent, I don't care if I get defrocked. I really don't. If people don't want me in this, I'll do something else. I might try and do hospital chaplaincy.
>
> I'm really not afraid of anything coming as a result [of these interviews]. I'm not afraid of being defrocked just because I'm not interested in being afraid.

Adam, Church of Christ—A Hunger for Learning

Adam decided to obtain a Master of Arts in Religion to be a minister in the Church of Christ, a denomination that does not require master's level education for its clergy:

> I hungered to continue learning; I felt like it was very applicable; I felt like it would prepare me more to minister. And I was very focused on the practical ministry side. I wasn't so much into deep theology or—world missions, or—philosophy of religion. . . . I mean, there were theology classes and philosophy classes and all that. And I had to have one year of Hebrew, two years of Greek.

Over 20 years later, that same desire to learn led him away from religious belief. It started when he read David Kinnaman and Gabe Lyons' (2007) *unChristian: What a New Generation Thinks About Christianity—and Why It Matters*, a Barna Group publication that rebuts common criticisms people have about Christianity. His intention was to become more skilled at defending his faith, but as he tried to "step back" to look at Christianity from a non-believer's perspective, he found that he became more swayed to that point of view:

> If God is God, he's big enough; he can handle any questions I've got. Well, he didn't. He didn't measure up! And that sounds, you know, so

> funny, because if I heard somebody else saying that a year ago, I'd have thought, "You are such a sacrilegious person. God's going to strike you dead by lightning or something!" I've actually thought and tried to pinpoint, but I can honestly say that intellectually, from within the first few weeks of my studies, I thought, "Wow! Could this be true?" So almost from that point on, it's almost been downhill if you're Christian; uphill if you're a non- believer. Coming to the truth—and I always thought there was absolute truth out there. Now I'm a lot more relativistic.
>
> I tell you, the book that just grabbed my mind and just twisted it around, was Christopher Hitchens' *God is Not Great*. It was shocking, some of that stuff—the throws and jabs against faith and stuff. I would think, "He's crazy." But then I'd say, "No. Step back and read it for what it is." And that's also the same time when I thought, "I'm going to balance my study. I'm not going to over-balance myself with atheist writers."

In the past year, Adam has absorbed over 60 books, videos or podcasts addressing a wide variety of views. He was especially impressed by debates on religion:

> Probably one of the most mind-opening things was listening to all these debates from top people of Christianity; or believers vs. non-believers. And I tried to do the same thing: be open and listen, and use my mind and reason, I guess. And almost undeniably, even being a believer and knowing the Christian claims and scripture, you know what? This guy won in the debate. He's a non-believer. Why?

Wanting a Life that Mattered

Adam is a 43-year-old worship minister and church administrator currently working in a large Church of Christ congregation in South Carolina. He was raised Presbyterian and became involved with conservative Christianity while dating his future wife. He decided to enter the ministry not because he felt a "calling" or had a "mystical experience" but because he wanted "a purpose that was beyond just existing":

> I wanted my life to matter. To connect. For something bigger and better, beyond what I was doing.

Even in seminary, when confronted with questions and contradictions in the study of academic Christianity, he stayed focused on his desire to help people live a Christian life that would ultimately lead them to eternal life:

> OK, here's what Biblical scholars are saying, and there's some questions over here, but I just trust God, and know he's guiding me, and I'm learning this so I can be a minister and help people. When I was working with people, it was a lot more practically focused on, "OK, here's what the Bible says, how do we live it out? How do we encourage other people? What's the whole evangelistic side of Christianity? How can we win more people into Christ." I mean you're sincere; that's what your goal is. You don't want anybody to miss out and to go to hell.
>
> I don't remember stressing a lot over doubts that were raised by the study, undergraduate or graduate. At the graduate level, I was challenged a little bit more by the theology and the philosophy—like suffering in the world. Which in the last year was probably one of my major wake-up calls. Like, how can there be a living God with the world in the shape that it's in? But looking back at it, I learned what I learned to get through so I could focus on things. My intentions were the greatest and the purest.
>
> During the time when I was introduced—even in undergraduate to textual criticism—looking at how we got the scriptures that we have, and the textual variances. I just kind of learned what I needed to learn to pass the test, and didn't really—I mean, I thought, "Well, how do we know what was the right variant that was chosen that we now have as the scripture?" But I really didn't—I had way too much going: I was too busy working full-time and going to school, and a family, and small children.

Now, when Adam thinks about leaving the ministry, one of the hardest things to contemplate giving up is the rich community life that his religion has provided:

> I will say one strong aspect of any religion, I'd guess, that I've been in is the community life. You have great friends who are close; you can depend on them. When there's hard times, financially, emotionally, whatever, you've got a support group.

Anguishing about Change

He also fears for the effect leaving could have on his family, because his wife and teenage children are very religious. While he has conducted his current religious study surreptitiously, he has expressed some of his changing views to his wife. At her urging, he has been talking about it with an old seminary professor. However, their meetings have not affected Adam's changing ideas:

> He's done everything he knows to do. He's prayed for me; he's shared with me. And I said, "One of the fears is that I'm going to sway you, and you're going to lose your faith. If I see that happening, I'll back off."

Adam does not want to make trouble in his friend's life or to let down the people in his church:

> And if they knew what I believe right now . . . some would [be against me] and some would try to keep working with me, and minister to me, and help me.

At the same time, he thinks there could be a benefit to his church family knowing about how he has changed:

> And the other part of me thinks: "You know what? It'd be good for people to grow up and to think things through at least. If they decide to keep their faith, that's fine. But if they don't, let's be real about it."

But he also wonders if he should leave well enough alone:

> Even if Christianity isn't true, is it best to leave the people alone in their ignorance? And I struggle with that feeling of superiority intellectually, which I've read all kinds of faith literature, and they say that's just a struggle you've got to deal with. But is it better to leave them—? And they're happy, and they have hope in a life to come, and so it helps them through their suffering, which is a strong selling point of Christianity. You know what I'm saying? I look at things a lot more in kind of a marketing form now.

Meanwhile, he struggles through his job, hiding his beliefs:

> Here's how I'm handling my job on Sunday mornings: I see it as play acting. I kind of see myself as taking on a role of a believer in a worship

> service, and performing. Because I know what to say. I know how to pray publicly. I can lead singing. I love singing. I don't believe what I'm saying anymore in some of these songs. But I see it as taking on the role and performing. Maybe that's what it takes for me to get myself through this, but that's what I'm doing.

He'd like to get out of this situation, but hasn't yet figured out how to do it:

> I'm where I am because I need the job still. If I had an alternative, a comfortable paying job, something I was interested in doing, and a move that wouldn't destroy my family, that's where I'd go. Because I do feel kind of hypocritical. It used to be the word "hypocritical" was like a sin. I don't hold that view anymore: there is goodness, and there is sinfulness; it's one or the other. It's black or white. That there's ultimate absolute truths that are mandated in scripture or given by a supernatural being. I don't see those anymore, so I use the word "hypocritical" differently, as in, I'm just not being forthright. But, at the same time, I'm in the situation I'm in, and rationally thinking about it is what I've got to do right now.

He considers himself an "atheistic agnostic" and wonders how non-believers fill the void left by loss of faith, or even if they feel a loss. For his part, he says:

> I've got to the point where I can't find meaning in something that I don't think is real anymore. I guess mostly inside I do toy with the fact that, "OK, what's driving me to get up every morning?" I used to be very devotional-minded. Get up, and maybe read a passage of scripture; say a prayer; ask God to guide me through the day, totally believing that he would. Now it's like, "You don't have that." So there's a lack of guidance. But at the same time I find it more free, where I create my own day.

He thinks of himself as being through with religion. He's not interested in a more liberal form of Christianity or in a non-supernatural concept of God:

> I've thought I could stay in church work, and I could become more liberal. But it's like, what have you become at that point? It's really like

> any other organization. . . . I mean, if you take God out of it, I don't understand why you would go to the trouble of being religious.... If it's only your natural abilities, why mask it as something religious? Other than the fact you don't want to make waves; you want to fit in with society without causing problems for yourself.
>
> I don't see nature as a God; I just see nature as nature. I can admire the beauty and the horror in it at the same time and don't have to cast a religious tone on it.

Right now, he is still studying and wondering where it all will lead:

> Honestly, there's been times when I thought, "You're going to drive yourself crazy dealing with all this." It's like, I just—I get through it, kind of keep plugging along even though I don't know what is ultimately going to happen. So it's just kind of like—take a day at a time; a week at a time. Kind of look at certain things. Keep studying; keep my options open.

Jack, the Southern Baptist—A Bunch of Bunk

Jack, age 50, has been a Southern Baptist minister for 15 years, serving mainly as a worship leader in churches in various southern states. He has a bachelor's degree in religion from a liberal Baptist Christian college and a master's in church music from a Southern Baptist seminary. He's been married for 25 years and has three teen-aged children.

He was raised nominally Christian, but his parents, who were abusive to each other and their children, did not attend church. As a child, he did not know the basic tenets of Christianity and did not think of Christmas as a Christian holiday. He first became involved in church activities in high school at the invitation of a classmate. He stayed involved, as he put it, because of the love:

> My attraction was the talk of love. So I said, "OK, I'm going to go toward this. I'm going to explore this. I want this. The greatest love of all." Who wouldn't want that, as a human? Especially one who had been deprived of it, of some of the basic needs of love, you know, from your parents.

About 10 years ago, he decided to read through the Bible very carefully. He did this completely on his own, as a way to get closer to his faith. However, his study has had the opposite effect:

> The pursuit of Christianity brought me to the point of not believing in God. Not that somebody did something mean to me. Let me tell you; ain't nothing anybody did in a church can compare to what my parents did to me, OK?
>
> I didn't plan to become an atheist. I didn't even want to become an atheist. It's just that I had no choice. If I'm being honest with myself.
>
> I've just this autumn, started saying to myself, out loud, "I don't believe in God anymore." It's not like, I don't want to believe in God. I *don't* believe in God. And it's because of all my pursuits of Christianity. I want to understand Christianity, and that's what I've tried to do. And I've wanted to be a Christian. I've tried to be a Christian, and all the ways they say to do it. It just didn't add up.
>
> The love stuff is good. And you can still believe in that, and live a life like that. But the whole grand scheme of Christianity, for me, is just a bunch of bunk.

He initially resisted his changing views:

> I wanted it to be true. And I kept telling myself, "I don't understand." And, you know, I devoted my whole life trying to understand. And finally I got to the point where—I've got to admit to myself this is how I feel. I can't pretend any longer. You know, this is probably just—I really started getting this way probably in the last 10 years. Realizing, "Hmmm, you know you've really given this one a chance, OK?" It's not like on a whim I decided to do something that didn't work out. You know what I mean? I've given it a good chance.

He related numerous examples of biblical thought that did not make sense to him, for example:

> OK, this God created me. It's a perfect God that knows everything; can do anything. And somehow it got messed up, and it's my fault. So he had to send his son to die for me to fix it. And he does. And now I'm supposed to beat myself to death the rest of my life over it. It makes no sense to me. Don't you think a God could come up with a better plan than that?
>
> What kind of personality; what kind of being is this that had to create these other beings to worship and tell him how wonderful he is? That makes no sense, if this God is all-knowing and all-wise and all-wonderful. I can't comprehend that that's what kind of person God is.

> Every church I've been in preached that the Jonah in the Whale story is literally true. And I've never believed that. You mean to tell me a human was in the belly of that whale? For three days? And then the whale spit him out on the shoreline? And, of course, their convenient logic is, "Well, God can do anything."
>
> Well, I think most Christians have to be in a state of denial to read the Bible and believe it. Because there are so many contradicting stories. You're encouraged to be violent on one page, and you're encouraged to give sacrificial love on another page. You're encouraged to bash a baby's head on one page, and there's other pages that say, you know, give your brother your fair share of everything you have if they ask for it.
>
> But if God was going to reveal himself to us, don't you think it would be in a way that we wouldn't question? . . . I mean, if I was wanting to have . . . people teach about the Bible . . . I would probably make sure they knew I existed. . . . I mean, I wouldn't send them mysterious notes, encrypted in a way that it took a linguist to figure out.

Even before he rejected belief in God, he rejected aspects of Christianity that didn't make sense to him:

> I do remember this a couple of years down the road after being a Christian—this concept and idea of hell. I was going, "Hell? What do you mean I was going to hell? Why? What's hell, and where is it?" And I've never believed in hell. I just never bought it. There's a place where people go when they die, and they burn eternally? No.
>
> The whole heaven thing makes no sense either. Why would I want to walk on streets of gold? I know people think that's literally how it's going to be. If we have no value system in heaven, as far as monetary or value system like we have here on earth, why would I want to walk on streets of gold? And I have people who believe they're going to have a physical body, and we're going to be in the new Earth . . . and we're not going to die, and we're not going to grow old, and we're not going to have pain. Why? That all makes no sense to me.

Settling into the Ministry

After traveling the country with a theater group, and marrying a woman of strong Christian faith, he decided to become a minister. It seemed like a natural fit. He and his wife were very involved in the life of the church, he felt he could make a special contribution to the church through his musical abilities and he was known for being sensitive and compassionate.

> And that's what people told me my best skills were—dealing with people. . . . I can be with somebody and genuinely have empathy with them, and concern and love and help them get through a difficult situation. And every time that I did it, those people thought that I was wonderful. And they would just bend over backwards to tell me, "Thank you." That was one of my strengths. . . . Being with somebody when their husband died. And just holding their hand, or putting my arm around them. But I never said "Now, he's in heaven. Aren't you glad for him?"

He felt the education he received in religion was high quality and objective, even though it was limited to Christianity:

> You know, where my degree says "Religion", it really should say "Christianity", because it wasn't a degree in religion because we did not study any other religion. But it still was an academic approach to Christianity rather than, "You will believe *this*."

Looking back on his education, he remembers other students being very upset about what they were learning:

> We had people that would cry in class because they were challenged on what they were thinking. And I'm going, "That's what we're supposed to be doing. Why are you so upset?" I could never get that. And actually, some professors got in trouble because they challenged the students' belief systems. Well, that's what it's about. That's part of what a philosophy class does.

He also recalls that he simply compartmentalized information that he didn't understand:

> I just attributed [biblical inconsistencies] to the fact that I didn't understand, and I compartmentalized it. I probably learned that as a child, because that's a survival technique. You know, my parents are the source of all my pain, physical, emotional, and otherwise. But then, they're my parents.

Once he was ordained, he took on the role of worship leader rather than pastor. This allowed him to focus on doing readings and music for the services. He much preferred this to preaching, which he has avoided as much as possible throughout his career:

> I didn't enjoy it [giving sermons] because of the issue of, "OK, what am I going to talk about, and what I'm *not* going to talk about?" This was very tricky. . . . I kept it very broad. And I didn't say, "You've got to believe in Jesus or you're going to hell."
>
> When I read a prayer, they're generic. They usually border on making people feel good. You know, "May we think these thoughts and do these kinds of things." I've never prayed out loud even, "May all these people be saved from hell." . . . I like to leave them open to their own interpretation.

Ongoing Empathy for Believers

While personally rejecting Christianity, he understands why others find it appealing and has no desire to change their views:

> I kind of understand where all those people are coming from. You know—of wanting to believe in God and wanting some higher power that's really looking after me. Especially me coming from the childhood that I had. I can understand that. It'd be nice if I had an omniscient big brother up there, wouldn't it? Saying, "Don't worry about it. I got it covered. I know they were mean to you. But don't worry; I'm going to take care of it." But that's not reality. I wished it was God still, but it's not. I wished it was like that.
>
> I don't think less of them for being a Christian. . . . Matter of fact, I understand them, because I was there too.
>
> Well, I'm not going to go on a campaign to try to convince people to become an atheist. It's my journey. . . . Everybody has their own journey; and this is my journey. And how I kind of look at it, I journeyed through it and came here.

Still, even when he was a believer, he had difficulty identifying with others' experience of God:

> [People would say] "I had this wonderful experience with God." I'd say, "I want that. Give it to me." Why didn't God ever give it to me? I think they're making it up in their mind. I never had one of those. I never

> heard God speak. I don't know how many people, I can tell you, come up and told me, "God told me to tell you this." I feel like saying, "Well, I think he could probably tell me himself, couldn't he? Because I've got my ear open."

Planning His Exit

He is firm about his decision to leave religion entirely, stating that, "I took many years making my mind up on this issue; I don't need to try another brand of it." He is planning to leave the ministry as soon he finds another way to support his family. He would leave sooner, if he had enough money to pay off his debts:

> If somebody said, "Here's $200,000," I'd be turning my notice in this week, saying, "A month from now is my last Sunday." Because then I can pay off everything.

In the meantime, he is quietly pursuing another career. His wife is aware of his plan to switch careers, but he hasn't told her yet of his reason for the change. He thinks she will be both upset and supportive of whatever he wants to do. Mutual support has been the pattern in their marriage:

> I couldn't ask for a better wife. I was very fortunate. We get along great. We support each other, and always give each other words of encouragement, and just support each other in every way we can think about.
>
> She doesn't need to hear this right now. It's not going to serve any of us. I feel like when the time's right, I can talk to her about it. She won't like it, but I will share it with her. And after I share it with her, I will start sharing it with other people. But she's going to be first. Because I know it's going to be—it's going to turn her life upside-down . . . she's a very dedicated Christian. Very devout.

He thinks she is aware that he has been changing, but she doesn't press him about it and he has no intention of trying to change her beliefs:

> I think she definitely sees me pulling away from it though. And we've talked about it, but in very superficial ways. I don't get into details about it.
>
> I'm not going to try to force her to change her mind. And if she

> wants to continue to live her life that way, I'll be supportive of her. And I'm not going to try to demean her or belittle her or belittle her beliefs.

He thinks his children won't have a problem with his change in beliefs. They haven't seemed to notice or care that he no longer says prayers before meals. Recently, he was very open with his son who asked him about some Bible passages:

> We were talking about some scriptures in Revelation and some other things. He said, "Dad, do you really believe?" Before I could think, I said, "Son, I don't believe any of it. No way." He just smiled.

Discussion

The Not So Tender Trap[1]

All of our pastors were grateful for the opportunity to talk candidly about their quandaries with an interested outsider who would challenge and probe them without judging them. This was, in most cases, the first time in their lives that they could speak aloud about these matters. As Wes said:

> So it's been very helpful, and—I was concerned at first that it might reawaken in me some of my old anxieties and depression about maybe I shouldn't be doing this for a living, and stuff like that. But it has not done that. If anything, it's—it's kind of convinced me that I'm over that stage in my life.

The loneliness of non-believing pastors is extreme. They have no trusted confidantes to reassure them, to reflect their own musings back to them, to provide reality checks. As their profiles reveal, even their spouses are often unaware of their turmoil. Why don't they resign their posts and find a new life? They are caught in a trap, cunningly designed to harness both their best intentions and their basest fears to the task of immobilizing them in their predicament. Their salaries are modest and the economic incentive is to stay in place, to hang on by their fingernails and wait for retirement when they get their pension:

> I think I'm doing it now because financially I don't have a choice. I could quit and go in there today and say today, "I'm not coming back."

> But it would cause a huge financial burden on me. I mean, how would I continue to make my house payment and support my family? (Jack)

Pastors who are provided a parsonage to live in are even more tightly bound: they have no equity to use as a springboard to a new house. But economic worries are not the only, or even the primary, consideration, in the eyes of some of our five:

> Because there have been times when I'd say, "You know what? I'm just going to tell everybody, and whatever happens happens." And then I think, "Gosh, I can't do that." I think I could handle it, but it's other people that I'm worried about. And I think, "by gosh, do I still care too much about what other people think of me or something?" (Adam)
>
> I'm thinking if I leave the church—first of all, what's that going to do to my family? And I don't know. Secondly is, I have zero friends outside the church. I'm kind of a loner. (Jack)

As Jack says about telling his wife: "It's going to turn her life upside down."

Another says it's his wife's family that is holding him back. They didn't approve of him in the first place, and will make her miserable. The tangle of conflicting motives is vividly captured in a single rambling reflection from Adam:

> . . . right now is a time of limbo, because there is so much more at stake than just my peace, or my intellectual pursuit. Because it's practically going to affect a lot of people that I really care about. And I've even thought, "Gosh, just keep doing it." I've thought, just keep along with it, buckle down and tell yourself that this is for the greater good for the people I care about, even though I don't believe it. Just stick with what you're doing; it pays good. It—you're not harming anybody, I don't think [chuckle]. You're doing good in your community; you're respected. But it's just gnawing away inside.

Confiding their difficulties to a superior is not an appealing option: although it would be unlikely to lead swiftly and directly to an involuntary unfrocking. No denomination has a surplus of qualified clergy, and the last thing an administrator wants to hear is that one of the front line preachers is teetering on the edge of default. More likely, such an acknowledgment of doubt would put them on the list of problematic clergy and secure for them the not very helpful advice to soldier on and work through their crises of faith. Speaking in confidence with fellow clergy is also a course fraught with danger, in spite of the fact that some of them are firmly convinced that many, and perhaps most, of their fellow clergy share their lack of belief.

What gives them this impression that they are far from alone, and how did this strange and sorrowful state of affairs arise? The answer seems to lie in the seminary experience shared by all our pastors, liberals and literals alike. Even some conservative seminaries staff their courses on the Bible with professors who are trained in textual criticism, the historical methods of biblical scholarship, and what is taught in those courses is not what the young seminarians learned in Sunday school, even in the more liberal churches. In seminary they were introduced to many of the details that have been gleaned by centuries of painstaking research about how various ancient texts came to be written, copied, translated, and, after considerable jockeying and logrolling, eventually assembled into the Bible we read today. It is hard if not impossible to square these new facts with the idea that the Bible is in all its particulars a true account of actual events, let alone the inerrant word of God. It is interesting that all our pastors report the same pattern of response among their fellow students: some were fascinated, but others angrily rejected what their professors tried to teach them. Whatever their initial response to these unsettling revelations, the cat was out of the bag and both liberals and literals discerned the need to conceal their knowledge about the history of Christianity from their congregations.

A gulf opened up between what one says from the pulpit and what one has been taught in seminary. This gulf is well-known in religious circles. The eminent biblical scholar Bart D. Ehrman's widely read book, *Misquoting Jesus* (2005), recounts his own odyssey from the seminary into secular scholarship, beginning in the Moody Bible Institute in Chicago, a famously conservative seminary which required its professors to sign a statement declaring the Bible to be the inerrant word of God, a declaration that was increasingly hard for Ehrman to underwrite by his own research. *The Dishonest Church* (2003), by retired United Church of Christ minister, Jack Good, explores this "tragic divide" that poisons the relationship between the laity and the clergy. Every Christian minister, not just those in our little study, has to confront this awkwardness, and no doubt there are many more ways of responding to it than our small sample illustrates. How widespread is this phenomenon? When we asked one of the other pastors we talked with initially if he thought clergy with his views were rare in the church, he responded, "Oh, you can't go through seminary and come out believing in God!" Surely an overstatement, but a telling one. As Wes put it:

> . . . there are a lot of clergy out there who—if you were to ask them—if you were to list the five things that you think may be the most central beliefs of Christianity, they would reject every one of them.

One can be initiated into a conspiracy without a single word exchanged or secret handshake; all it takes is the dawning realization, beginning in seminary, that you and the others are privy to a secret, and that they know that you know, and you know that they know that you know. This is what is known to philosophers and linguists as mutual knowledge, and it plays a potent role in many social circumstances. Without any explicit agreement, mutual knowledge seals the deal: you then have no right to betray this bond by unilaterally divulging it, or even discussing it.

Don't Ask; Don't Tell

Circumstances conspire to encourage everyone to cooperate with this arrangement. The bishop, as already noted, is certainly not motivated to expose any doubters or outright atheists among his subordinates. For instance, Adam did confide his difficulties to a pastor in another church who counseled him on several occasions, and said:

> Well, first of all, I know the trouble you're going through. I know you're sincere in it. I'm praying you're going to come out OK on the end of it. So I don't see you as a non-believer still.

And of course Mother Theresa encountered the same response from those to whom she confided her loss of faith. Nobody in any church wants to learn that a person of God has lost their belief in God. Even parishioners who harbor suspicions about their pastor's doctrinal commitments may well decide to leave well enough alone, especially if he or she is doing a fine job holding the congregation together. This incuriosity begins at ordination, when the candidate for a pulpit is examined. Nobody in our small sample was asked by their inquisitors if they actually believed in God. That would be rude, of course, and officially unnecessary. Indeed, it's likely that none of our pastors has *ever* been asked point-blank, by anyone—parishioner, fellow minister, or superior—if they believed in God. "The 'borderline fundamentalists' ask you about your beliefs, but never about whether you believe in God" (Wes).

This is a relief to them, since an honest answer would set off an avalanche of problems. There is variation in the severity of the ordination questioning, with more conservative churches asking more pointed questions about doctrine, but even here there are circumlocutions that pass muster. Candidates are typically well aware of what will be expected from them at the hearing, and Rick, the UCC minister, having recounted a successful dodge that slid him into a college chaplaincy, remarked: "Now I might not have been able to get away with that in, say, Kansas." As Wes puts it, "There are poisonous questions that have no business being asked. And one of those questions might be, 'Do you believe in the virgin birth?'"

Among their fellow clergy, they often develop friendships, and suspecting that their friends share their views, they gingerly explore the prospect, using all the ploys that homosexuals have developed over the centuries: "And I let on like I do have an uncle who's a non-believer, and he always said, 'You know, it's . . .'" (Adam). Probably both knew that this was no uncle he was talking about.

Recall Wes saying of his friendship with a parish leader who had attended seminary:

> He would joke about things. I mean, some of the times—I think some of the times he was taking a little risk with me. We kind of felt each other out over the course of time, and he could tell that I was joking. The things I would joke about were not the kinds of things he was accustomed to hear joked about. And so he just kind of—just a little bit of self-revelation at a time. And we got to the point, you know, where he felt comfortable saying things to me.

Plausible deniability is maintained by both parties, just in case either of them is making a dangerous mistake. It seems that atheist "gaydar" is not yet a well-developed sensitivity among the clergy, and one of our pastors acknowledged that his efforts at sounding out his friends struck him as much like the forays of homosexuals in earlier times, when so much calamity could be triggered by coming out.

Creative Wiggle Room

> Most clergy take beliefs metaphorically, not as literally true. Given that assumption, there is quite a lot of creative wiggle room. (Wes)

None of our five pastors has come up with any particularly original ways of evading or softening the issue of God's existence, but they all exploit many of the available moves. Among the favorites are variations on what a philosopher would call a "use-mention error": conflating the name (or concept) of a thing with the thing itself. When Karen Armstrong writes *A History of God* (1993), she is talking, of course, about the history of the *concept* of God, a topic that is as readily researchable by atheist scholars as, say, the history of (the concept of) Santa Claus. And when Robert Wright publishes *The Evolution of God* (2009), this must be the concept of God he is writing about, not God himself (or itself), but it is convenient for authors to blur the distinction. A nice example comes from Rodney Stark's *One True God: Historical Consequences of Monotheism* (2001):

> All of the great monotheisms propose that their God works through history, and I plan to show that, at least sociologically, they are quite right: that a great deal of history—triumphs as well as disasters—has been made on behalf of One True God. What could be more obvious? (p1)

"Sociologically" apparently means, here, that Stark is writing about the concept of God, and the role it plays, not the role that God plays (if any). Sometimes our pastors produce inadvertently comical versions of this popular obfuscation: "God is literally what we would call a metaphor" (Wes) (Think about it). ". . . the difference between me and an atheist is basically this. It's not about the existence of God. It's do we believe that there is room for the use of the word 'God' in some context?" (Wes again). But even atheists find plenty of room for *using* the word "God"; it is well-nigh indispensable, for instance, in denying the existence of God.

Another familiar theme borrows heavily from postmodernism, with its attempt to subvert the very idea of truth. For instance:

> When I lived in New Mexico, I heard these Native American story tellers tell creation stories. Or other stories about their tribe. Then they'd say, "Maybe it didn't happen this way, but the story's true." Meaning there's truths *in* the story, but they're not literally true. (Rick)

Where, we wonder, did the Native American story tellers get this idea?

Somewhat more inventive is this nice twist on literalism: "If you read the Bible literally, you're not taking the Bible seriously" (Darryl). And Rick has a deft way of using quotation marks to save him from assertion: "But when I say the creed, what I say is 'Let us remember our forefathers and mothers in the faith who *said*, "dot, dot, dot, dot".' Again, it's the historical connection that I kind of appreciate."

The Slipping Ratchet

This constant spin doctoring takes its toll, apparently, but it also subverts a mission that the liberal pastors claim for themselves: staying in the church in order to liberalize it, in order to make it a saner, wiser, more tolerant institution. "My goal is to become obsolete," says Wes. And according to Rick:

> One of my strategies to stay in the church, is to *change* the church. I mean, I want the church to hear this stuff! I want the church to deal with me. I want the church to know that there's a progressive way of thinking out there. I want the church to know that there are people who are thinking really radical stuff about theology.

Bit by bit, day by day, they would like to lift their parishioners closer to their own way of seeing the world, but by not speaking their minds, their *sincere* minds, they squander most of the opportunities to lead their congregations to new ways of thinking. In fact, there is a sort of Hippocratic Oath that all five seem to follow: *In the first place, do no damage to any parishioner's beliefs*. Sometimes this is obviously the right thing to do, what anyone would do:

> But he's still dying of cancer; [his faith is] not changing the situation. It's changing his acceptance of things; it's allowing him to cope with it. And I'm certainly not going to pull that rug out from under him. (Darryl)

And sometimes concern for others is arguably the dominant motive:

> I say I never try to take away from somebody something they believe unless I can put something better in its place, as opposed to just attacking. (Rick)

But other times this policy seems more self-protective than altruistic:

> So it's like you want to build their faith, not tear down their faith. So you do your work carefully. (Adam)

Do they *ever* volunteer their radical ideas to parishioners? One tactic they have discovered is the book club or study group, where self-selected parishioners get to read one of the controversial books by Bart Ehrman (2005) or Bishop John Shelby Spong (1994; 1998), or even Sam Harris (2004; 2006a), or to watch the 21 week Lutheran DVD series *Living the Questions*, a carefully open-ended exploration of the issues. Those who participate are alerted to the nature of the materials in advance and are then gently encouraged to discuss the ideas, in an unusually tolerant atmosphere, a sort of holiday from the constraints of dogma. Here the pastors can demonstrate their open-mindedness and willingness to take these shocking ideas seriously, and let the authors be the mouthpieces for what is in their hearts. Again, they need to have plausible deniability: they aren't *preaching* these ideas, just acquainting their parishioners—those who are interested—with them. Not surprisingly, they draw a sharp distinction between what they can say from the pulpit, and what they can say in these less official circumstances:

> Well, because on the pulpit, on a Sunday morning, you get people in all different stages. And if I laid that out there, then again, people would not hear the point of the sermon. (Wes)

Those in the congregation who are already liberal can easily tolerate the otherwise incredible assertions, because they have internalized the message that whenever they need to, they can treat what they hear as merely metaphorical. Those of less liberal, more literal, creed are reassured that their pastor is still four-square on their side—and so the whole spectrum of congregants can "hear the point of the sermon."

But still, the pastors often find themselves put on the spot. When asked what he would say to a new widow who says, "Now he's in heaven," Jack replied, "I'm very good at holding my tongue." And if a parishioner volunteers that he's been born again, or just talked to God, Rick says, "I let them talk about it. I let it be meaningful. I don't try to dissuade them from their opinion, or evangelize my better, broader understanding of the Lord to them." And then there are noncommittal responses designed to go unnoticed. Jack's favorites are, "Well, it's good to see you today" and "Well, that's nice of you to say that."

So in spite of their best intentions, these pastors do not manage to exert very much pressure on their congregations to evolve their own beliefs in liberalizing directions. Instead, they find their own ways of dealing with the widening gap between what they find they can say, and what they know their parishioners take them to be saying:

> I don't feel like a hypocrite. I feel very authentic and very credible when I say things to my people. . . . The real truth of the matter is that I'm not being more honest with you than I am with my church. I'm not being more candid here. I'm just in a different context that requires a different kind of conversation. Because I don't ever have the feeling at church of withholding, or . . . playing . . . I feel very authentic; very genuine with them. I don't feel like I'm being more of myself here than I would be there. And in some ways, I feel like perhaps I'm more of myself there than I'm being here. It's really strange. (Wes)

What Will Happen to These Pastors?

Are they, in fact, in a good position to lead their congregations towards their own understandings, or are they condemned by their own commitments—to parishioners, their families, their colleagues—to perpetuate the double standards of sincerity that they have crafted so unwittingly over the years? We all find ourselves committed to little white lies, half-truths and convenient forgettings, knowing tacitly which topics not to raise with which of our loved ones and friends. But these pastors—and who knows how many others—are caught in a larger web of diplomatic, tactical, and, finally, ethical concealment. In no other profession, surely, is one so isolated from one's fellow human beings, so cut off from the fresh air of candor, never knowing the relief of getting things off one's chest.

These are brave individuals who are still trying to figure out how to live with the decisions they made many years ago, when they decided, full of devotion and hope, to give their lives to a God they no longer find by their sides. We hope that by telling their stories we will help them and others find more wholehearted ways of doing the good they set out to do. Perhaps the best thing their congregations can do to help them is to respect their unspoken vows of secrecy, and allow them to carry on unchallenged; or perhaps this is a short-sighted response, ultimately just perpetuating the tightly interlocking system that maintains the gulf of systematic hypocrisy between clergy and laity. Perhaps new institutions will arise, siphoning off the congregants into more open allegiances, in which creeds need no special defense or interpretation, since they are already so credible and honorable. Perhaps congregations can transform themselves into such institutions. Only then will Wes get his wish and become obsolete, and in the meantime, we can expect that many others will go through the trials and temptations that our five clergy have weathered.

Acknowledgments: We would like to thank Pamela Blake, Rosina Maiers, and Carmen Vaughan for their invaluable personal and professional support in this project.

Received 18 March 2010; Revision submitted 25 March 2010; Accepted 26 March 2010

Notes

1. One of our five informants, Rick, on reading this report, told us that while he found his profile accurate, he himself has never felt trapped, so we wish to correct the impression that all of our pastors consider themselves caught in a trap.

References

Armstrong, K. (1993). *A History of God*. New York: Albert A. Knopf.

Armstrong, K. (2009). *The Case for God*. New York: Albert A. Knopf.

Dennett, D. C. (2006). *Breaking the Spell: Religion as a Natural Phenomenon*. New York: Viking Penguin.

Ehrman, B. D. (2005). *Misquoting Jesus: The Story Behind Who Changed the Bible and Why*. New York: HarperSanFrancisco.

Good, J. (2003). *The Dishonest Church*. Scotts Valley, CA: Rising Star Press.

Harris, S. (2004). *The End of Faith: Religion, Terror and the Future of Reason*. New York: W.W. Norton.

Harris, S. (2006a). *Letter to a Christian Nation*. New York: Albert A. Knopf.

Harris, S. (2006b). 10 Myths—and 10 Truths—About Atheism. *Los Angeles Times*, December 24.

Hitchens, C. (2007). *God is Not Great: How Religion Poisons Everything.* New York: Hachette Book Group.

Kinnaman, D., and Lyons, G. (2007). *unChristian: What a New Generation Thinks About Christianity—and Why It Matters*. Grand Rapids, MI: Baker.

Procter-Murphy, J., and Felten, D. *Living the Questions*, DVD series, www.livingthequestions.com.

Maher, B. (Writer/Producer), and Charles, L. (Director). (2008). *Religulous* [Motion picture]. United States: Thousand Words.

Spong, J. S. (1994). *Resurrection: Myth or Reality? A Bishop's Search for the Origins of Christianity*. New York: HarperCollins.

Spong, J. S. (1998). *Why Christianity Must Change or Die: A Bishop Speaks to Believers in Exile*. New York: HarperSanFrancisco.

Stark, R. (2001). *One True God: Historical Consequences of Monotheism.* New Jersey: Princeton University Press.

Updike J. (1996). *In the Beauty of the Lilies.* New York: Fawcett Books.

Wright, R. (2009). *The Evolution of God.* New York: Little, Brown and Company.

NOTES

Chapter I: Introduction

1. "Preachers Who Are Not Believers," *Evolutionary Psychology* 8, no. 1 (2010): 122–50, http://www.epjournal.net/articles/preachers-who-are-not-believers/.

2. Finding seminary professors willing to participate was more difficult than finding nonbelieving clergy; out of twenty-six professors we contacted, only three volunteered.

3. See The Clergy Project's Web site, http://www.clergyproject.org/.

4. The piece was originally posted at http://newsweek.washingtonpost.com/onfaith/Non-Believing-Clergy.pdf in March 2010. However, FaithStreet acquired On Faith from the *Washington Post* in 2013, thus the piece no longer appears at this link. The piece, along with a series of response essays to "Preachers Who Are Not Believers" initially posted to the On Faith Web site, is now available at http://ase.tufts.edu/cogstud/dennett/papers/On_Faith_essays.pdf.

5. Laurie Goodstein, "Evangelicals Fear the Loss of Their Teenagers," *New York Times*, October 6, 2006.

6. Michael Spencer, "The Coming Evangelical Collapse," *Christian Science Monitor*, March 10, 2009.

7. John S. Dickerson, *The Great Evangelical Recession: 6 Factors That*

Will Crash the American Church . . . and How to Prepare (Grand Rapids, MI: Baker Books, 2013).

8. "Why You Can't Make a Computer That Feels Pain," reprinted in Daniel C. Dennett, *Brainstorms: Philosophical Essays on Mind and Psychology* (Pepperell, MA: Branch Line Press, 1979).

9. Daniel C. Dennett, *Breaking the Spell: Religion as a Natural Phenomenon* (New York: Penguin, 2006).

10. Daniel C. Dennett, *Consciousness Explained* (Boston, MA: Little, Brown, 1991); *Intuition Pumps and Other Tools for Thinking* (New York: W. W. Norton, 2013).

11. The previous two paragraphs are drawn with revision from *Breaking the Spell.*

12. Adrian Raine, *The Anatomy of Violence: The Biological Roots of Crime* (New York: Pantheon, 2013), 122.

Chapter II: Seven Sketches

13. John Michael Talbot, from the album *The Troubadour Years*, Troubadour for the Lord Records, 2008.

14. Frederick Buechner, *Wishful Thinking: A Theological ABC* (New York: Harper & Row, 1986).

15. Marcus J. Borg was a well-known author and New Testament scholar. Originally Lutheran, he was active in the Episcopal Church. For more, see http://www.marcusjborg.com/.

16. For example, see *South Park*, "Red Hot Catholic Love," Season 6, Episode 8, July 3, 2002, http://www.southparkstudios.com/full-episodes/s06e08-red-hot-catholic-love. For clips of various *South Park* episodes dealing with religion, see "Top 10 South Park Episodes about Religion," Huffington Post, February 23, 2011, http://www.huffingtonpost.com/2011/11/17/top-10-south-park-episode_n_824696.html#slide=480114.

17. One prominent example is Mitt Romney, former governor of Massachusetts and Republican presidential candidate who served as a Mormon bishop in Belmont, Massachusetts, from 1981 to 1986.

Chapter III: Breaking the Shell

18. For more on this, see Daniel C. Dennett, "The Social Cell: What Do Debutante Balls, the Japanese Tea Ceremony, Ponzi Schemes and Doubting Clergy All Have in Common?" *New Statesman*, April 13, 2012.

19. See Daniel C. Dennett, *Darwin's Dangerous Idea: Evolution and the Meanings of Life* (New York: Simon & Schuster, 1995).

20. Words by Sam M. Lewis and Joe Young, music by Walter Donaldson. Published 1919, by Waterson, Berlin & Snyder Co., Music Publishing.

Chapter IV: From the Ivory Tower to the People in the Pews

21. John Dart, "The Value of a Theological Education: Is It Worth It?" *The Christian Century*, February 22, 2003, 32–5.

22. James P. Wind and David J. Wood, *Becoming a Pastor: Reflections on the Transition into Ministry*, Special Report (Durham, NC: Alban Institute, October 2008).

23. Jonathan Haidt, *The Happiness Hypothesis: Finding Modern Truth in Ancient Wisdom* (New York: Basic Books, 2005).

24. Steven Pinker, *The Blank Slate: The Modern Denial of Human Nature* (New York: Viking, 2002).

25. Robert Wright, *The Moral Animal: Why We Are the Way We Are: The New Science of Evolutionary Psychology* (New York: Pantheon, 1994).

26. David Sloan Wilson, *Evolution for Everyone: How Darwin's Theory Can Change the Way We Think about Our Lives* (New York: Delacorte Press, 2007).

27. See the ReligionLink Web site, http://www.religionlink.com/.

28. "Clergy Burnout: Who Shepherds the Shepherds?" ReligionLink, October 8, 2012, http://www.religionlink.com/tip_121018.php.

Chapter V: Emerging Themes

29. See "'Nones' on the Rise," Pew Research Religion & Public Life Project, October 9, 2012, http://www.pewforum.org/2012/10/09/nones-on-the-rise/.

30. Laurie Goodstein, "Some Mormons Search the Web and Find Doubt," *New York Times*, July 20, 2013.

31. Marcus Borg, "Don't Tell Them Anything They'll Need to Unlearn," On Faith, *Washington Post*, December 6, 2006, http://www.faithstreet.com/onfaith/2006/12/06/dont-tell-them-anything-theyll/5605.

32. "For as Jonah was three days and three nights in the whale's belly, so shall the Son of man be three days and three nights in the heart of the earth." (Matthew 12:40)

33. See Dennett, *Breaking the Spell*, 229–30.

34. The audio of his talk at the 2012 American Atheists convention was played on the *Living After Faith* podcast, Episode 55, March 25, 2012, http://www.livingafterfaith.com/LAF00055AAJerryDewitt.mp3. See also Jerry DeWitt, *Hope After Faith* (Boston, MA: Da Capo Press, 2013).

35. The film *The Truman Show* (1998) conveys other aspects of the immorality of systematic and involuntary illusion.

36. Even atheists can love the concept of God without contradicting themselves. Dan is quite fond of the concept of the Largest Prime Number, knowing full well that nothing is, or could be, the Largest Prime Number. In fact, that's why he likes the concept so much; it makes a fine example in philosophical discussions.

37. Karen Armstrong, in an interview on *Fresh Air* with Terry Gross, National Public Radio, September 21, 2009, http://www.npr.org/2009/09/21/112968197/karen-armstrong-builds-a-case-for-god.

Chapter VI: Where Are They Now?

38. Yonat Shimron, "Pastor Sticks up for Modern View of God," *News & Observer*, August 2, 2010.

39. The foundation gave a $100,000 grant to The Clergy Project to provide outplacement services to formerly religious clergy. The program provides each individual with six months of assistance, including skills-assessment, résumé preparation, and connection with a local recruiter to help in the search for sustainable employment.

40. For a transcript, see "Atheist Ministers Struggle With Leading the

Faithful," ABCNews.com, November 9, 2010, http://abcnews.go.com/WN/atheist-ministers-leading-faithful/story?id=12004359.

41. On June 21, 2012, "Adam" appeared on *Tapestry* with Mary Hynes in an episode titled "Preachers Who No Longer Believe in God." This episode later won a gold medal at the 2012 New York Festivals competition for world's best radio programs, http://www.cbc.ca/tapestry/episode/2012/06/21/preachers-who-dont-believe-in-god-2/. He appeared again on *Tapestry* on April 26, 2013, in a follow-up episode titled "The Exit Ramp," http://www.cbc.ca/tapestry/episode/2013/04/26/the-exit-ramp/.

42. See, for example, Teresa MacBain, interviewed by Barbara Bradley Hagerty, "From Minister to Atheist: A Story of Losing Faith," National Public Radio, April 30, 2012, http://www.npr.org/2012/04/30/151681248/from-minister-to-atheist-a-story-of-losing-faith; Mike Aus, interviewed on *Up with Chris Hayes*, "Pastor Comes Out as a Non-believer," MSNBC, March 25, 2012, http://www.nbcnews.com/video/up/46848396#46848396; Jerry DeWitt, interviewed by Robert Worth, "From Bible-Belt Pastor to Atheist Leader," *New York Times Magazine*, August 26, 2012, http://www.nytimes.com/2012/08/26/magazine/from-bible-belt-pastor-to-atheist-leader.html?pagewanted=all&_r=0.

43. For information about Julia Sweeney's *Letting Go of God*, see http://juliasweeney.com/letting-go-of-god/.

44. See "'Nones' on the Rise," http://www.pewforum.org/2012/10/09/nones-on-the-rise/.

45. See http://www.patheos.com/blogs/rationaldoubt/.

46. For example, see the Sunday Assembly, http://sundayassembly.com.

47. The video of the interview is available at http://www.nbcnews.com/video/up/46848396#46848396.

48. "Unbelieving Pastor Justifies Staying in the Pulpit," *Rational Doubt* blog, July 10, 2014, http://www.patheos.com/blogs/clergyproject/2014/07/unbelieving-pastor-justifies-staying-in-the-pulpit/

49. Mark Rutledge, "'Non-believers'—Who Are They and What Will Become of Them?" *Rational Doubt* blog, May 19, 2014, http://www.

patheos.com/blogs/clergyproject/2014/05/non-believers-who-are-they-and-what-will-become-of-them/.

50. See Sarah Knapton, "Richard Dawkins: 'I Am a Secular Christian,'" *Telegraph*, May 24, 2014, http://www.telegraph.co.uk/culture/hay-festival/10853648/Richard-Dawkins-I-am-a-secular-Christian.html.

51. Jeff Falick, "Humanistic Judaism: Modernizing an Ancient Religion," *Rational Doubt* blog, September 8, 2014, http://www.patheos.com/blogs/rationaldoubt/2014/09/humanistic-judaism-modernizing-an-ancient-religion/.

52. See Samuel G. Freedman, "Minister Admits Overstating Her Credentials," *New York Times*, September 26, 2013, http://www.nytimes.com/2013/09/27/us/minister-admits-overstating-her-credentials.html

53. Marcus Borg, "Disbelief or Just Different Beliefs?" On Faith, *Washington Post*, March 16, 2010, http://www.faithstreet.com/on-faith/2010/03/16/when-pastors-move-beyond-belief/3298.

54. Philip Kitcher, "Militant Modern Atheism," *Journal of Applied Philos*ophy 28, no. 1 (2011): 1–13.

55. Dennett, "The Social Cell."

Chapter VIII: What's Next?

56. One might wonder how Linda finds herself so often in the presence of clergy. Some of them were clergy she met at events supporting liberal causes. Also, she is acquainted with numerous clergy in the DC area, as an active member of two Episcopal churches in Washington from 1989 to 2006.

57. Philip Kitcher, "Militant Modern Atheism."

58. This paragraph draws on my "What to Do While Religions Evolve Before Our Very Eyes," forthcoming in a collection of essays on Kitcher's work edited by Mark Couch.

59. John L. Allen, Jr., "Catholic Bishops Soften Tone on Same-Sex Unions," *Boston Globe*, October 14, 2014.

60. William J. Cromie, "Prayers Don't Help Heart Surgery Patients; Some Fare Worse When Prayed For," *Harvard University Gazette*, April 6, 2006, http://news.harvard.edu/gazette/2006/04.06/05-prayer.html.

For the full study, see Herbert Benson et al., "Study of the Therapeutic Effects of Intercessory Prayer (STEP) in Cardiac Bypass Patients: A Multicenter Randomized Trial of Uncertainty and Certainty of Receiving Intercessory Prayer," *American Heart Journal* 151, no. 4 (April 2006): 934–42, http://www.ncbi.nlm.nih.gov/pubmed/16569567.

Appendix B: About Qualitative Research

61. The text in this appendix comes from the Qualitative Research Consultants Association, http://www.qrca.org/?page=whatisqualresearch

Appendix C: Linda's Personal Story

62. Marcus J. Borg, "Me & Jesus—The Journey Home," *The Fourth R* 6, no. 4 (July–August 1993), available at http://www.westarinstitute.org/resources/the-fourth-r/me-jesus-the-journey-home/.

63. Daniel C. Dennett, "The Agnoy of Misplaced Ecstasy," On Faith, *Washington Post*, August 30, 2007, http://www.faithstreet.com/onfaith/2007/08/30/the-agony-of-misplaced-ecstasy/4714.

REFERENCES AND RESOURCES

Here we list both the books and articles referred to or quoted in the book and other selected resources: books, Web sites, and podcasts our study participants drew to our attention.

As a group, participants were information seekers and enjoyed gaining knowledge and insights. For some, their exploration played a major role in their initial movement away from religious belief. For others, the exploration came later and served as reinforcement for what they had already determined based on their own ideas and experiences.

Participants often started by seeking out the respected, bold voices from their own traditions, then branched out to atheist thinkers. Bishop Spong had a major influence on liberals, but not on conservatives. Conservatives tended to seek out the milder voices from their own tradition, such as Rob Bell, before moving on to atheist sources, such as Richard Dawkins. Both conservatives and liberals enjoyed hearing about clergy who had left religion and learning about science, particularly cognitive science and evolution.

Taking a fresh look at the Bible also had an impact. While rereading and rethinking the Bible affected the beliefs of both liberals and conservatives, the effect was greater and swifter on the conservatives, who did not have metaphorical meanings to fall back on. Once they applied logic and scientific thinking to Bible stories, their beliefs began to fall away.

Study participants cited the following resources as being influential in their movement away from religious belief.

Achtemeier, Paul, J. 1980. *The Inspiration of Scripture: Problems and Proposals (Biblical Perspectives on Current Issues)*. Louisville, KY: Westminster John Knox.

Allen, John L., Jr.. 2014. "Catholic Bishops Soften Tone on Same-sex Unions," *Boston Globe*, October 14.

Armstrong, Karen. 1994. *History of God*. New York: Ballantine Books.

____. 2000. The Battle for God: A History of Fundamentalism. New York: Knopf.

____. 2009. Interview on *Fresh Air* with Terry Gross, National Public Radio. http://www.npr.org/2009/09/21/112968197/karen-armstrong-builds-a-case-for-god.

Barbour, Ian, G. 1974. *Myths, Models and Paradigms: A comparative Study in Science and Religion*. New York: HarperCollins College Division.

Barker, Dan. 1992. *Losing Faith in Faith: From Preacher to Atheist*. Madison, WI: Freedom From Religion Foundation.

____. 2008. *Godless: How An Evangelical Preacher became one of American's Leading Atheists*. New York: Ulysses Press

____. 2010. *The Good Atheist: Living a Purpose-Filled Life Without God*. New York: Ulysses Press

____. 2015. *Life-Driven Purpose: How an Atheist Finds Meaning*. Durham, NC: Pitchstone Publishing.

Bayer, Lex, and John Figdor. 2014. *Atheist Mind, Humanist Heart: Rewriting the Ten Commandments for the Twenty-first Century*. Lanham, MD: Rowman & Littlefield.

Bell, Rob. 2005. *Velvet Elvis: Repainting the Christian Faith*. Grand Rapids, MI: Zondervan.

____. 2011. *Love Wins: A Book about Heaven, Hell, and the Fate of Every Person Who Ever Lived*. San Francisco, CA: HarperOne.

Bonhoeffer, Dietrich. 1966. *The Cost of Discipleship.* New York: MacMillian.

Borg, Marcus. 1994. *Meeting Jesus Again for the First Time.* San Francisco: HarperCollins.

____. 1997. *The God We Never Knew: Beyond Dogmatic Religion to a More Authentic Contemporary Faith.* San Francisco, CA: Harper San Francisco.

____. 2001. *Reading the Bible Again for the First Time: Taking the Bible Seriously But Not Literally*. New York: HarperOne.

____. 2004. *The Heart of Christianity.* San Francisco: HarperCollins.

____. 2010. commentary in *Washington Post* Web site "On Faith" http://newsweek.washingtonpost.com/onfaith/marcus_borg/2006/12/dont_tell_them_anything_theyll.html

Bradley, Martha Sontagg. 2000. *Four Zinas.* Salt Lake City: Signature Books.

Brodie, Fawn. 1995. *No Man Knows My History: The Life of Joseph Smith.* Free download at http://ebookee.org/No-Man-Knows-My-History-The-Life-of-Joseph-Smith_1874923.html.

Buechner, Frederick. 1986. *Wishful Thinking: A Theological ABC*. New York: Harper & Row.

Bushman, Richard, L. 2006. *Joseph Smith: A Cultural Biography of Mormonism's Founder: Rough Stone Rolling*. New York: Knopf.

Chaucer, Geoffrey. 1475. *The Canterbury Tales*. Free at http://www.canterburytales.org/canterbury_tales.html.

Cline, Eric, H. 2007. *From Eden to Exile: Unraveling Mysteries of the Bible*. Washington, DC: National Geographic.

Compere, John, S. 2010. *Towards the Light*. Writers Cramp Publishing.

Cox, Harvey. 2002. *The Future of Faith*, New York: HarperOne.

Coyne, Jerry, A. 2009. *Why Evolution is True*. New York: Viking.

Crossan, Dominic. 1993. *The Historical Jesus: The Life of a Mediterranean Jewish Peasant*. New York: HarperOne.

____. 1998. *The Birth of Christianity: Discovering What Happened in the Years Immediately After the Execution of Jesus*. New York: HarperOne.

Cupitt, Don. 2008. *Above Us Only Sky*. Oregon, CA: Polebridge Press.

Daily, Steven. 1993. *Adventism for a New Generation*. Better Living Publishers.

Daly, Mary. 1974. *Beyond God the Father: Toward a Philosophy of Women's Liberation*. Boston, MA: Beacon Press.

Daniel, Lillian and Martin B. Copenhaver. 2009. *This Odd and Wondrous Calling: The Public and Private Lives of Two Ministers*. Grand Rapids, MI: William Eerdmans Publishing Company.

Daniels, Kenneth, W. 2009. *Why I Believed: Reflections of a Former Missionary*. Dallas, TX: Kenneth W. Daniels.

Dart, John. 2003. "The Value of a Theological Education: Is It Worth It?" *The Christian Century*, February 22.

Dawkins, Richard. 1976. *The Selfish Gene*. Oxford University Press.

____. 1986. *The Blind Watchmaker*. New York: W. W. Norton.

____. 2006. *The God Delusion*. New York: W. W. Norton.

de Botton, Alain. 2012. *Religion for Atheists: A Non-believer's Guide to the Uses of Religion*. New York: Pantheon.

Dennett, Daniel C. 1978. "Why You Can't Make a Computer that Feels Pain." *Synthese* 38: 415–56, reprinted in Daniel C. Dennett, *Brainstorms: Philosophical Essays on Mind and Psychology*, Cambridge, MA: MIT Press.

____. 1991. *Consciousness Explained*, Boston, MA: Little, Brown.

____. 1995. *Darwin's Dangerous Idea*. New York: Simon and Shuster.

____. 2006. *Breaking the Spell: Religion as a Natural Phenomenon*. New York: Viking.

____. 2012. "The Social Cell: What Do Debutante Balls, the Japanese Tea Ceremony, Ponzi Schemes and Doubting Clergy All Have in Common?" *New Statesman*. April 13.

____. 2013. *Intuition Pumps and Other Tools for Thinking,* New York: W. W. Norton.

Dennett, Daniel and Linda LaScola. 2010. "Preachers Who Are Not Believers," *Evolutionary Psychology* 8, no. 1: 122–50. http://www.epjournal.net/wp-content/uploads/EP08122150.pdf.

DeWitt, Jerry. 2013. *Hope After Faith,* Boston, MA: Da Capo Press. See also his 2012 American Atheists talk, available at *Living After Faith* podcast, Episode 55, March 25, 2012. http://www.livingafterfaith.com/LAF00055AAJerryDewitt.mp3.

Diamond, Jared. 1997. *Guns, Germs, and Steel: The Fates of Human Societies*. New York: W. W. Norton.

Dickerson, John S. 2013. *The Great Evangelical Recession: 6 Factors That Will Crash the American Church . . . and How to Prepare.* Grand Rapids, MI: Baker Books.

Dunphy, Catherine. 2015. *From Apostle to Apostate: The Story of the Clergy Project*. Durham, NC: Pitchstone Publishing.

Ehrman, Bart, D. 2005. *Misquoting Jesus: The Story Behind Who Changed the Bible and Why*. San Francisco, CA: HarperSanFranscisco.

____. 2008. *God's Problem: How the Bible Fails to Answer Our Most Important Question—Why We Suffer*. San Francisco: HarperOne.

____. 2009. *Jesus, Interrupted: Revealing the Hidden Contradictions in the Bible (and Why We Don't Know About Them)*. San Francisco: HarperOne.

____. 2011. *Forged: Writing in the Name of God. Why the Bible's Authors Are Not Who We Think They Are*. San Francisco: HarperOne.

Epstein, Greg, M. 2009. *Good Without God: What a Billion Nonreligious People Do Believe*. New York: William Morrow.

Falick, Jeff. 2014. "Humanistic Judaism: Modernizing an Ancient Religion." *Rational Doubt* blog. September 8. http://www.patheos.com/blogs/rationaldoubt/2014/09/humanistic-judaism-modernizing-an-ancient-religion/.

Finkelstein, Israel, and Neil Asher Silberman. 2001. *The Bible Unearthed: Archaeology's New Vision of Ancient Israel and the Origin of Its Sacred Texts*. New York: Free Press.

Frankl, Viktor, E. 1946. *Man's Search for Meaning*. Boston, MA: Beacon Press.

Gish, Duane, T. 1997. *Evolution? The Fossils Say No!* Houston, TX: Master Books.

Good, Andrew, J. (Jack). 1998. *The Dishonest Church*. St. Louis, MO: Chalice Press.

Goodstein, Laurie. 2006. "Evangelicals Fear the Loss of Their Teenagers." *New York Times*, October 6.

____. 2013. "Some Mormons Search the Web and Find Doubt." *New York Times*. July 20.

Haidt, Jonathan. 2006. *The Happiness Hypothesis: Finding Modern Truth in Ancient Wisdom*. New York: Basic Books.

Harris, Sam. 2004. *The End of Faith: Religion, Terrorism and the Future of Reason*. New York: Norton.

____. 2006. *Letter to a Christian Nation*. New York: Knopf.

____. 2010. *The Moral Landscape: How Science Can Determine Human Values*. New York: The Free Press.

Hitchens, Christopher. 2007. *God Is Not Great: How Religion Poisons Everything*. New York: Twelve.

Hurlin, Stephen, J. 2009. *Courage to Doubt*. Raider Publishing International.

Jeskin, Alan. 2010. *Outgrowing God: Moving Beyond Religion*. CreateSpace Independent Publishing Platform.

Johnson, Mary. 2011. *An Unquenchable Thirst: A Memoir*. New York: Random House.

Kitcher, Philip. 2011. "Militant Modern Atheism," *Journal of Applied Philosophy* 28, no. 1: 1–13.

Kugel, James L. 2007. *How to Read The Bible: A Guide to Scripture, Then and Now*. New York: Free Press.

Kuhn, Thomas. 1962. *The Structure of Scientific Revolution*. Chicago: University of Chicago Press.

Kushner, Harold S. 1978. *When Bad Things Happen to Good People*. New York: Random House.

Lax, Eric. 2010. *Faith Interrupted: A Spiritual Journey*. New York: Knopf.

Lewis, Sam M. and Joe Young. 1919. *"How 'ya gonna keep 'em own on the farm?"* New York: Waterson, Berlin & Snyder Co., Music Publishing.

Lobdell, William. 2009. *Losing My Religion: How I Lost My Faith Reporting on Religion in America and Found Unexpected Peace*. New York: Harper Collins.

Loftus, John W. 2008. *Why I Became an Atheist: A Former Preacher Rejects Christianity*. Amherst, NY: Prometheus Books.

____, editor. 2010. *The Christian Delusion: Why Faith Fails*. Amherst, NY: Prometheus Books.

____, editor. 2011. *The End of Christianity*. Amherst, NY: Prometheus Books.

McDowell, Josh. 1972. *Evidence that Demands a Verdict*. San Bernardino, CA: Here's Life Publishers.

McLaren, Brian. 2011. *A New Kind of Christianity*. New York: HarperOne.

McNaught, Brian. 1997. *Now that I'm Out What Do I Do?* New York: St. Martin's Press.

Merla, Patrick. 1997. *Boys Like Us: Gay Writers Tell Their Coming Out*

Stories. New York: William Morrow Paperbacks.

Merton, Thomas. 1948. *Seven Storey Mountain*. New York: Harcourt Brace.

Monette, Paul. 1992. *Becoming a Man: Half a Life Story*. New York: Harcourt Brace Jovanovich.

Paine, Thomas. 1794, 1795, 1807. *The Age of Reason*. Free download at http://www.deism.com/images/theageofreason1794.pdf

Pinker, Steven. 2002. *The Blank Slate: The Modern Denial of Human Nature*. New York: Viking.

Quinn, Michael D. 1998. *Early Mormonism and the Magic World Views*. Salt Lake City: Signature Books.

Raine, Adrian. 2013. *The Anatomy of Violence: The Biological Roots of Crime*. New York: Pantheon.

Ray, Darrel. 2009. *The God Virus: How Religion Infects Our Lives and Culture*. IPC Press.

Real, Terrance. 1998. *I Don't Want to Talk About It: Overcoming the Secret Legacy of Male Depression*. New York: Fireside Simon & Schuster.

Robinson, John, A.T. 1963. *Honest to God*. Louisville, KY: Westminster John Knox.

Ruether, Rosemary Radford. 1974. *Religion and Sexism: Images of Woman in the Jewish and Christian Traditions*. New York: Simon & Schuster.

____. 1983. Sexism and God Talk: *Toward a Feminist Theology*. Boston, MA: Beacon Press.

____. 1985. *Women-Church: Theology and Practice of Feminist Liturgical Communities*. New York: Harper & Row.

Rutledge, Mark. 2014. "'Non-believers'—Who Are They and What Will Become of Them?" *Rational Doubt* blog. May 19. http://www.patheos.com/blogs/clergyproject/2014/05/non-believers-who-are-they-and-what-will-become-of-them/.

Semple, Patrick. 2008. *The Rector Who Wouldn't Pray For Rain*. Cork, Ireland: Mercier Press.

Shimron, Yonat. 2010. "Pastor Sticks up for Modern View of God," *Raleigh News & Observer*, August 2, 2010.

Shermer, Michael. 2012. *The Believing Brain: From Ghosts and Gods to Politics and Conspiracies---How We Construct Beliefs and Reinforce Them as Truths*. New York: St. Martin's Griffin.

Spencer, Michael. 2009. "The Coming Evangelical Collapse," *Christian Science Monitor*, March 10, 2009.

Spong, John, Shelby. 1991. *Rescuing the Bible from Fundamentalism: A Bishop Rethinks the Meaning of Scripture*. HarperSanFrancisco.

____. 1998. *Why Christianity must Change or Die: A Bishop Speaks to Believers in Exile*. HarperSanFrancisco.

____. 2005. *The Sins of Scripture: Exposing the Bible's tests of Hate to Reveal the God of Love*. HarperSanFrancisco.

____. 2009. *Jesus for the Non-Religious*. New York: HarperCollins.

Strobel, Lee. 1998. *The Case for Christ: A Journalist's Personal Investigation of the Evidence for Jesus*. Grand Rapids, MI: Zondervan.

Talbot, John Michael. 2008. "Be Not Afraid." From the album The Troubadour Years. Troubadour for the Lord Records.

Thomson, J. Anderson, Jr., and Clare Aukofer. 2011. *Why We Believe in God(s)*. Charlottesville, VA: Pitchstone Publishing.

Tillich, Paul. 1951. *Systematic Theology: Volume I*. Chicago, IL: University of Chicago Press.

Uhl, Stephen Frederick. 2007. *Out of God's Closet: This Priest Psychologist Chooses Friendly Atheism*. OroValley, AZ: Golden Rule Publishers.

Unamuno, Miguel. 1930. *San Manuel Bueno, Martir*. Free online English translation available at http://www4.gvsu.edu/wrightd/SPA%20307%20Death/SaintManuelBueno.htm.

Updike, John. 1996. *In the Beauty of the Lilies*. New York: Random House.

Walsh, Michael, editor. 1991. *Butler's Lives of the Saints: Concise Edition Revised & Updated*. San Francisco: Harper Collins.

Weatherhead, Leslie, D. 1944. *The Will of God*. Reprint, Abingdon Press, 1987.

____. 1965. *The Christian Agnostic*. Abingdon/Nashville, KY: Festival Books.

Wilkerson, David, with Elizabeth and John Sherrill. 1962. *The Cross and the Switchblade*. New York: Penguin.

Wilson, David Sloan. 2007. *Evolution for Everyone: How Darwin's Theory Can Change the Way We Think about Our Lives*. New York: Delacorte Press.

Wind, James P., and David J. Wood. October 2008. *Becoming a Pastor: Reflections on the Transition into Ministry*. Special Report. Durham, NC: Alban Institute.

Wright, Robert. 1994. *The Moral Animal: Why We Are, the Way We Are: The New Science of Evolutionary Psychology*. New York: Vintage.

____. 2009. *The Evolution of God*. New York: Little, Brown and Company.

"Andy's List"

The following resources were provided by study participant "Andy." They influenced him as he moved from Southern Baptist to United Church of Christ to agnostic.

Altizer, Thomas J. J. 1966. *The Gospel of Christian Atheism*. Philadelphia: Westminster.

Aronson, Ronald. 2008. *Living Without God: New Directions for Atheists, Agnostics, Secularists and the Undecided*. Berkeley, CA: Counterpoint.

Bellinzoni, Arthur. 2006. *The Future of Christianity: Can It Survive?* Amherst, NY: Prometheus.

Berger, Peter L., and Thomas Luckmann. 1966. *The Social Construction of Reality: A Treatise in the Sociology of Knowledge*. New York: Doubleday.

Freeman, Charles. 2008. *A.D. 381: Heretics, Pagans, and the Dawn of the Monotheistic State*. New York: Overlook.

Geering, Lloyd. 2002. *Christianity Without God*. Santa Rosa, CA: Polebridge.

Meyers, Robin. 2009. *Saving Jesus from the Church: How to Stop Worshiping Christ and Start Following Jesus*. New York: Harper.

Neusch, Marcel. 1977. *The Sources of Modern Atheism*. New York: Paulist.

Van Buren, Paul. 1963. *The Secular Meaning of the Gospel, Based on an Analysis of its Language*. New York: Macmillan.

Internet Resources: Web sites, Blogs, Podcasts

Loosely alphabetized and with some brief descriptions

"Adam Mann's" Study List—http://wp.production.patheos.com/blogs/rationaldoubt/files/2015/01/Adam-Study-List-2008-to-2012-revised.pdf: 32-page list compiled by pilot study participant.

Seth Andrews' The Thinking Atheist—http://www.thethinkingatheist.com

The Bible—http://www.kingjamesbibleonline.org/

The Book of Mormon—http://mormon.org/discover/002/07-book-of-mormon.html?gclid=CKTe7dDH6roCFa1QOgodnA8AEg&CID=99110386&ef_id=UogNHQAABe-PagXb:20131117002605:s

Rudolf Bultmann—http://www.theopedia.com/Rudolf_Karl_Bultmann: "Rudolf Karl Bultmann (1884–1976) was a German Lutheran theologian. He is well known for his "demythologizing" of the New Testament, and was influenced by the existentialism of Martin Heidegger. Educated at the universities of Tübingen, Berlin, and Marburg, Bultmann taught at the universities of Breslau and Giessen and from 1921 to 1950 was professor at the University of Marburg."

Joseph Campbell Web site—http://www.jcf.org/new/index.php: "Joseph John Campbell was an American mythologist, writer and lecturer, best known for his work in comparative mythology and comparative religion. His work is vast, covering many aspects of the human experience. His philosophy is often summarized by his phrase: 'Follow your bliss.'" http://en.wikipedia.org/wiki/Joseph_Campbell

Tony Campolo Web site—http://tonycampolo.org/: "speaker, author, sociologist, pastor, social activist and passionate follower of Jesus!"

The Center for Progressive Christianity—http://progressivechristianity.org/

The Clergy Project—http://www.clergyproject.org/

Common Sense Atheism—http://commonsenseatheism.com/

Debunking Christianity Web site, written by former minister John Loftus —http://debunkingchristianity.blogspot.com/

Episcopal Prayer Book: The Ordination of a Priest—http://www.bcponline.org/EpiscopalServices/ordination_of_a_priest.htm

Ex-Mormon Web site—http://www.exmormon.org/

Freethought Today—http://ffrf.org/publications/freethought-today: "Freethought Today covers timely news related to state/church separation and includes articles of interest to freethinkers."

The writings of *Bruce Gerenscer*, former Evangelical preacher—http://brucegerencser.net/

The Great Courses Network: The New Testament, by Bart D. Ehrman— http://www.thegreatcourses.com/tgc/professors/professor_detail.aspx?pid=150

Stephen Hawking, Discovery Channel, Curiosity Show, "Did God Create the Universe?" August 7, 2011—http://dsc.discovery.com/tv-shows/curiosity/topics/did-god-create-the-universe.htm

The Jesus Seminar, founded by Robert W. Funk—http://www.westarinstitute.org/projects/the-jesus-seminar/: "The Jesus Seminar was organized in 1985 to renew the quest of the historical Jesus and to report the results of its research to the general public, rather than just to a handful of gospel specialists."

The writings of Orthodox American-Israeli *Rabbi Meir Kahane*—http://www.jewishvirtuallibrary.org/jsource/biography/kahane.html

The writings of *Rabbi Mordecai Kaplan*, Orthodox turned Reconstructionist—http://www.jewishvirtuallibrary.org/jsource/biography/kaplan.html

The work of *Karen King*, professor, Harvard Divinity School—http://www.hds.harvard.edu/people/faculty/karen-l-king

Opus Dei—http://www.opusdei.org/: "Opus Dei is a Catholic institution founded by Saint Josemaría Escrivá. Its mission is to help people turn their work and daily activities into occasions for growing closer to God, for serving others, and for improving society."

Stephen J. Patterson—http://www.willamette.edu/cla/religion/faculty/patterson/: "Dr. Patterson is an historian of religion specializing in the beginnings of Christianity. His research and writing have focused on the Gospel of Thomas, Q, and various aspects of the historical study of Jesus."

Paul's Letters—http://tyndalearchive.com/scriptures/www.innvista.com/scriptures/compare/letters.htm

Bishop Carlton Pearson—http://www.bishoppearson.com/: "As a result of what Carlton calls 'Expanded Consciousness', he strongly advocates personal evolution, transformation and Self Actualization. He says his deep roots in Pentecostalist transcendance have informed his embrace of a more Metaphysical approach to life, scriptural interpretation and spirituality."

Pew Research Religion & Public Life Project, 2012, "'Nones' on the Rise," October 9, 2012—http://www.pewforum.org/unaffiliated/nones-on-the-rise.aspx

Rational Doubt: With Voices from The Clergy Project—http://www.patheos.com/blogs/rationaldoubt/

Reasonable Doubts Web site—http://freethoughtblogs.com/reasonabledoubts: "Reasonable Doubts is an award winning radio show [WPRR Reality Radio (Grand Rapids, MI)] and podcast for people who won't "just take things on faith." RD's mission is to investigate the claims of religion from a fair-minded yet critical perspective."

ReligionLink—http://www.religionlink.com/: "the ultimate source for journalists reporting on religion" and "a non-partisan service of Religion Newswriters Association and Religion News LLC . . . created by journalists, for journalists.

Sojourners Web site (Jim Wallis)—http://sojo.net/: "Sojourners is a national Christian organization committed to faith in action for social justice. We seek to inspire hope and build a movement to transform individuals, communities, the church, and the world."

Bishop John Shelby Spong—http://johnshelbyspong.com/: "A New Christianity for a New World"

Sunday Assembly—http://sundayassembly.com: "A Global Movement for Wonder and Good"

Julia Sweeney, Letting Go of God Monologue—http://juliasweeney.com/letting-go-of-god/:

TED Talks—http://www.ted.com/pages/about ("Technology, Entertainment, Design—Ideas worth Spreading); http://www.ted.com/topics/atheism; http://www.ted.com/topics/religion

ABOUT THE AUTHORS

Daniel C. Dennett is the Austin B. Fletcher Professor of Philosophy at Tufts University and the codirector of the Center for Cognitive Studies. He is the author of numerous books, including *Brainstorms*, *Breaking the Spell*, *Consciousness Explained*, *Darwin's Dangerous Idea*, *Elbow Room*, *Freedom Evolves*, and *Intuition Pumps*. He lives in North Andover, Massachusetts.

Linda LaScola has been a qualitative researcher for more than 25 years and has traveled around the United States interviewing people on numerous subjects, including health, mental health, public policy, and religion. She lives in Washington, DC.